THE SOUTH

vs.

THE SOUTH

Other Oxford Books by
William W. Freehling

Prelude to Civil War
The Nullification Controversy in South Carolina, 1816–1836

Willie Lee Rose
Slavery and Freedom
(Editor)

The Road to Disunion, Volume I
Secessionists at Bay, 1776–1854

Secession Debated
Georgia's Showdown in 1860
(Co-editor with Craig M. Simpson)

The Reintegration of American History
Slavery and the Civil War

THE SOUTH

vs.

THE SOUTH

How Anti-Confederate Southerners
Shaped the Course of the Civil War

William W. Freehling

OXFORD
UNIVERSITY PRESS

OXFORD

UNIVERSITY PRESS

Oxford New York

Auckland Bangkok Buenos Aires Cape Town Chennai
Dar es Salaam Delhi Hong Kong Istanbul Karachi Kolkata
Kuala Lumpur Madrid Melbourne Mexico City Mumbai
Nairobi São Paolo Shanghai Taipei Tokyo Toronto

Copyright © 2001 by William W. Freehling

First published by Oxford University Press, Inc., 2001
First issued as an Oxford University Press paperback, 2002
198 Madison Avenue, New York, New York 10016

www.oup.com

Oxford is a registered trademark of Oxford University Press, Inc.

Library of Congress Cataloging-in-Publication Data
Freehling, William W., 1935-
The South vs. the South : how anti-Confederate southerners shaped
the course of the Civil War / William W. Freehling
xv, 238 p. : ill., maps ; 25 cm.
Includes bibliographical references (pp. 207-230) and index
ISBN 0-19-513027-8 (cloth) ISBN 10-19-515629-3 (pbk)
1. Confederate States of America—Politics and government.
2. Confederate States of America—Social conditions.
3. Slaves—Southern States—Political activity—History—19th century.
4. African Americans—Southern States—Politics and government—19th century.
5. Unionists (United States Civil War).
6. Whites—Southern States—Politics and government—19th century.
7. United States Army—Southern Unionists.
8. United States—History—Civil War, 1861-1865—Social aspects.
I. Title.
E487 .F83 2001
973.7'1—dc21   00-51678

3 5 7 9 8 6 4 2

Printed in the United States of America

For
Alison Freehling Johnson
and
William Goodyear Freehling

Contents

Maps and Illustrations

Preface

Civil War battles invite vivid storytelling. Sagas of courageous soldiers, of colorful generals, of bloody combat, with a nation's fate at stake—here is stuff for riveting epics. Yet battlefield tales alone cannot solve even the main military puzzle, why the Confederacy lost the Civil War. A satisfying Civil War narrative must also illuminate the home front. Events beyond the battlefields partially determined military verdicts. Furthermore, home front and battlefront, when their stories become intertwined, unveil defining aspects of Civil War America, beyond the soldiers' ordeals.

Work on my two-volume history of the Old South, *The Road to Disunion*, compelled these thoughts, for my designated home-front road continued after disunion. Divisions within the South helped pave the path toward war. The same divisions behind army lines helped turn the war against the slaveholders. That wartime epilogue adds depth and credibility to my prewar story. Before the Civil War, a showdown between Southerners remained largely a potentiality, a possible rift that key folk feared might be fatal. During the Civil War, the potential became actual, unmistakably demonstrating a southern house divided—and freshly illuminating the nation's divided house as well.

The University of Texas provided the occasion to add this wartime perspective to *Road to Disunion*. The University's Littlefield Lecture Committee sought a debate between successive lecturers. The previous Littlefield Lecturer, Professor Gary Gallagher, had discounted divisions among southern folk and denied that home-front dissensions determined battlefield verdicts. I welcomed the Littlefield Committee's invitation to develop the opposing case.

In his lectures, Professor Gallagher skillfully discussed half the Slave South's population: whites who lived within the eleven Confederate states. He concluded that "southern white society" maintained "remarkable resiliency until the last stage of the war." Thus "contrary to what much recent literature proclaims, defeat in the military sphere, rather than dissolution behind the lines, brought the collapse of the Confederacy." Professor Gallagher added that "Confederate arms" could "have won the war"—indeed "more than once almost" did.[1]

While I dissent from that addendum, I admire Professor Gallagher's portrait of his selected Southerners' pro-Confederate passions. I concur that white Confederates' plunge in zeal (including white wives' plummeting commitment) largely came late in the war, after battlefield results had turned irretrievably against the rebels. True, the earlier Confederacy could ill afford its tens of thousands of white draft resisters, guerrilla saboteurs, and army deserters, to say nothing of its 100,000 whites who fought in the Union army. Still, if all the Slave South's inhabitants had emulated Confederate state whites, southern battlefield commitments would have trumped home-front defections.[2]

But unfortunately for white Confederates, blacks throughout the South and whites in the four nonseceding Border South states made up the other half of the southern population (with slaves representing 40 percent of the Confederate population). While the vast majority of Confederate state whites long supported their new nation, the vast majority of other Southerners either opposed the rebel cause or cared not whether it lived or died. Precisely because white Confederates were only half the Southerners, the divided southern home front crippled Confederate battlefield heroes.

Statistics indicate other Southerners' ability to cool white Confederates' ardor; and the numbers illuminate but the tip of the iceberg. Southern blacks supplied close to 150,000 Union soldiers and sailors (northern free blacks provided another 50,000). Border South whites added 200,000 and Confederate state whites 100,000 soldiers to Union troop strength. The resulting total of 450,000 Southerners who wore Union blue, half as many as the 900,000 Southerners who wore Confederate gray, replaced every one of the Federals' 350,000 slain men and supplied 100,000 more men besides — a number greater than the usual size of Robert E. Lee's main Confederate army. White Confederates developed no such replacements for their mounting casualties; and in addition, anti-Confederate Southerners piled on psychological, economic, and geographic burdens that ultimately helped flatten white Confederates' resiliency.

While I focus on a different race and a different southern region than did Professor Gallagher, a fully told tale of the South versus the South must move beyond the question of where to look for the Slave South's most destructive divisions, indeed beyond purely southern subjects. Such nonsouthern phenomena as President Abraham Lincoln's statescraft, the Union's "anaconda" military strategy, Northern Democrats' and Englishmen's attitudes — all these seemingly tangential matters bore vitally on southern anti-Confederates' capacity to influence the battlefields and to illuminate important characteristics of Civil War America.

The tale of the southern house divided, when told in lockstep with intertwined tales of the American house divided, highlights underappreciated gems of Civil War lore, including revealing code words ("contraband," "refugeeing," "garrisoning"), colorful luminaries (Patrick Cleburne), key battles (Fort Henry, Fort Donelson, Chattanooga), and vital military orders (Henry Halleck's General Orders #3, William Tecumseh Sherman's Special Field Orders #15). The interlocking epics centered on the Southerners versus Southerners theme help solve pivotal puzzles about the American sectional controversy — not just why Confederates lost but also why the Civil War came, how American free labor and slave labor societies differed, how whites (not just masters) dominated slaves, and how slaves helped shatter whites' dominion. This multifaceted narrative illuminates key issues in American racial history, including the power of national (not just southern) racism to delay national reform, why that forbidding power momentarily eased during the Civil War, why Abraham Lincoln started out as the great delayer and ended up as the Great Emancipator, how Lincoln's Emancipation Proclamation emancipated, and why the Union used the resulting mass of black soldiers in revealingly limited (and telling) ways.

This analysis uncovers antecedents of Martin Luther King's nonviolent resistance. It illuminates the history of Americans' antibureaucratic bias against the national state. It deepens understanding of Augustus Saint-Gaudens's sculptural depiction of Robert Gould Shaw and black troops, one of America's greatest artistic masterpieces. By moving back and forth from southern home front to battlefront, from South to North, even from America to England, I hope this new-style Civil War narrative will give new meaning to military stories cherished by Civil War "buffs"—and new understanding to those who cherish other aspects of American civilization.

As I explored these potentialities of a fresh Civil War epic in my Littlefield Lectures, I thoroughly enjoyed the intellectual community at the University of Texas. I think especially of Dave Bowman, Neil Kamil, Jim Sidbury, Bob Olwell, Sally Clarke, Howard Miller, George Forgie, Frank Goodyear, Anne Collins Goodyear, and Michael Parrish. As I expanded my Littlefield Lectures into this book, Mike Parrish continued to give me the benefit of his awesome Civil War knowledge. Mike, both a longtime friend of Gary Gallagher and a good friend of this book, epitomizes the unusually supportive camaraderie among Civil War scholars, no matter their different viewpoints. A memorable conversation with Mike Holt also exemplifies why I relish my work within this circle of historians.

Mark Summers, John Cawelti, George Herring, Steve Weisenburger, William Campbell, Jean Baker, Benjamin Franklin Cooling, David Williams, David Carlson, and Mike Parrish criticized all or part of my draft and immensely improved it. My wonderful secretary, Lynn Hiler, enabled a computer-illiterate Neanderthal to remain a publishing scholar. My scribbles on legal pads continue to draw on research conducted as a Guggenheim Foundation Fellow. My new editor at Oxford, Peter Ginna, continues the splendid tradition of Sheldon Meyer. My new mapmaker, Professor Donald Frazier, has "written" his own fine book within my book on the importance of Civil War anacondas. My new Singletary Chair in the

Humanities at the University of Kentucky provided indispensable support for much of this collective labor.

In Texas as everywhere, Alison shared my adventure. All my books should be dedicated to her. But she will applaud a dedication to the two people who mean more to us than every sentence we have written.

William W. Freehling
Lexington, Kentucky
Christmas Day, 1999
The Last Christmas of the Twentieth Century!

In this paperback edition I have corrected a few minor errors in the hardback edition. I thank those who suggested the corrections, especially Larry Kohl and Richard McMurray.

WWF
Christmas Day, 2001

part one

The Other House Divided

The Union's Task　1

Military surrenders invite a simple explanation: The heavier battalions swept the battlefield. Supposedly, the combatant that can bring more men, more material, more sophisticated weapons to military points of contacts will defeat the less well endowed foe.

Assuredly, the free labor North wielded weightier resources than the slave labor South. The North's immense Civil War task, however, bade fair to outweigh the section's larger power. If the Confederacy could have marshaled all the slave labor states' people and resources, free labor states might have been insufficiently richer, especially in manpower, to afford the Union's costly strategy to complete its difficult conquest.

1

In 1860, the free labor states' population outnumbered the slave labor states' by 19 to 12 million, a more than three to two margin. Free labor states also contained two times more railroad tracks, three times more bank deposits, and five times more industrial output. Yankees sported 90 percent of the nation's boot and shoe production, 93 percent of its pig iron production, 94 percent of its factory-made clothing, 96 percent of its manufacture of locomotives, 97 percent of its output of firearms, 98 percent of its construction of ships, and 100 percent of its production of rolled iron, essential for railroad tracks. With more railroad tracks, more ships, more firearms, more locomotives, more iron, more boots, more shoes, more cloth, and more fighting men, it might appear that free labor states should have easily crushed underindustrialized, underpopulated slave labor states.[1]

But if the North's resources were greater, its task was greater still. Rebel armies won if they stood still. Lincoln's soldiers lost unless the entire Confederacy surrendered. The Slave South's land mass, as large as Western Europe's and 10 percent more extensive than the North's, required Yankee troops to trudge thousands of miles, to storm hundreds of fortifications, to expose themselves ever farther from the North's better railroads and factories.

As Union soldiers advanced, conquered miles behind often remained as treacherous as unsubdued miles ahead. Some careless Civil War analysts ask why Confederates shunned guerrilla tactics. The answer: Rebels *did* use irregular warfare, very successfully. By exploding railroad tunnels, torching railroad bridges, and twisting railroad tracks, rebel raiders such as Nathan Bedford Forrest and John Hunt Morgan threatened to cut off invaders from the Yankee home base, isolate Federals from reinforcements, and subject them to the revenge of an enraged citizenry, wild to redeem hearth and home from detested Yankees. This guerrilla warfare often delayed Union advances for weeks, in one case for months. It always forced the advancing force to leave behind a large army of occupation.[2]

The need to conquer, occupy, and pacify endless Confederate terrain often offset the Union's huge advantages. Yankee superiority only loomed sufficiently immense in the most complicated manufactured products and plants. Among complex American mid-nineteenth-century products, steam-powered ships ranked first and railroads second. Just as naval supremacy eased Yankee infantrymen's advance into the Slave South, so railroad supremacy eased dangers behind the infantry.

Confederate Guerrilla Warfare

John Hunt Morgan.
Courtesy of the Valentine Museum,
Richmond, Virginia.

Nathan Bedford Forrest.
Courtesy of the United States Army
Military History Institute, Carlisle
Barracks, Pennsylvania.

Confederate guerrillas' railroad devastation.   Courtesy of the Minnesota History Society,
St. Paul, Minnesota, photograph by Sweeny.

2

Throughout the Civil War, Northerners controlled almost all the nation's largest warships and all but one of the plants to produce them. (The Confederate navy controlled the exception, Norfolk, Virginia's, Gosport Navy Yard, for only thirteen months.) Yet on water as on land, plucky rebels refused to concede defeat. The Civil War's most famous naval incident illustrated how cleverly (and futilely) the Confederate navy tried to catch up.

Using ingenuity that Yankees supposedly monopolized, southern tinkerers fashioned a sea monster from a buried corpse. They raised a steam frigate, the *U.S.S. Merrimack*, from its watery grave. They stripped this ex-titan naked above the water level. They slapped above the hull a cap, shaped like a barn roof. They plated the roof with iron, four inches thick. They thus concocted the world's first ironclad, power-driven warship and proudly renamed it the *C.S.S. Virginia*.

For two months, the *Merrimack/Virginia* seemed a threat to sink the Federals' Atlantic fleet. On her initial March 1862 sortie, the "*Thing*," as Yankees called her, sank two Union wooden warships, the *Congress* and the *Cumberland*, then drove the steam frigate *Minnesota* aground. Federal officials rushed forth their own weird thing, the *U.S.S. Monitor*, with its central cap resembling a tin can. The Federals' iron can and the rebels' iron roof clashed once, inconclusively. Soon thereafter, the *Merrimack/Virginia's* engines, damaged by their sunken interlude in pre-ironclad days, could not adequately budge the ship's armored coat. The stricken vessel repeated the plight of the medieval knight who tripped and could not arise, crushed down as he was by his protective armor. So Confederates had to sink their "*Thing*."

The trouble: the industrially retarded Confederacy could not leap far enough into the industrial age, having already jumped incredibly far. Rebels mustered the resources and ingenuity to raise and plate a drowned behemoth. These industrial unsophisticates, however, could not fabricate adequate engines for the raised *Merrimack/Virginia*. Subsequently, Confederates constructed two dozen smaller ironclads. But lighter ironclads also remained too heavy for Confederate-made engines. With their limited range, they could be effective only in relatively stationary positions, guarding several Confederate ports that held out until near the end of the war. While never-say-die rebels never ceased trying to match the Union's more numerous and better powered gunboats, Yankee factories always retained their supremacy.[3]

The Union's naval supremacy inspired its first blueprint for victory. Lincoln's first overall military planner, the army's Winfield Scott, prayed that the navy could largely win the war. General Scott envisioned a choking watery ring around the eastern Confederacy. The Union should conquer all Confederate ports on the Atlantic and Gulf, thus blocking European aid. Federals should also seize dominion over the Mississippi River, thus severing the Trans-Mississippi states of Louisiana, Texas, and Arkansas from the eastern Confederacy. A surrounded, isolated eastern Confederacy, Scott hoped, would seek reunion. The alternative appalled him. If we have to "conquer the seceding States by invading armies," Scott warned a month before the war, the North's "waste of human life" would be "enormous" and "the destruction of life and property on the other side would be frightful."[4]

Winfield Scott's prayer for a relatively undestructive water war rather than a frightful land war resembles late-twentieth-century Americans' preference for air wars over land wars. But in its own time, the Union's early "soft war" mentality created the apparent plausibility of Scott's so-called Anaconda Plan. Federal officials long erroneously believed that Confederates, if softly chided, would return to gentle Union, for Lincoln seemed too indistinct a menace to slavery, hard-core disunionists too small a southern minority, the Confederate majority too fond of the Union. Only a little southern blood need be shed. No Confederate property—least of all slaves—should be confiscated. To administer the little reprimand, Lincoln initially called up only 75,000 men for only three months. Scott prayed that few of the 75,000 would be necessary, and only to help the navy reduce Confederate ports.

The soft war prayer long persisted. Ulysses S. Grant somewhat retained the illusion until April 1862 (until the Battle of Shiloh), Lincoln until the end of 1862 (when he finally realized that a soft emancipation policy would not lure Confederates back). After the soft war chimera evaporated, Scott's watery anaconda endured, but long only as another semifantasy. Union seamen for years failed to conquer several Confederate ports, not least because slow-moving rebel ironclads blocked the way. Unconquered harbor installations long stymied soldiers too. Vicksburg would not be reduced until mid-

1863, Mobile Bay until mid-1864, and Fort Fisher (guarding Wilmington, North Carolina) until January 1865.

Half an anaconda remained better than none. On the Atlantic Ocean and the Gulf of Mexico, federal warships early established a semiclosed embargo against Confederate overseas trade. Rebels, semi-isolated on the Western World's Atlantic fringe, had as much trouble receiving outside supplies as did Yankee invaders, semi-isolated in the Confederacy's ocean-sized terrain.

The federal navy not only policed the Atlantic and Gulf but also steamed up Virginia's James River, establishing a presence on the war's first, eastern front. Here, ships menaced the flank of Robert E. Lee's Virginia army. While Grant's infantrymen would have to surround Lee's other sides, the navy had shrunk the miles to complete a strangling circle.

The payoff from Union naval dominance (and thus indirectly from Union industrial dominance) reduced the Confederate miles still more dramatically on the war's second, western front. In 1862, Union ships steamed up the Mississippi River, conquering New Orleans (the Confederates' largest city), Baton Rouge, and Natchez. Another fleet sped down the great river, conquering Memphis. In 1862, the two fleets together could not conquer their point of intersection, Vicksburg, Mississippi, towering above the river. But naval vessels indispensably helped Ulysses S. Grant's successful siege of Vicksburg in mid-1863. By thus at last securing the great river, the Union reduced its need to conquer the Trans-Mississippi third of the Confederate land mass. Union military operations still occurred in Texas, Louisiana, and Arkansas. Federal armies, however, did not have to press that offensive relentlessly, for Confederate power west of the Mississippi could no longer stream eastward.

The Union navy also helped the Union's western infantrymen to establish and spread their landed front. Instead of having to fight their way down to western Tennessee, many soldiers caught a relatively safe river ride into the Confederacy's Mississippi Valley breadbasket. During the ensuing eighteen months of frustrating combat, before Vicksburg finally surrendered, the naval contribution of water transportation and river gunboats proved indispensable to the long-stymied army.

Once Union troops belatedly secured Vicksburg and thus the Mississippi Valley, they turned toward the Atlantic, to add a landed anaconda

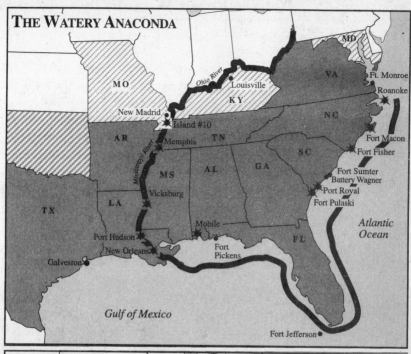

The Watery Anaconda

MD

MO

Ohio River

Louisville

KY

VA

Ft. Monroe

Roanoke

New Madrid

Island #10

NC

AR

Memphis

TN

Fort Macon

Fort Fisher

SC

MS

AL

GA

Fort Sumter

Battery Wagner

Vicksburg

Port Royal

Fort Pulaski

TX

LA

Mobile

Atlantic
Ocean

Port Hudson

New Orleans

Fort
Pickens

FL

Galveston

Gulf of Mexico

Fort Jefferson

Mississippi River

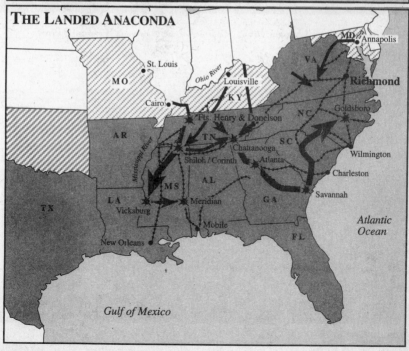

The Landed Anaconda

MD

Annapolis

St. Louis

VA

Richmond

MO

Ohio River

Louisville

Cairo

KY

Goldsboro

NC

Fts. Henry & Doneison

AR

TN

Wilmington

Shiloh / Corinth

Chattanooga

SC

Atlanta

Charleston

MS

AL

Vicksburg

Meridian

GA

Savannah

TX

LA

New Orleans

Mobile

FL

Atlantic
Ocean

Gulf of Mexico

Mississippi River

Yankee Repair Wizardry

Union railroad repairs, October 1863.   Courtesy of the Minnesota Historical Society,
photograph by Sweeny.

Repairs finished, January 1864.   Courtesy of the Minnesota Historical Society.

around Robert E. Lee's Virginia theater of war to the watery anaconda around the eastern Confederacy. River transports eased infantrymen's eastward way to Nashville and Chattanooga. Thereafter, the navy usually could not speed landed warriors toward Lee. Instead, the most significant late-war naval transportation of troops carried Union soldiers away from their circle around Lee to counter Jubal Early's July 1864 campaign against Washington, D.C. Yet a second sophisticated industrial resource that the Confederacy could not match, Yankee railroad expertise, helped complete the landed anaconda around Lee's theater of war.

The Mississippi Valley's conquerors could not ride their own railroads toward the Atlantic. Those superior rails and locomotives lay up North. But thanks to Yankees' railroad expertise (and their army of occupation), Union infantrymen used southern rails to maintain supply lines to home base.

When Yankee armies conquered a Confederate area, Yankee engineers often rebuilt its railroads. Sherman's soldiers, so it was said, carried railroad bridges in their knapsacks. Southern rails supplied precarious lines to northern terrain, with emphasis on the precarious. Kentucky's John Hunt Morgan and Tennessee's Nathan Bedford Forrest, "that devil Forrest" as Union soldiers called the Confederates' prize guerrilla warrior, perfected the mounted assault on railroads. But not even this Satan on horseback could tear all invaders off southern rails. Union troops deterred guerrillas from most tracks, and engineering wizards repaired sabotaged rails. Meanwhile, ahead of would-be conquerors lay many hundred miles and several hundred thousand rebel troops, armed with another revolutionary weapon. Modern rifles stretched the difficulty of conquering interminable miles almost as much as modern ships and railroads shrank the task.[5]

3

Yankee invaders would have advanced more easily in the pre-rifle early nineteenth century, the so-called Napoleonic Era of European warfare. Then the smoothbore musket and its attached bayonet sword reigned as shoulder arm of choice. With flashing swords, heavier battalions could triumph inside undermanned defenders' fortifications. To stymie more numerous bayonet-bearing infantrymen, less numerous defenders needed to shoot down advancing troops before the attackers reached the fortifications.[6]

But infantrymen's Napoleonic Era firearm, that smoothbore musket, lacked the range, accuracy, and loading speed for sharpshooters to stop chargers. A gun barrel's inner surface is called its "bore." The bore of the old-fashioned musket was left smooth for the same reason that its bullet was left round: to help jam a missile down the tightly fitting inner barrel. The slightly eased entrance, however, caused a more innocuous exit. As the fired ball exploded down the bore, it rubbed only against smoothness, acquiring only a forward spin before it flew against atmospheric deterrence. Then crosswinds easily deflected a flight without sideward spin, just as air resistance easily slowed a rounded ball.

The resulting missile thudded to earth prematurely, erratically. Attackers could safely drag cannon within a hundred yards of musket-bearing defenders. Heavy artillery then softened defensive fortifications. When smoothbores' answering volley fell futilely short, bayonet-bearing assaulters charged double time, leaping atop their prey before smoothbores could be reloaded. The offensive advantage soared when cavalrymen galloped on infantrymen's flanks, riding down fleeing defenders.

Defenders fled less often when rifles replaced smoothbore muskets, a transformation sped along by the Crimean War of the 1850s. Where the smoothbore's bullet had been round and approximately the same diameter as the musket's inner barrel, the rifle's new bullet was pointed, hollow at its nonpointed end, and smaller in diameter than the new bore. Where the musket's bore had been smooth, spiral ridges ran down the rifle barrel's inner surface. Where the old rounded ball had to be jammed into its tightly fitting bore, the new bullet slipped more easily inside its slightly larger bore.

When a rifleman fired, gas filled the new bullet's hollow end, expanding the missile to the size of the bore. By rubbing against the new bore's spiral ridges, the fired projectile acquired a sideward spin as it raced toward the atmosphere. Where the musket's exiting ball, tumbling only forward, could not fight deflecting crosswinds, the rifle's bullet spun against deflection. Where resisting air slowed the musket's rounded ball, the rifle's pointed projectile cut through resistance. Where the musket's ball veered after 80 yards and dived after 300 yards, the rifle's bullet found the target precisely for 300 yards and flew toward the kill for 1,000 yards. Where the smooth-bore took thirty second to reload, the rifle took twenty.

The consequence: Whereas attackers could charge the last eighty yards while suffering only two smoothbore volleys, chargers' final dash against rifles had to cover 300 yards and endure some ten blasts from sharpshooters. Bayonets became less lethal, since chargers less often reached defensive forti-fications. Artillery became less helpful, since heavy guns had to be kept far-ther from defenders' positions. Cavalry became less supportive, since a horse galloping inside 300 yards of defensive fire might soon carry a savaged rider.

The new missile's premodern material destroyed as savagely as its modern technology. The twentieth-century bullet, encased in hard steel, remains intact as it slices in and out of the victim's body. The Civil War bullet, fashioned in soft lead and hollow inside, smashed against bone and blew apart. If the mushrooming projectile managed to depart the body, it left a gaping hole. More often the foreign body remained inside, contaminating bony rubble.

The contamination routed premodern medical care. To treat smashed limbs, doctors usually sawed off the disfigured mess. Surgeons, lacking modern antiseptic theory, almost never cleaned amputating saws from pre-vious sawings. Splintering bullets plus filthy saws added up to doubled in-fections. Sharpshooters, now able to fire more accurately, did not need to be as accurate. A shot aimed at a head and crushing a knee killed almost as often as a bull's-eye.

The new rifle reduced the more industrialized North's military advan-tage. When the transforming new weapon had been a sophisticated behe-moth, the ironclad ship or the locomotive, slaveholders' cruder industrial plants could not match Yankees' advances. But the spiral-grooved shoulder firearm and its expanding bullet required a simple technology and com-manded an affordable price. The new killer cost $20, compared to $250,000 for an ironclad frigate. Rifles could be mass produced in the South, mass purchased in England, and mass confiscated from Yankee corpses. Two years into the Civil War, the otherwise-underequipped Confederacy ade-quately possessed the new weapon that boosted undermanned defenders' power. Federal invaders had to subdue a landmass almost as extensive as Napoleon had conquered, despite facing a post-Napoleonic rifle that might have stopped Napoleon long before Moscow.

In the new rifle-haunted tactical situation, the offensive charge became a very costly, usually counterproductive strategy to annihilate a defensive army. Civil War generals, including Grant and Lee, learned that truth the hard way, when they learned it at all. The charge toward total victory remained a tantalizing illusion: Find the enemy's weak point, charge through it, and keep charging until retreaters surrendered. Occasionally, a Civil War charge yielded a military breakthrough. More often, the charge against protected riflemen yielded too many slain attackers and too little conquered terrain. Frustratingly often, defenders would abandon one set of earthworks only to dig another. Then rifle-bearing defenders subjected assaulters to another round of higher casualties. Eventually (and usually after the first exhausting charge), attackers paused rather than pursued.

Assaulters' pauses provoked second guessing, then and since. Supposedly, if Civil War armies had kept charging after retreaters, an offensive army would have ended the war much sooner (and, some think, with a Confederate victory). But the armchair quarterback's gospel of relentless charging ignores how exhausting the charge became, to mind and spirit. Attackers badly needed pauses, to bury their dead, dress their wounds, and summon the nerve to dare withering rifles again.

Since rifles made a charge *through* a Civil War army psychologically and physically forbidding, the movement *around* a defensive army usually became the path toward unconditional surrender.[7] An offense with superior manpower need not charge suicidally ahead. Instead, a larger army could move sideward, outflanking a smaller army. As defenders spread their line to counter the football-like end run, more numerous assaulters could sweep wider still. Assaulters' movement *around* rather than *through* avoided the horror of storming down the throat of stationary earthworks. Successive end runs could also stretch undermanned defenders' lines vulnerably thin. Best of all, continual movement *around* could end in a strangling circle, a killing siege. Then the assaulting army could crouch behind earthworks, forcing defenders to charge or starve.

Starving sieges required superior manpower. To outflank defenders continually and then to fortify the encirclement thoroughly, a troop advantage of around two to one was usually mandatory. Moreover, to secure its most important encirclement, the Union found a single siege insufficient. Only three circles around Robert E. Lee could trap the master.

For three years, Lee reigned as the seemingly unbeatable star of the Virginia theater of war. Lee's stage stretched over the highly publicized 106 miles between Washington, D.C., the Federals' capital, and Richmond, the rebels'. So confined a battle zone with such excellent (for the Confederacy) interior railroad lines enabled a supple maneuverer to drive the Federals wild. Darting here, dashing there, now charging, now retreating, Lee kept Union generals far from pinning him in any siege for more than three years.

To sweep both arms around the Confederate genius, the Union needed to render the lightning-fast defender heavy-footed. Lee would not be nimble if Union armed forces isolated their nemesis from his nation and from Europe, leaving his army with little food and few reinforcements. The Union implicitly sought to encircle Lee's Virginia theater long before early 1864, when Ulysses Grant explicitly articulated the climactic anaconda plan.

Grant hoped to complete Winfield Scott's watery anaconda around the eastern Confederacy, thus choking Lee off from European or Trans-Mississippi aid. In addition, the Union hoped to march its western army from the Mississippi River across the Middle South (with a detour to Atlanta). Another Union army would hopefully conquer Virginia's Shenandoah Valley. Then conquering armies would form a landed anaconda, choking Lee's theater of war off from other southern areas. Inside these watery and landed anacondas, yet another Union army might move around and around Lee's flank, eventually forming a third encirclement around the weakened titan.[8]

This blueprint for triumph potentially shrank the Confederacy's largest advantage. With a triple siege in place, Federals would need to conquer only half as many Confederate acres. The three Trans-Mississippi and seven Lower South states could be left largely uninvaded, once anacondas made these areas unhelpful to Lee. Yet the anaconda solution bore an outlandish price tag, especially extravagant in its manpower requirements. Federals needed to keep Lee busy in Virginia, *plus* conquer very tough Confederate Gilbraltars (especially Vicksburg and Fort Fisher), *plus* move down the Mississippi Valley from free labor states to Vicksburg and across the Middle South from the Mississippi River to the Atlantic Ocean, *plus* everywhere leave behind armies of occupation (often as large as advancing armies), *plus* continually bring to major sieges the requisite two to one advantage. Those requirements for a triple siege could overwhelm the free labor states' three to two edge in manpower.

Southern residents' allegiances thus became critical. If southern inhabitants everywhere refused to be beaten or stay beaten, the Union's grasp for a triple siege might exhaust Yankee resources. But if a large fraction of slave labor state inhabitants added large quantities of acreage, troops, and material to free labor states' advantages, invaders' shrinking margin of superiority would bulge again, up to the requirements for an exhaustingly ambitious half continent of sieges. Abraham Lincoln knew that the costly solution depended on rallying Southerners against Southerners. Lincoln also knew that much about the prewar South invited a divide-and-conquer strategy.

Fault Lines in the Pre-Civil War South 2

The Old South! Those words call to mind cotton and slaves, masters and mansions, heat and humidity, plantations and lashes. A myth? Not wholly. *The* reality? Only in the southernmost Old South, and only during the final quarter of slavery's U.S. history.

During the eighteenth century, slavery's North American center lay hundreds of miles north of its future Lower South home base. The institution dominated the upper two-thirds of the South and peppered northern areas that would eventually contain only free laborers. Then at the end of the century, Eli Whitney and others perfected a cotton gin, and the land seemed to tilt toward the upstart Cotton Kingdom. Slaves drained north to south, with the institution eliminated from the North and diluted in the northernmost South. As the southernmost South belatedly became the Old South, *our* Old South, the northernmost South became ambiguously southern. That ambiguity created the potential, still latent in prewar times, for a war of Southerners against Southerners.

1

In the colonial New World, Europeans faced a non-European problem: too few laborers, too many resources.[1] Throughout Europe's colonies, seventeenth- and eighteenth-century capitalists used slavery to ease labor shortages. In 1790, future free labor states contained 10 percent of North American serviles. A little farther south, 69 percent of the thirteen colonies' slaves toiled in tobacco-dominated Virginia, North Carolina, Maryland, and Delaware. Deepest in North America, only 20 percent of U.S. serviles endured the South Carolina/Georgia rice-producing swamps. That sliver of land lay within thirty miles of the Atlantic coast. West of this first Lower South, only .5 percent of North American slaves labored, for the habitat was too steamy for tobacco, too cool for coffee, and too dry for rice. How could slavery thrive in North America's lush, empty tropics?

The cotton gin crowned King Cotton to preside over the answer. Soon King Sugar reigned over much of Louisiana. Lower South areas west of the Carolina/Georgia coastal rice belt soared from their .5 percent of North American slaves in 1790 to 56 percent in 1860. In those seventy years, the percentage of U.S. slaves in the rice swamps, usually too wet for cotton, plummeted from 20 percent to 2.5, while the figures in tobacco belts, too cool for cotton, plunged from 69 percent to 28 percent and in the North from 10 percent to zero.

A pivotal federal law helped channel the southward drain of black folk. In 1807, the U.S. Congress barred slave importations from overseas. Thereafter, King Cotton had to draw most of his serviles from more northern slave locales. Between 1790 and 1860, white owners dispatched some 750,000 slaves toward sugar- and especially cotton-growing tropics.

The slave drain left in its wake three mid-nineteenth-century southern zones, piled atop each other. Farthest south lay the system's new titans, the seven Lower South states. This most tropical North American area stretched westward from South Carolina, Georgia, and Florida on the Atlantic Ocean through Alabama and Mississippi to Louisiana and Texas across the Mississippi River. The Lower South, having contained 20.5 percent of U.S. slaves in 1790, possessed 58.5 percent in 1860. On the eve of the Civil War, when slaves made up 46.5 percent of its population, the

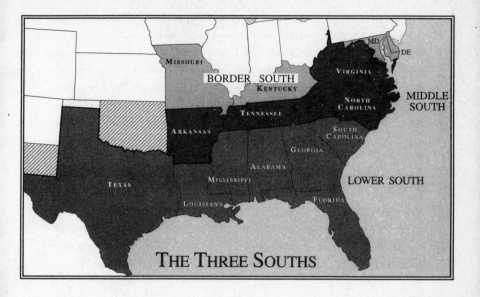

THE THREE SOUTHS

Lower South grew 85 percent of the South's cotton, 96 percent of its sugar, and 100 percent of its rice.

Farthest north in the South in 1860, bordering on free labor states, lay the newly attenuated top of the slave system, the four Border South states. This coolest tier of mid-nineteenth-century U.S. enslaved areas stretched westward from Delaware and Maryland on the Atlantic Ocean through Kentucky to Missouri across the Mississippi River. The Border South, having contained 19.9 percent of U.S. slaves in 1790, dropped to 11.3 percent in 1860. On the eve of the Civil War, when slaves made up only 12.7 percent of its population, the Border South grew almost none of the South's cotton, sugar, or rice.

Sandwiched between Lower and Border Souths, the four Middle South states stretched westward from Virginia and North Carolina on the Atlantic Ocean through Tennessee to Arkansas across the Mississippi River. The Middle South, having contained 59.6 percent of U.S. slaves in 1790, plunged to 30 percent in 1860. On the eve of the Civil War, when slaves made up 31.7 percent of its population, the Middle South grew almost none of the South's sugar and rice and only 15 percent of its cotton.

Not so much proportions of slaves as proportions of thickly enslaved neighborhoods distinguished these three tiers of slave states. Compared to the Middle and Border South, the Lower South contained many more black belt neighborhoods (locales with 20 percent or more of their population enslaved) and many fewer white belt neighborhoods (locales with 5 percent or fewer slaves). The Border South, while containing a large predominance of white belt neighborhoods, featured some significant black belts, just as the Middle South, while most dominated by black belts, contained some significant white belts. Silently, ceaselessly, like a glacier, the slave drain chiseled black belts so extensively into the southernmost South as to form the New World's mightiest slave empire—the only one that felt mighty enough to save slavery in a civil war. The glacial change also carved white belts so extensively into the northernmost South as to create one of the New World's most attenuated slavocracies—and one growing ever slacker in fighting the forces of attenuation.

2

Nothing was slack or attenuated about the brotherhood of whites in black belts.[2] In thickly enslaved areas, fancied racial dangers united white classes and sexes. Whites in black belts shared horror images about freed blacks as rioters, rapists, arsonists, and cannibals. These whites characteristically thought that using slavery to control alleged barbarians meant saving civilization.

Whites in black belts shared not only obsession with racial salvation but also involvement with slave control. Not husbands but wives usually directed house servants. Not planters but nonslaveholders, so-called overseers, usually directed plantation slaves. Not patriarchs but plebians numerically dominated neighborhood patrols. These mounted police punished blacks who left plantations without permission.

Whether poor whites lashed rich whites' supposedly unequal blacks as patrolmen or as overseers, slaveless plebians eased their own discomfort about inequality. American egalitarianism invites a nasty question: If all men are born equal, why am I less successful than you? A possible answer, less ability, corrodes self-esteem. Inequality especially distressed poor whites in black belts. Allegedly, only blacks could perform so-called nigger work under the brutal southern sun. White dirt farmers, however, sweated under the same sun, performed many so-called nigger tasks, and lived in shacks sometimes cruder than slaves' dwellings.

The sting intensified when indiscreet proslavery theorists declared that all inferiors, even white inferiors, needed a master. That nonracial haughtiness offended the nonslaveholding majority that could vote down pretentious squires. So wiser patriarchs declared that only blacks needed a master. With that more common racial proslavery argument, rich men raised poor men to equality in the brotherhood of white men, dedicated to keeping blacks unequal.

Economically no less than racially and psychologically, many black belt nonslaveholders prized black slavery. Only about one in three Lower South families owned slaves. Many black belt nonslaveholders, however, profitably served slaveholders, including overseers, lawyers, preachers, merchants, physicians, bankers, and artisans. Some poor whites in slaveholders' neighborhoods aspired to become slaveholders. Some rich squires gave aspiring yeomen small loans or aid in ginning and marketing a little cotton. Because of the omnipresence not only of slaveholders but also of would-be slaveholders, overseers for slaveholders, merchants for slaveholders, lawyers for slaveholders, doctors for slaveholders, preachers to slaveholders, borrowers from slaveholders, and users of slaveholders' cotton gins, most whites in black belt neighborhoods possessed an economic stake in the regime.

Impoverished black belt whites saw scant reason to assault the stakeholders. Some heretics claimed that slaveholders monopolized the lushest land, leaving poor men only scruffy plots. But grimy folk suspected that well-scrubbed squires would always snatch the gorgeous acres, whether tenants, hired hands, or slaves worked the dirt. Other heretics pointed out that white wage earners sometimes had to compete with despised slaves for menial jobs. But while white employees cursed slave competitors, free black competitors would double the curse. Thus in the late 1850s, white urban proletarians demanded not that slave competitors be freed but that free black competitors be enslaved. That lower-class demand did not provoke an upper-class shudder, not with many slaveholders wishing that free blacks could be enslaved or ousted.

Northern abolitionists provoked slaveholders to fury rather than shudder. Uniquely in the Americas, zealous crusaders labeled slaveholders as insufferable sinners. In almost pornographic diatribes, northern abolitionists excoriated masters for supposedly raping black "wenches," siring bastard offspring, and selling children from mothers, whoever was the father. Nonslaveholders, added abolitionists, served Satan by tolerating the monstrosity.

This diatribe assaulted Southerners' self-respect and sense of honor. Outraged squires responded with a ferocious defensiveness, also unique in New World slavery arguments. Uneasily unequal nonslaveholders shared slaveholders' outrage. They resented those who would raise lowly blacks to lowly whites' level.

This fury at condescending tormentors become an emotional wildfire. Its flames, fueled by shared economics, shared racism, and shared control of blacks, melted rich men and poor men into a revolution and an army. Why did most white Confederates in black belts bitterly fight Yankee intruders until the fighting became obviously hopeless? An observer of the prewar black belt would have found the question absurd.

3

In the vast southern white belt areas with few or no slaves, nonslaveholders felt less brotherhood with slaveholders.[3] The geographic point cannot be overemphasized. Before fault lines between nonslaveholders and slaveholders could open wide, physical separation of the classes usually had to compound class differences. Even when geographic spaces separated the classes, little prewar contention over slavery exploded. White belt folk usually remained neutral rather than hostile about far-off slaveholders, until the black belts' disunion obsessions threatened white belts' Unionist priorities.

A startling Slave South phenomenon encouraged diverging impulses: Many southern whites rarely saw a slave. In almost lily-white portions of the South, whites had little economic interest in slave ownership to protect, little prospect of free blacks to fear, no slaveholders to ask for a loan, no slaveholders' cotton gin to use, no slaveholders' product to market or lawsuits to settle or slaves to cure, no slaveholders' patrols to join or slave gangs to oversee or human property to aspire to own. It was almost like living in the North, with the important exception that the slavocracy lived closer.

Because of that relative proximity, border whites deplored national abolitionism. Most white belt Southerners, like most Northerners, harbored no love for blacks and little disposition to abolish the ruling American double standard: slavery for blacks, democracy for whites. White belt Southerners loved white men's Union. They scorned outside meddlers who might provoke that other, fanatical South into disunion.

Aside from shared outrage at holier-than-thou outsiders, southern white and black belts often seemed like severed realms. Mountains imposed the most visible barrier. Wherever the land heaved high, percentages of blacks usually drooped under 5 percent. Northern Alabama and Georgia, eastern Tennessee, and western Virginia contained especially widespread white belts. More often, heat and humidity invisibly cleaved Dixie, especially separating the steamy Lower South, with its predominant black belts, from the milder Border South, with its predominant white belts.

Within the South's northernmost states, the few black belts usually could be found in the southernmost areas. These atypical borderland plantation regions included one-fourth of Kentucky (especially the Bluegrass region, running southwest from Lexington in midstate to Bowling Green), one-fifth of Maryland (especially southern Maryland), and one-tenth of Missouri (especially the Missouri River/Mississippi River basins, running down the state's eastern and western borders and in a thin line across its center). In contrast, white belt areas controlled far more of the border states and consumed their northern halves.

At the South's northern extremities, the great border cities thrived: Baltimore, Louisville, and St. Louis. All three resembled northern more than Lower South cities. All contained few slaves, more free blacks, and many more foreign immigrants. All traded predominantly with the North. All developed Yankee-style factories and growth rates. All grew far larger than every southern city except New Orleans. All generated Yankee-style politics, often centered on disenfranchising immigrants rather than defending slavery. All these booming cities, surrounded by largely slaveless farmers, made the upper ninth of the South primarily an a-southern hinterland of the North.

Borderites seemed especially a-southern in their tolerance for softness on slavery, particularly when the softheart was a softspoken native rather than a belligerent Yankee. Private manumissions of slaves, having helped remove the institution from free labor states, had diluted border slavery too. In 1860, only 1.5 percent of Lower South blacks were freed. In contrast, 21.2 percent of Border South blacks lived as freedmen in 1860, including 92.5 percent of Delaware's blacks and 49 percent of Maryland's. Delaware, with only 1,798 slaves in a state population sixty-two times greater, remained scarcely a slave state. Maryland had become as much a free black as a slave state.

Borderites sometimes tolerated public discussion of antislavery ideas as well as private manumissions. South of the Border South, intolerant southern politics featured a defining contradiction. On the one hand, democracy for white males must be pristine, with no trace of dictatorship. On the other hand, white men's discussion of slavery must be dictatorially suppressed, with no republican procedures encouraging white heretics or black resisters. Antislavery advocates must be gagged in legislatures; their newspaper presses thrown in rivers; their pamphlets seized from the post office; their persons tarred, feathered, and expelled.[4]

Only once did Lower or Middle South states tolerate a full-scale democratic discussion of abolition. In 1831–32, after the Virginia slave insurrectionist Nat Turner brought off the largest U.S. slave revolt, for two weeks the Virginia legislature debated whether slavery should be abolished. The legislators' conclusion was a rather qualified no to antislavery. The Lower and Middle South's conclusion: This convulsive discussion must never be repeated.[5]

The Border South periodically did repeat the convulsion. Not that Border South discussion of slavery was exactly wide open. Cassius Clay, Kentucky's most successful heretic, suffered a mob that confiscated his printing press before he used his famed bowie knife to fight free of censorship. Partly as a result of Cassius Clay's brawls, debates on pushing slavery out of the border states transpired in Kentucky in 1849 (during the crafting of a new state constitution), in Missouri cities in the mid and later 1850s (during Kansas-Nebraska excitements), in Maryland in 1859-60 (amid proposals that free blacks be reenslaved), and frequently in Delaware. Always, border reformers proposed removal of blacks, either by dispatching freedmen to Africa or by selling slaves to Lower South customers.[6]

To hasten slave sales southward, some Kentucky and Missouri reactionary reformers proposed a delayed legislative edict, declaring slavery illegal in the state in five or ten years. Then border slaveowners would supposedly sell their investment at Lower South slave auctions before the day when the property could walk free in Kentucky or Missouri. The proposal displayed no sympathy for blacks, who would be enslaved down river. The proposition instead sought to make Border South neighborhoods into lily-white utopias. This glimpse of paradise, chauvinistic white style, offered borderites a boon unavailable in the Lower and Middle Souths: a seductive case for eliminating an institution that was slowly fading out of the least enslaved South.

That southern rarity, a politically auspicious case for pushing slaves out of a state, together with that other southern rarity, a relatively open opportunity to agitate for the heresy, handed border heretics their chance to attack orthodoxy the slow democratic way. These politicians still lacked that American mainstream necessity, connection to a national party. If northern politicians gave southern heretics patronage and an honored place inside a national party, heresy might take off.

Border reformers remained grounded in 1860. Cassius Clay won only 10 percent of his state's vote for governor. Frank Blair, Missouri's version of Cassius Clay, won St. Louis's congressional seat, then lost his bid for re-election. More comforting still for slowly dwindling border slaveholders, slaves' most open road to liberty, the one most capable of opening the way for white heretics, apparently could be closed—if Northerners could tolerate national arbitrary arrest and return of fugitive slaves.

4

Current conventional wisdom errs in calling slaves' counterculture back at the slave quarters their most successful resistance. The error does not lie in celebrating that counterculture. After three decades of masterful historical reconstructions, no American story seems more remarkable than the saga of a people exploited, lashed, and exhausted by day, yet coming back to each other at night to love, to create, and to build a redemptive world.

Resourceful slaves devised black ways of singing spirituals, telling tales, weaving baskets, formulating language, defining families, constructing theologies. With such achievements, blacks gained semi-autonomy, a modicum of self-respect, and endurance as a folk scarred but not destroyed.[7] By day, slaves also preserved a degree of self-esteem. Field hands somewhat undermined masters by pretending to be sick, pretending not to understand orders, spreading poison, burning barns, sowing crookedly, breaking tools.[8]

But slaves' important day-to-day sabotage and night-to-night counterculture could only make the exploitative system less damaging, more endurable. The most successful resistance to exploitation helps end the system. While slavery ended in a war between whites, fugitive slaves helped provoke that combat and helped turn it into an antislavery war. Those pivotal consequences of runaways' resistance have eluded superb historians only because their histories of slavery end in 1860, before Civil War fugitives' agency in emancipation became unmistakable and shattering.[9]

An individual who ran away may seem less shattering than a group of slaves who slit their masters' throats. In the Old South, however, whites annihilated slave insurrectionists every time, and almost every time before blacks killed a single white person. The faintest whiff (often a false whiff) of black uprising set off whites' murderous panics. The ensuing reigns of terror cut like scythes through the slave quarters. On scarcely a half dozen occasions during the century before the Civil War, a scant few dozen black rebels began slitting throats. The end result even then: far more blacks than whites were slaughtered.

Black insurrectionists faced double deterrence. On the one hand, violent black resistance fused a panicky white majority against the minority race. On the other hand, black insurrectionary planning enabled the consolidated white majority to divide and conquer the slave minority. To pull off insurrection, slave groups had to meet and solicit others to join. To abort such plotting, whites rewarded slaves who informed on rebels. A wary slave, when recruited by would-be rebels, could best win freedom not by joining but by ratting on freedom fighters.

In contrast to slave insurrectionists, a slave runaway could outplay whites in the divide-and-conquer game. When an individual slave ran away without informing others, no group could betray the resister. Since the individual fugitive resisted nonviolently, the runaway gave no cause for panicky whites to mass for slaughters in the slave quarters. Better still, some northern whites aided unarmed runaways.

Few Lower South slaves could reach such helpers. Potential runaways from the southernmost South knew that many miles, inhabited by many suspicious whites and guarded by many southern patrols, separated them from freedom's ground. The odds improved the farther north the potential fugitive lived. Up near the top of the Border South, potential fugitives saw better chances, in precisely the region of the Slave South where white heretics enjoyed better opportunities.

Of the more than 5,000 runaways a year who made it to the North, border slaves formed the vast majority, with Frederick Douglass the archetype. Douglass, a Maryland slave, first attempted to flee with several black compatriots. The group's plan failed when a supposed ally told the slaveowners about the impending flight. Subsequently, Douglass dashed for freedom the most productive way, all by himself. He had to overcome great perils, including patrolmen seeking to nab fugitives and bounty hunters paid to capture runaways. But he reached the North. There he used his prodigious talents as writer, speaker, and editor to publicize the fugitive as supreme freedom fighter.[10]

How could a freedom fighter be called supreme when he left afflicted slaves behind? Because Maryland's Douglass utilized slaves' most plausible way to undercut the slave system—in the Border South zone where runaways could best elude capture and could most undermine slavery's staying power. If border slaves' escapes to the North increased, prudent borderland capitalists would increase their slave sales to the Lower South. As border slavery diminished, already slack borderland commitments to the institution could grow slacker still. Then the Cassius Clays and Frank Blairs could better sell their proposal that border legislatures quicken the slave drain and thus produce a totally white population. In the face of slaves' most auspicious resistance in the most auspicious place for it, the more committed border slaveholders sought to toughen deterrence to the Frederick Douglasses.

5

Northern abolitionists described slaveholders' deterrence in a word: terror. According to Yankee crusaders, Southerners deterred disobedient slaves with lashes, in the manner of impersonal tyrants. Masters answered with their own one-word summary of their deterrence: paternalism. They claimed to cherish their "people" (their revealing word for slaves) not primarily as property, laborers, or investments but as familial servants. They claimed a parallel between directing black servants and raising white children. In both cases, they claimed to mix strictness and kindness in the manner of uplifting patriarchs. Did they use the lash? Of course, to correct both slaves and sons. Because they allegedly punished fairly, slaves supposedly consented to their paternalistic authority, in the manner of corrected sons. Slave consent, concluded patriarchs, yielded a familial friendship between master and man that Yankee fanatics could never fathom.[11]

Affection assuredly did abound between some masters and some house servants. Yet other aspects of the prewar South raised doubts about how thoroughly paternalism suffused master-slave relationships, especially relationships between owners and far-off field hands. Slaves who met supposedly paternalistic dictation with day-to-day petty sabotage did not seem to consent to paternalistic rule. Masters who met financial adversity by selling individual slaves for top dollar, sometimes breaking up black families, did not seem to treasure paternalism as their bottom line. Overseers who met slaves' misbehavior with forty-nine lashes, brutally administered, did not seem to be treating masters' slaves as family friends.

Whether impersonal terrorizing or paternalistic chastisement best characterized prewar masters' deterrence (the Civil War evidence would help answer that either/or), both conceptions shared the same error (an error impossible to make once analyses touch wartime slave resistance). Proponents and ridiculers of slaveholders' paternalism presumed that slaveholders alone deterred slaves. They missed runaways' great lesson: The Slave South's survival hinged on effective deterrence *between* as well as inside masters' private realms. Controlling slaves depended not only on masters, whether they were terrorizers or paternalists, but also on police power beyond the estate.

Slave runaways could easily sneak out their masters' gates. Plantation managers could not incessantly watch every black, every day and every night. Once beyond their owners' property, the fugitives' greatest problem became not the masters they had left behind but slave patrolmen ahead, farther ahead, yet farther ahead.[12] For the Slave South to deter its most potentially destructive slave resistance, potential fugitives had to dread coercion outside as well as inside their masters' estate. The history books, with their debate about paternalism inside the gates, miss that overriding truth. The wartime dissolution of slavery makes the truth inescapable.

Illinois' U.S. senator Stephen A. Douglas especially grasped the necessary white coerciveness beyond masters' acres. At Freeport, Illinois, in 1858, at a defining moment of the Lincoln-Douglas Debates, Abraham Lincoln asked how slavery could be abolished, if the Supreme Court declared abolition edicts unconstitutional. Douglas answered that a community could abolish slavery by passing no edict at all. Failure to establish police deterrence of fugitives accomplished something vital: It left coercive voids beyond slaveowners' gates. "Slavery cannot exist a day or an hour anywhere," climaxed Douglas, "unless it is supported by local police regulations."[13]

Slaveholder police regulations ended at the South's northern border. While a slave dash across the border to a free labor state required enormous will and courage, nearby exits enticed. If border slaves' sprints to the North increased, border slaveholders' sales to the South might multiply. Frank Blair's and Cassius Clay's credibility might then advance.

In 1850, realizing that fugitives might hasten the dilution of the borderland's incrementally diminishing institution, the border slaveholders who were more zealously proslavery counterattacked. They demanded that the federal government close the open border. With a new federal fugitive slave law, they would strengthen the transplantation deterrence to future Frederick Douglasses. They prevailed in Congress. They thereby helped push their beloved Union down their most dreaded path: the road to disunion.

6

The U.S. Constitution empowered Congress to pass a fugitive slave law. The Border South, however, needed not only a law but also law enforcers. Such creatures remained scarce. After American colonists' experience with and outrage at England's distant government, far-off bureaucrats seemed enemies of citizens' control and citizens' liberties. Thus, when Americans created their own government, they crafted a tiny federal apparatus with slim capacity to eradicate, regulate, or protect social institutions. In the early-nineteenth-century National Bank, for example, the national government appointed only one-fifth of the board of directors. Jacksonian banking reform replaced that small federal involvement with no involvement, depositing the government's gold and silver under the treasury building. The antibureaucratic animus meant no national economic regulators, no national police, no national security system, only a handful of clerks, not even a handful of secretaries. The post office became the biggest federal bureaucracy. Postmasters remained busy delivering the mails and running local politics. When Abraham Lincoln had to enforce his Emancipation Proclamation, he would find no nonmilitary bureaucrats to help.

Since slaveholders wanted no Great Emancipators, they usually considered no federal bureaucrats the right number. But no bureaucrats was the wrong number to police the border between North and South. To enforce its early fugitive slave laws, the federal government had to depend on state governments' bureaucrats. Northern state officials' capture of southern runaways worked tolerably well for decades. Then in the late 1830s, some northern states refused to provide the nation's slave capturers. In *Prigg v. Pennsylvania* (1842), the U.S. Supreme Court upheld states' right to refuse to help enforce federal laws. After the decision, a nation with scant bureaucrats could not enforce a law that closed border fugitives' gateways to the North.

In 1850, borderites in Congress, led by U.S. Senator James Mason of western Virginia, secured a new means of enforcement while still avoiding that dreaded permanent national bureaucracy. Mason's Fugitive Slave Law, passed as part of the Compromise of 1850, empowered a master seeking an alleged runaway to secure a northern commissioner to enforce the law this one time only. The one-case bureaucrat could force Yankee citizens to serve as one-case slave-nabbers. After the alleged fugitive had been captured, the commissioner alone tried the case, with no other judge, no jury, no right of appeal, no writ of habeas corpus, no defendants' right to call witnesses in their own behalf.

The new national law brought southern limits on white men's democracy to the North. Nationally as in the South, liberty for whites had to be curtailed, wherever danger to black slavery began. Draconic southern-style patrols became the federal device for deterring fugitives, with Northerners coerced into slave-catching and no democratic process protecting patrolmen's prey. Slaveholders here increased not only their coerciveness but also Yankees' discomfort. Few northern antiabolitionists enjoyed being dragooned into personally enslaving a fellow human.[14] Few northern detesters of blacks wished to have *their* white men's liberties curtailed, to keep blacks enchained.

Four years later, the Kansas-Nebraska Act increased northern distress about white liberty lost. Missouri's U.S. senator, David Atchison, leader of Missouri River slaveholders, began the 1854 controversy with his demand that Congress allow previously barred slaveholders to enter Kansas and Nebraska territories. Atchison sought slaveholder opportunity to cross over the Missouri border, secure a Kansas majority, and pass antifugitive edicts. Otherwise, warned Atchison, Missouri slaves would be the ones dashing over the border toward freedom in free soil Kansas. By thereby weakening Missouri slaveholders, fugitives would strengthen Missouri's heretics such as Frank Blair.[15]

After a complicated legislative process, involving more than Atchison's preoccupation with fugitives, Congress turned Atchison's remedy for Missouri slaveholders' exposure into the Kansas-Nebraska Act. Then Davy Atchison led his constituents over the Kansas border to vote for the first territorial legislators. Missouri's one-day Kansans won the election, controlled the Kansas territorial legislature, and passed the most draconian slave code in the Americas, making agitation for antislavery and aid to slave runaways illegal. In defense of these not-so-democratic Kansas edicts, secured by not-so-democratic one-day settlers, slaveholders called debate and majority decision on slavery, in the presence of slaves, not a democrat's right but an insurrectionist's madness and a thief's attempt to steal fugitive property. A rising northern Republican Party replied that to protect black slavery, slaveholders must not destroy white democrats' right to discuss and decide in open republican processes, whether on the hustings, in legislatures, or in civil courts.

Two regions, two labor systems, two conceptions of whether white men's democracy should be shuttered, whenever an opening for abolition intruded. The Fugitive Slave and Kansas Controversies, by bringing clashing conceptions of white men's democracy to the fore, pitched the nation toward a shattering secession crisis. While whites conducted these congressional controversies, blacks had precipitated the fugitive crises in the first place. The tritest and truest sentence about the road to disunion is that without fugitive slaves, there could have been no fugitive slave issue. Black runaways who supposedly freed only themselves in reality played divide and conquer—masterfully although unintentionally. They helped provoke angry congressional crises between northern and southern whites, leading to a slavery-ending Civil War.

A white men's dialectic intensified the fugitive slave controversies that black runaways first provoked. The more the slave drain made the Lower South a thicker black belt, the more the Border South became a thinner black belt, with slacker commitments to slavery. The more border slaveholders felt their hold weakening, the more they sought to strengthen their diluting control with national laws, true to southern white men's version of democracy but not to the northern variant. The more Northerners raged that Southerners' expanding defenses of black slavery enslaved the white republic, enslaved *them*, the more Middle and Lower South black belts raged at Yankee critics. This fury above and below the Border South left border folk caught in the middle—and, like fugitive slaves, perhaps in a position to determine the victor if a secession crisis yielded a civil war.

The Secession Crisis 3

In November 1860, the Republican Party's Abraham Lincoln won the national presidential election. Thereafter, one question predominated: Would the president-elect likely menace slavery inside southern states? Had the answer been clear, the post-election secession crisis would have taken a clear-cut form. If Lincoln had been indisputably an immediate menace, with obvious intention of imposing federal antislavery on sovereign states, the whole Slave South would have seceded, and long before the president-elect's March 4, 1861, inauguration. On the other hand, if Lincoln had clearly posed no threat to slaveholders, no southern state would have departed the Union.

So much for clarity and a united southern decision. The president-elect's antislavery position had always been guarded, politic. His ambiguity helped divide the southern house against itself throughout the secession crisis.

1

Guarded, politic, ambiguous—those Lincolnian mainstream virtues seemed intolerable vices to America's post-1830 antislavery extremists. On New

Year's Day, 1831, when William Lloyd Garrison first issued his abolitionist newspaper, *The Liberator*, he proclaimed that he would "not equivocate," that he would "not excuse," that he would "not retreat a single inch," and that he would "BE HEARD." Heard or not, he insisted until 1865 that abolishing America's worst sin trumped every other priority.

Some listeners rallied to Garrisonian priorities, including white women and free blacks, previous nonactors in American politics; rich Yankees such as Benjamin and Louis Tappan, who previously believed that prostitution was the intolerable sin; and eloquent revivalists such as Theodore Dwight Weld, previously a fanatic for improving human memory. These converts and more formed the American Antislavery Society in 1833. Their political cells across the northern countryside became local beehives, full of stinging antisouthern invective. They spread fury at slaveholders as American political rage had never before been advanced.

Then as the 1830s ended, so did the most radical abolitionists' advance. In 1840, support for Garrisonian extremism peaked at around 2 percent of the northern voting population. The other 98 percent of northern citizens considered immediate abolition too extreme to be American, too problack to be tolerable, too keen on seizing property to be capitalistic, and too antisouthern to be safe for the Union. Antiabolitionists preferred saving the Union, saving property values, saving white supremacy—and remembering that moderation alone would save the American mainstream way.

Twenty years before the Civil War, abolitionists needed a boost from some nonabolitionist source to capture the national mainstream. Their best boosters turned out to be their most livid opponents. An aggressively defensive slavocracy demanded that the white democratic process be shackled, lest blacks or whites be aroused. That insistence changed the issue. No longer did the national slavery debate focus sheerly on that unpopular radicalism, snapping black men's chains. Now debate swerved to that popular conservatism, preserving white men's liberties. Slaveholders thus helped create what abolitionists alone could not forge—a potentially victorious antisouthern political party.

Northerners invented two words to describe slaveholders' offensive-minded defense: Slave Power. The term alleged that slaveholders, to silence antislavery agitation, dictatorially suppressed white men's democratic rights. Northern critics pointed out that in a Southland supposedly based on pure democracy for whites and pure slavery for blacks, slaveholders undemocratically gagged white men's criticism of slavery. Beyond the South, southern politicians secured congressional gag rules in the mid-1830s, silencing discussion of antislavery petitions.

While national gag rules fell before northern attack in 1844, Southerners still sought to prevent white republican procedures from harming black slavery. In 1850, the Fugitive Slave Law established dubiously democratic procedures for capturing runaways in the North. In 1854, the Kansas-Nebraska Act enabled Missouri's one-day Kansans to establish dubiously democratic proslavery barricades in that territory. In 1856, in the symbolic climax of the Slave Power's tactics, South Carolina's Preston Brooks smashed Massachusetts's Charles Sumner unconscious to the U.S. Senate floor. Sumner's crime: declaring that Preston Brooks's cousin, South Carolina's U.S. senator Andrew P. Butler, "had chosen a mistress . . . chaste in his sight—I mean the harlot, slavery." Brooks's justification for closing debate inside democracy's open chamber: I will not debate slurs on my kinfolk. As the South Carolinian crashed his cane again and again against the Yankee debater's skull, the thuds epitomized an issue transformed from whether black Southerners should be freed to whether white Southerners could lash white Northerners into silence.[1]

In 1856, the new northern Republican Party almost won the presidency with an anti-Slave Power agenda. Republicans distinguished between antislavery radicalism and anti-Slave Power conservatism. They eschewed all proposals to impose abolition inside southern states. They embraced all efforts to stop the Slave Power from imposing minority law on northern majorities. They would allow the southern minority no more national proslavery laws. They would permit no further slaveholder expansion into national territories. They would subsequently hope that the nation's restriction of slavery to southern states would someday, somehow, lead to the institution's extinction.[2]

Abraham Lincoln perfectly represented a Republican Party full of soft somehows on extinction of slavery inside southern states but hard as nails on containing the Slave Power from spreading antimajoritarian governance beyond the South. No softness tempered Lincoln's or any Republicans' verbal antislavery fury. Early and often, the Illinois Republican insisted that slavery must "be treated as a *wrong*," for the institution perpetuated "the same tyrannical principle" as "the divine right of kings." Nor was Lincoln ambiguous about the central slavery issue of the 1850s, the expansion of slavery into new U.S. territories. Treating slavery "as a wrong," he continually reemphasized, meant making *"provision that it shall grow no larger."*[3]

By containing slaveholders from enlarging their terrain, Lincoln would place the institution "where the public mind will rest in the belief that it is in the course of ultimate extinction."[4] Still, whatever the public mind believed, how would containment lead to slavery's extinction in the fifteen states where the institution still existed? On that question, Lincoln, like his party, offered no answers. The president-elect saw no constitutional power for the U.S. government to force abolition on southern states. He expected that slavery might last a century. He hoped that freed blacks would be dispatched to Africa. But Southerners alone would have to decide about emancipation inside their states, after Northerners imprisoned slavery's moral horror inside the South.

With Republicans such as Lincoln silent on how imprisonment might lead to extinction, Southerners had to guess. They often guessed that although Republicans might allow caged Southerners to decide about slavery, those outside the cage might open up white men's democracy inside the prison. The Republican Party, having overturned unrepublican protections of slavery in the nation, might unleash republican debate against the institution in the South. If a national Republican administration showered patronage on Kentucky's Cassius Clay and Missouri's Frank Blair, the heretics might be transformed from gadflies into mainstream politicians. If freshly empowered southern critics attacked slavery from a position inside the national political establishment, they might win more Border South votes; more border slaves might run away; and more border slaveowners might sell out to the Lower South. If the beleaguered institution collapsed in the borderland and if free labor controlled all new states, Republicans could secure enough states to pass a constitutional amendment. Then the federal government could impose abolition on holdout slave states. Thus might the Lincolns begin to nudge slavery toward extinction just by distributing rewards of office inside southern areas slack in their commitment to the institution.

2

In their presidential election campaign in the fall of 1860, Republicans offered no evidence that they intended to transform border slackness into a southern antislavery movement. Republicans insisted only on slavery's containment. They demanded only the extinction of the Slave Power's grip on national politics, on northern whites. On that anti–Slave Power program (with much thundering against slavery's sins sweetening the northern political appeal), Lincoln swept to the presidency in November 1860. The question now became, would this anti–Slave Power hater of slavery become a menace to the institution inside southern states?

Southern disunionists preferred to dwell on more certain matters. They called Lincoln's antislavery insults bad enough. No honorable Southerner could tolerate the castigation. Some secessionists claimed that no institution could endure without expanding. Some ridiculed northern protestations about never interfering in the South. But disunionists also faced the immediate menace question squarely. They warned that Lincoln would immediately appoint border heretics to office. They claimed that he would but lightly enforce the fugitive slave law. They predicted that Republicans would abolish slavery in Washington, D.C., located uncomfortably close to southern Maryland's black belts. They prophesized that within a decade, slavery would wither away in Maryland and throughout the Border South. They calculated that within twenty-five years, the North and the liberated Border South would possess a three-fourths free labor state majority. Then would come the knockout punch, the antislavery constitutional amendment.[5]

In early 1861, for example, Georgia's Henry L. Benning told the Virginia state convention, called to consider secession, that Lincoln could immediately begin poisoning slavery. This former state Supreme Court jurist noted that "the North hates slavery." When haters can abolish the hated, they "will do it." The North could end supposedly hateful slavery by admitting only free labor states into the Union and by speeding up the process whereby "some of our own slave States are becoming free states already." Benning cited Maryland, Delaware, and "other States in the same [border] parallel." Because of close-by Yankee antislavery prejudices, "owners of slave property in these States have a presentiment that it is a doomed institution, and the instinct of self-interest impels them to get rid of" doomed property. Thus slave property will be sold "lower and lower, until it gets to the Cotton States—until it gets to the bottom." Benning feared "that the day is not distant when the Cotton States, as they are called, will be the only slave States." Then free labor states "will have the power to amend the Constitution, and say that slavery shall be abolished." If masters wait until then to secede, weakened rebels will "be hung for disobedience."[6]

Benning's speculation that Lincoln would immediately begin to fasten a hangman's noose around slaveholders remained only a guess. The huge majority of Southerners deplored the prospect of smashing their Union over a guess. They preferred to wait and see whether Lincoln would attack slavery inside the South. They pointed out that the new chief executive would control only the presidency, that Democrats would control Congress and the Supreme Court, that the president could enforce only laws that Congress passed and the Court upheld. The president-elect announced his intention of enforcing the Fugitive Slave Law. If Lincoln lied—if he failed to enforce slavery-protecting laws or if he sought to jam antislavery on southern states—*then* the South could secede. But why secede now, over the mere possibility of some overt antislavery act later?

That question initially appeased many Upper South slaveholders who would later become Confederate heroes. John Hunt Morgan of Kentucky, for example, would imminently emerge as Confederates' arch Border South raider. But on November 19, 1860, Morgan wrote that "the election is now over & Lincoln is certainly elected. . . . Both Congress & the Senate are Democratic, so he could do nothing even if he wished." Eight days later, Morgan again hoped that "our state will not . . . secede. Have no doubt but Lincoln will make a good president—at least we ought to give him a fair trial."[7]

Lincoln begged Southerners for a fair trial. True, he would ensure that the white majority, not the Slave Power minority, would rule the nation. True, he would forbid expansion of slavery onto national terrain. But he sought to guarantee, now and forever, that only Southerners could abolish slavery inside their states.

After Lincoln's election, congressional compromisers had introduced an unamendable constitutional amendment, forever banning the federal government from abolishing slavery within a state. The necessary two-thirds majority of Congress had passed this amendment and several states had swiftly ratified it before Lincoln spoke in its behalf. This proposed amendment, Lincoln noted in his inaugural address, declares "that the federal government shall never interfere with the domestic institutions of the States." Lincoln approved this "express, and irrevocable" language, for "I have no purpose, directly or indirectly, to interfere with the institution of slavery in the States where it exists. I believe I have no lawful right to do so, and I have no inclination to do so."[8]

"Never interfere," "no lawful right," "no inclination," not "directly or indirectly"—words could not further repudiate an assault on slavery inside the South. Nor could Lincoln further preclude Republicans' supposed plot to turn present containment into future emancipation by eventually plastering an antislavery constitutional amendment on intransigent slave states. I will not compromise on the extension of slavery or on the preservation of the Union, the new president in effect announced. I will, however, make the North's surrender on touching slavery inside southern states total, perpetual, irrevocable. Do I sound like an immediate menace or a Great Emancipator? The vast majority of southern voters did not think so.

3

Secessionists possessed a trump card to rout a southern majority deaf to Lincoln's alleged menace. According to the southern version of American republicanism, a majority of the people *in any state* could withdraw their consent to be governed. One majority in one slave state could force a secession crisis that a Southwide majority deplored. South Carolina had long aspired to be that state. As A. P. Aldrich, one of the most important South Carolina secessionists, exclaimed, "whoever waited for the common people when a great move was to be made—We must make the move and force them to follow."[9]

Aldrich and his compatriots saw a need to force even South Carolinians to follow. Secession in South Carolina required a two-thirds majority. In

1832–33 and again in 1850–51, disunionists had failed to persuade that large a majority of Carolinians. Secessionists did not wish to bet their 1860 revolution on persuasion alone. So when U.S. Senator James Hammond wrote a long public letter, seeking to persuade his state against secession, the Aldrich contingent suppressed it. Whenever hostility to secession surfaced, armed militiamen appeared in neighborhoods, calling dissent disloyal. Posterity cannot tell whether in a free and open democratic election, South Carolina secessionists would have secured their two-thirds majority. We know only that disunionists took no chances. On December 20, 1860, South Carolina's Aldrich followers swept their state out of the Union, in defiance (this we do know) of a large southern majority's unionism.[10]

South Carolinians thereby canceled other Southerners' debate on whether a revolution should be started. Now antisecessionists had to decide whether an accomplished revolution should be joined. South Carolina's neighbors could either stand with southern brothers or with Yankees insulters. After the disunion decision took this Carolina-altered form, disunionists secured 56 percent of the key vote in Georgia as well as 54 percent in Alabama and Louisiana. Elsewhere in the Lower South, South Carolina's precipitancy galvanized more comfortable disunion majorities. When 77 percent of Texas voters went for secession on February 23, 1861, the entire Lower South stood with South Carolina.[11]

But the eight Border and Middle South states (together called the Upper South) stood against the new Confederacy when Abraham Lincoln assumed the presidency. In the four Middle South states, only Arkansas and Virginia called a state convention to consider secession before the Civil War began. The Arkansas convention rejected disunion on a close thirty-nine to thirty-five vote in mid-March 1861. The Virginia convention concurred on a not-so-close vote of ninety to forty-five in early April. In February popular referendums on calling a convention, Tennessee voters shouted no, 69,675 to 57,798, and North Carolina voters whispered no, 47,323 to 46,672. If war began, the Lower South could hope for no more than a Middle South contingent of initially very reluctant Confederates.[12]

The Border South offered Confederates less hope. Above the Middle South, only Missouri called a state convention. In that conclave, Unionists outnumbered secessionists three to one. In the three other Border South states, only the Kentucky legislature even considered calling a convention before the Civil War, and the lower house rejected the idea by a three to two margin.[13] Thus as Abraham Lincoln began his presidency, two-thirds of southern whites remained rooted in the Union, at least until some outbreak of war forced them to decide whether to shoot Yankees or secessionists.

No shooting would begin unless Lincoln attempted to enforce federal laws or to protect federal property inside Confederate states.[14] Here Lincoln faced the prewar version of his midwar predicament as administrator of the Emancipation Proclamation. While no pre–twentieth-century president commanded many civilian administrators, the Civil War president commanded none in rebel-controlled areas. There, only federal soldiers could enforce federal laws and protect federal property. In March and April of 1861, Union troops protected only two Lower South sites: Fort Sumter outside Charleston, South Carolina, and Fort Pickens outside Pensacola, Florida. Neither fort contained sufficient troops or food. If Lincoln sent reinforcements, he might be seen as provoking a civil war. Upper South states, wishing to avoid that combat, might punish the precipitator for initiating the horror. Yet if the president ordered both forts evacuated, not one federal official would be left in the Confederacy to enforce federal law and thereby to demonstrate that election winners must govern.

Upper South leaders asked Lincoln to relinquish both indefensible forts peaceably. Then in time, the Lower South minority of Southerners might return to majoritarian Union. But Lincoln felt compelled to enforce majoritarian laws at least symbolically at Sumter or Pickens, lest he symbolically accept rebels' destruction of majority rule. The president also meant to avoid firing the first shot at Sumter or Pickens, lest he alienate the southern majority that clung to Union.

Lincoln faced trouble no matter who fired the first shot, for many Southerners would call any federal shot wrong. They believed that minorities could legitimately depart a majoritarian republic. Like American Revolutionaries (and like Confederate President Jefferson Davis in his inaugural address), they emphasized that the people of any state could withdraw their consent to be governed. So here was the (arguably unanswerable) question: When the minority exercises its right to withdraw consent and the majority exercises its right to rule, who is right?

Moderate Southerners saw virtue in both arguments. These men in the middle might blame the warrior who fired the first shot for turning a legitimate debate into an illegitimate war. In his inaugural address, Lincoln promised to fasten on the rebels "all the folly of being the beginners of a war," should war come. Five weeks later, President Lincoln moved to pin the folly on Confederates, if President Davis wanted to blast aside majority law.

In early April 1861, Lincoln wrote the South Carolina governor that he was sending ships to Fort Sumter. The ships would unload "provisions only," and no "men, arms, or ammunition," assuming that the "attempt be not resisted." Or as the president more graphically told Congress on July 4, 1861, he "expressly notified" Confederates that his naval expedition would only "give bread to the few brave and hungry men of the garrison."[15] Would rebels fire bullets against bread?

Confederate rulers saw no choice. The bread would sustain troops that by their very presence denied any right to withdraw consent to be governed. The South Carolina governor sped news of the coming expedition to Jefferson Davis in Montgomery, who rushed back orders to conquer the fort before Lincoln's bread-bearing expedition arrived. As first Confederate and then Union shots lit the sky above Fort Sumter, both sides endeavored to save their half of democratic theory. Just as Davis sought to show symbolically that consent to be governed could be withdrawn, so Lincoln sought to show symbolically that election winners must be obeyed.

To the men in the middle, now forced to decide which side best sustained democracy, the answer looked as uncertain as Lincoln's immediate menace to slavery. Again, the answer to so debatable a question hinged not on theoretical logic but on how deeply slavery had penetrated a given region. To the blackest belts, Davis seemed the supreme democrat, for a majority must never coerce a minority that withdrew its consent. To the whitest belts, Davis seemed democracy's destroyer, because he ordered the first shot and because a majority must enforce its laws.

In the Middle South, where black belts outnumbered white belts, the crucial facts seemed to be that Lincoln had sent the provoking ships and that he subsequently called up 75,000 troops to coerce provoked Confederates. In

May 1861, Virginia voters seceded by a six to one margin. The Arkansas convention concurred by a thirteen to one margin. The North Carolina convention agreed unanimously. In June, Tennessee voters followed by a two to one margin. Where only seven of the fifteen southern states (containing only 33 percent of southern whites) had left the Union after Lincoln's election, eleven southern states (containing 63 percent of southern whites) waved the Confederate flag after guns flared and Lincoln called out the militia.[16]

Even in the Middle South, however, two major white belt clusters of citizens voted against disunion. Both groups inhabited mountain habitats, akin to much of the Border South. Western Virginians favored Union, three to one, eastern Tennesseeans by over two to one. Here, Lincoln could hope for a war of Southerners against Southerners.[17]

The Border South offered richer hope. None came close to secession over Fort Sumter, just as none had come close to secession over Lincoln's alleged immediate menace. Few borderites saw themselves as subjects of an intolerable despot just because Lincoln had sent bread to hungry men stationed far from the Border South. Most raged at Davis for firing bullets against food. All hoped to stop the war. Their preferred strategy: neutrality. They would refuse to help either combatant. They would bar both sides' troops from crossing their neutral terrain. If both belligerents honored their neutral zone, neither could touch the other. Then neutrals might drag extremists back toward reconciling their differences with ballots instead of bullets.

part two

Southern White
Anti-Confederates

From Neutrality to Unionism 4

When President Lincoln recruited Southerners to help Northerners squelch the Confederacy, he had unyielding priorities: First go after whites; only then go after blacks. The first priority helped make Lincoln no Great Emancipator in the 1861–62 years. By rejecting federally imposed emancipation, the early Civil War president maneuvered to hold Border South neutrals in the Union and to lure Union supporters from the Confederacy's Middle South white belts. He succeeded on both scores. His double success with southern whites gave the Union greater manpower, a stronger economy, and a larger domain. These slave state resources boosted free labor states' capacity to shoulder the Union's heavier Civil War burden.[1]

1

As war began, Lincoln considered Border South neutrality as malignant as disunion. Yet Lincoln treated the malign with remarkable tact. Partly a border man himself (he had been born in Kentucky and had loved Henry Clay), he understood that if he governed with a light touch, border neutrals might tread the path back to the Union. But neutrality, Lincoln told Congress on July 4, 1861, must not lead to "disunion completed." If neutrals blocked Union or rebel forces from "passing one way . . . or the other, over their soil," the resulting "impassable wall" would secure the Confederacy's fondest dream, "disunion without a struggle." Neutrality thus equaled "treason."[2]

On April 19, 1861, a week after Confederates reduced Fort Sumter, neutrality's treasonous consequences endangered Lincoln himself.[3] Washington, D.C., lay across the Potomac River from Confederate Virginia. Since only a handful of northern troops guarded the capital, Abraham and Mary Todd Lincoln would have to flee if Virginians attacked. Northern reinforcements could reach Lincoln only through neutral Maryland, which wrapped around Washington from the north. The Baltimore railroad hub offered the best Yankee route through Maryland. In Baltimore, a traveler had to transfer railroads, each with its own station. Transfers between stations required passage through the city's streets, often plagued with rowdy gangs.

On April 19, 1861, some 700 members of the 6th Massachusetts Regiment disembarked at Baltimore's President Street Station, headed for Washington to protect the president. The train toward the capital left from the Camden Street Station. As horse-drawn cars bearing Lincoln's would-be saviors lumbered along Pratt Street, some civilians assaulted the "invaders" with shouts and stones. Then they heaved sand and anchors in front of the conveyances. The blockaded Yankee soldiers piled into the street and dashed toward the Camden Street Station. For a time, Mayor George William Brown raced ahead of them. Eventually, Police Marshal George Kane and a police line followed them. These protectors tried to deter the rowdies.

Rowdyism prevailed. Cobblestones pelted the Massachusetts troops. Bullets nicked them. Several soldiers fell. Compatriots fired at the trampling crowd. Baltimoreans' assaults continued as Massachusetts soldiers dashed, stopped, fired, dashed, stopped, fired. At last, the Camden Street haven loomed. After clambering aboard their Washington-bound train, troops fired from their windows. When their train rolled clear of the riot, nine soldiers and twelve civilians lay dead, casualties not of disunion but of neutrality.

Baltimore officials wanted no further slayings. The mayor and police board ordered Police Marshal George Kane to burn railroad bridges connecting Baltimore with the North. Policeman Kane gladly lit the pacifying torch. The telegraph wire, offering the best communication between the North and Washington, tumbled too.

The isolated president embraced the arriving Massachusetts volunteers. But 700 protectors would not suffice. Could more soldiers fight past Maryland's neutrals? A Pennsylvania regiment finessed the question; the corps turned and fled home. Their flight left Lincoln's new Washington home badly exposed. The lanky chief executive, shoulders slumped, lines already furrowing his long face above his new, straggly beard, looked even sadder than usual as he told his Massachusetts rescuers that no North existed. New York's regiments were a myth. "*You* are the only Northern realities."[4]

In the next couple of days, no further proof of northern reality reached Washington. Instead, Baltimore's police chief, mayor, and the president of the Baltimore and Ohio Railroad arrived at the White House. They lectured the president on how to enforce the laws. They demanded that northern troops march around, not through Baltimore, perhaps to catch a ride to Washington from Annapolis. Otherwise, Yankee "invaders" would provoke neutrals into becoming disunionists.

Lincoln could not fathom their logic. An "invasion" of Annapolis seemed as much an "invasion" of Maryland as an "invasion" of Baltimore. But maybe these neutrals understood something he missed. He would obey their orders on how to "invade" their state.

But neutrals must not touch his troops. "I have no desire to invade the South," he claimed, "but I must have troops to defend this Capital." My defenders must come over your territory. "Our men are not moles, and can't dig under the earth; they are not birds, and can't fly through the air." They could only "march across" Maryland, "and that they must do." Lincoln told his visitors to "go home" and "tell your people" to "keep your rowdies in Baltimore." Tell your nonrowdies that "if they will not attack us, we will not attack them."[5]

The Marylanders went home, told their people, and no more rowdies rioted. The nonrepetition of April 19 rowdyism showed where Baltimore really stood, which was hardly at the forefront of disunion. Slavery had long been slowly fading in Maryland, especially in northern Maryland and particularly in Baltimore. In 1860, slaves accounted for only 1 percent of 212,418 Baltimoreans. *Free* blacks outnumbered enslaved blacks eleven to one, and foreign immigrants outnumbered blacks two to one. Baltimore's predominantly free labor, heavily immigrant lower class resembled a Yankee city's proletariat. Also, far more Baltimore trade ran northward than southward.

Foreign intervention in Baltimoreans' affairs, not slavery or disunion, had long been the trigger that brought the city's rowdies out to riot. The so-called Know Nothing issues, centering on whether foreign immigrants should vote, had catapulted Baltimore to the forefront of northern-style urban disturbances in the 1850s.[6] When 700 soldiers from Massachusetts barreled into the metropolis on April 19, resentful natives considered the intruders another species of foreign meddler. To some of Baltimore's Democratic party politicians, especially those with Custom House patronage jobs, the Yankee presence also seemed the first unacceptable consequence of Republicans' triumph. The dispossessed politicos, some of them quite wealthy merchants, rallied some of their retainers, desperately poor Irishmen. Those foreign-born plebeians were the bane of the Know Nothings, also out to riot. A week into the Civil War, with so many different types of borderites aching to consider the war an anti-American mistake that must stay away from their neutral terrain, the mistake invaded Baltimore. The city's motley mob trampled all over the mistake and then with Yankee troops gone from center city, went back to trading with the North.

After Lincoln diverted troops around the Baltimore hotspot, the state's cool was like ice. By April 23, General Benjamin F. Butler (another Massachusetts man) had secured Annapolis. From this Union sanctuary, Washington-bound troops could bypass Baltimore via the Annapolis and Elkridge Railroad's branch lines to the capital. In a foretaste of the railroad wizardry that would overcome Confederate saboteurs, Butler's tinkerers also propped railroad bridges back up before Yankees arrived to cross them. Two weeks after Lincoln declared the Massachusetts 6th Regiment the only northern reality, so many Yankee soldiers paraded toward the White House that the morose president could not keep the smile off his face.

Frowning Maryland neutrals had one whimper left. On April 26, the state's General Assembly met in a special session in Frederick. (The state's capital, Annapolis, now General Butler's headquarters, hardly seemed the place to determine whether to declare war on Yankee troops!) Lincoln feared that Maryland's lawmakers would call a secession convention and assault federal law enforcers. Still, Lincoln decided to let the neutrals meet. Perhaps their action would be "lawful, and peaceful." If they instead declared war, then his men could slam them into prison.[7]

This position showed more shrewd Lincoln forbearance; more allowing traitors to hurt themselves by firing the first shot; and more inviting Marylanders to discover for themselves that neutrals they could not be and South Carolinians they were not. Legislators met. They called Ben Butler a beast. They proclaimed Lincoln a despot. They termed federal coercion a monster. But they raised no army. They called no secession convention. They fired nothing but insults at Abraham Lincoln.

So the president moved more troops into Maryland—to fortify passage around Baltimore, then to fortify Baltimore itself. Baltimoreans heaved no more cobblestones at "invaders." When fewer than three dozen legislators threatened to reconsider secession later in the year, Lincoln took no chances. He jailed verbal disunionists until after the state's voters resoundingly elected Unionists, ending even verbiage about secession.[8]

The endgame stimulated a myth with a charmed life among Maryland's southern gentry—that only Lincoln's arbitrary arrests kept this state from joining the Confederacy. Few Civil War myths have less reality.[9] We know how disunionist Civil War communities acted under the thumb of federal power. They endlessly rioted. They continually sabotaged. They relentlessly staged guerrilla warfare. Maryland had its day of guerrilla-like upheaval on April 19, then little unrest. Her April legislators, enraged by the first 700 Massachusetts invaders, had deliberately met far from Ben Butler's second wave of invaders. The representatives had still forfeited their chance to call a secession convention.

Their constituents subsequently forfeited their chance to continue the April 19 guerrilla war. Marylanders' true vote for unionism came not after Lincoln jailed a few loose talkers but after most citizens recognized that this war was theirs too. Then they voted with their feet to join either Union or Confederate armies. White Marylanders chose the Union army by almost a two to one margin.[10]

Lincoln had feared the reverse choice. Yet he had wisely little disrupted Marylanders' decision. His heavy-handed interference came only after they had unofficially chosen. As his earlier light-handed touch revealed, too many Maryland communities, and especially Baltimore, had too few slaves to choose disunion, once white belts reluctantly realized that neutrality was an illusion.

2

The neutrality illusion flickered longer in Kentucky.[11] Farther west, no emergency akin to the threatened loss of Washington, D.C., immediately required Yankee troops to cross neutrals' terrain. But eventually, Union soldiers had to march across Kentucky no less than across Maryland. From Kentucky, prime railroad and river routes aimed straight at the Confederate heartland. The state could thus help fulfill border neutrals' ambition: prevent the two nations' warriors from touching each other and thus force the two nations' politicians to reconstruct the Union.

Kentucky was the most enslaved and thus the most divided Border South state. Delaware's population contained only 1 percent slaves; West Virginia less than 4 percent; Missouri less than 10 percent; and Maryland less than 13 percent, with almost as many free blacks as slaves. Kentucky, in contrast, contained almost 20 percent slaves, less than 1 percent free blacks, and more slaveholders than any southern state except Georgia and Virginia. The state's Bluegrass black belt dominated an unusually large (for the Border South) minority of counties and contained an unusual amount (for the Border South) of Confederate partisans. Still, the Bluegrass consumed less terrain than the thicker, more populated white belts above and below the slaveholders' zone. Most Kentuckians saw themselves as Ohio Valley rather than Mississippi River folk; they traded far more with the North.

For so divided a state, neutrality seemed mandatory. On May 16, a month after Fort Sumter surrendered, the Kentucky House voted sixty-nine to twenty-six to "take no part in the civil war, now being waged, except as mediators and friends to the belligerent parties," and only from a "position of strict neutrality." The state senate concurred, thirteen to nine.[12] Governor Beriah Magoffin then issued a ferocious Neutrality

Proclamation, warning that death awaited belligerents who defied Kentucky's decision. Hundreds of Kentuckians enrolled in the "State Guard" to back up the governor's threat. From Maryland's verbal neutrality, Kentucky had progressed to armed neutrality.

Once again, Lincoln stayed away from the hotspot, in hopes that time and the impossibility of permanent neutrality would bring a border state to its largely unionist senses. Lincoln also hoped that if federal forces had the good sense to stay out, Confederate forces would have the poor sense to move in first. That scenario would repeat the Confederacy's first shot at Fort Sumter, so upsetting to borderites.

Lincoln's light touch again proved deft. As spring gave way to summer and then fall, Kentuckians increasingly saw for themselves that neutrality's time was passing. Federal and Confederate forces both massed on Kentucky's border. Both impatiently eyed Kentucky's gates to the Confederacy. Both sides recruited Kentuckians, who spilled over their state's borders to join Confederate or Union armies. Fewer Kentuckians enlisted to fight with the State Guard for the chimera of permanent neutrality.

While Kentuckians served both armies, Union recruiters fared far better. So did unionist politicians. In June, Unionists captured five of six U.S. Congress seats. In August, Unionists captured three of every four state legislative seats. Then an indiscreet first shot by the Confederates finalized the secessionists' rout, just as Lincoln had hoped. On September 4, 1861, Confederate general Leonidas Polk penetrated Kentucky. Two days later, Union commander Ulysses S. Grant entered, claiming he came to save Kentucky from rebel invaders.

That undiscourageable neutralist, Governor Beriah Magoffin, insisted that both belligerents withdraw from neutral terrain. The two houses of the Kentucky legislature instead insisted, in lopsided votes of sixty-eight to twenty-nine and twenty-five to eight, that only the first invader must withdraw. The Confederates' Polk defiantly stayed. The Union's Grant graciously accepted Kentucky's invitation to remain. A month later, Magoffin resigned. Kentucky's gateways to the western Confederacy were becoming as safe as Maryland's passageways to Washington, D.C.

But if the state of Kentucky was now safe for the Union, many Kentuckians' allegiances wavered. The so-called Jackson Purchase area of extreme southwestern Kentucky claimed a right to secede from the state and join the Confederacy (which welcomed the Kentucky fraction as its twelfth state). Kentucky's most famous Civil War military unit, the Orphans Brigade, orphaned itself from the home state to fight for the rebels. Twice as many white Kentuckians went the other way, toward Union soldiering. Yet 71 percent of Kentucky's white males of fighting age settled for inertia, a Southwide record for disinclination to fight for either army.[13]

That inertia, the natural successor to neutrality, especially undercut the Confederacy. Rebels desperately needed Kentucky combat troops, or at least guerrillas, to harass the Union soldiers who enjoyed a safe haven in the border's largest slaveholder state. But such slackness worried Lincoln too, for individuals' noncommitment could easily turn into hostility, especially if the Union did menace Kentucky's continued inclination to retain slavery. Until he had these Kentuckians under control, the Kentucky-born politician in the White House would be no Great Emancipator.

3

Unionists more swiftly dominated the three less enslaved Border South states.[14] Delaware, with 1,798 slaves, never needed a Union army to police its 587 slaveholders (out of 90,589 whites). Alone in the borderland, Delaware sent volunteers (albeit unofficially) when Lincoln called for his first 75,000 soldiers. Missouri, with under 10 percent of its population enslaved, and the new state of West Virginia, containing under 5 percent slaves, both decided for the Union as quickly as Delaware. In both Missouri and West Virginia, however, federal armies had to save unionist majorities' government of choice from a ferocious secessionist minority.

The Missouri minority's proslavery ferocity had first gained national notoriety after the Kansas-Nebraska Act of 1854. Then western Missouri slaveholders had deployed guerrilla tactics across their Missouri River border, in Bleeding Kansas. When the Civil War began, they moved their terrorizing inside Missouri. These proslavery intransigents, the most fiery in the border, faced a sea of Missouri white belts, especially eastward in the state, where St. Louis and Jefferson City contained the South's most powerful antislavery warriors.

Proslavery guerrillas' advantage in badly torn Missouri: the state's governor, Clairborne (Fox) Jackson, was one of their own. Their disadvantage:

the first skirmish occurred on enemy terrain. Missouri's Civil War commenced in antislavery-inclined St. Louis, for there sat the first prize, the U.S. arsenal, containing 60,000 firearms. Hoping somehow to prevail in this overwhelmingly unionist city, the governor trained around 900 troops at "Fort Jackson," a scarcely fortified grassland in the St. Louis suburbs.

Fox Jackson's thin ranks and motley fort proved no match for St. Louis's heavily unionist citizenry and the federal commander in St. Louis, Captain Nathaniel Lyon. This red-haired Connecticut Yankee first moved with Lincoln-like deftness to seize the U.S. arsenal's contents. One dark night, his men secreted most of the shoulder arms across the Mississippi River to Illinois. In the light of day, unfortunately, Lyon showed non-Lincolnian indiscretion. He ordered Fort Jackson reduced and its captives marched through St. Louis, with Germans guarding the rebels. When a Connecticut redhead and German immigrants unnecessarily made fools of southern boys, tension momentarily exploded in St. Louis, akin to Baltimore's momentary riot of April 19. Neither border city harbored much sympathy for slavery or rebels. Yet neither wanted New England foreigners parading through their streets.

The city's anti-Lyon riot did Fox Jackson little good. Fleeing St. Louis, the governor next met his Connecticut tormentor in the state's capital, Jefferson City. This antislavery-inclined town also wished no part of the pro-Confederate governor. Jackson and his few troops again fled, this time to friendly terrain, Missouri's western black belt. The retreat left Nathaniel Lyon in control of the rest of the state. The Missouri state convention, called to consider secession, rejected disunion, defrocked Fox Jackson, and declared itself, rather illegally, not a temporary convention but Missouri's permanent wartime government.

Fox Jackson and his henchmen answered with tactics as irregular as the convention's. They conducted bitter guerrilla raids against Unionists, in and out of Missouri. No Civil War area endured worse terrorizing. Some afflicted Missourians blamed the disorder on the indiscreet Lyon, and the redhead certainly did not calm an explosive situation. But take away the tempestuous Connecticut Yankee and no becalmed Missouri would have emerged. No Border South state had such entrenched antislavery and proslavery regions or such experience with the nighttime raid and the daytime ambush. While the state's thick white belts gave Unionists control over the state, its embittered black belt offered guerrillas their launching pad against the Federals' dominion.

In western Virginia, guerrillas lacked any black belt launching pad but possessed something better: an ideal topography for irregular warriors. Mountainous nooks and crannies abounded in western Virginia. From any of them, armed bushwackers might spring. Guerrilla raiders, however, had little chance to control a largely unionist populace, especially in the northernmost half of western Virginia, so long as federal soldiers provided defense against ambushes. Almost immediately after Virginia seceded from the Union, West Virginia seceded from Virginia, and Lincoln sent in troops to consolidate West Virginians' two to one support for the Union. Union and Confederate troops first clashed at Philippi, located up in north-central West Virginia, on June 3, 1861. The Confederates retreated so fast that the skirmish became derisively known as the "Philippi Races." Further Union victories impelled the Confederacy to speed Robert E. Lee to western Virginia.

Not even Virginia's future hero could save this Virginia situation. As in Missouri, federal troops could rout scant Confederate troops, so long as showdowns occurred in white belt areas where citizens overwhelmingly favored the Union. Like Fox Jackson, Lee swiftly realized that he could fight more successfully on friendlier terrain.

He fled from western Virginia's white belts to eastern Virginia's black belts in September 1861, almost on the same day that his future rival, Ulysses S. Grant, entered Kentucky. While Lee's flight and Grant's entrance prefigured things to come, the hero of the western Virginia campaign was none other than that future Union antihero, George McClellan. In contrast to his later infamous caution, McClellan here boldly secured avenues toward the Lower Shenandoah Valley, future breadbasket of Lee's Virginia army, just as the always bold Grant secured avenues toward the Mississippi Valley's heartland. Their September 1861 triumphs completed the Union's unbroken wall of Border South states, from the Atlantic Ocean past the Mississippi River.

Only a combination of some federal force and much Unionist sentiment could have swiftly erected that wall. If Lincoln's army had imposed no coercive force, fanatically determined secessionist troops might have intimidated Unionist majorities. But if Missouri's and West Virginia's citizens had been largely rabid Confederates, the relatively small federal armies would have been overwhelmed. The Federals' Nathaniel Lyon commanded all of 6,500 troops when he routed Missouri Governor Fox Jackson at "Fort" Jackson. In truly secessionist Upper South areas such as western Tennessee or eastern Virginia, Lyon's slim corps would have been crushed. In the huge border areas where slavery barely existed, a little federal repression sufficed to keep most borderites on their chosen, illusory course: keep hoping that other peoples' nasty war would fade away.

4

Some call the Civil War the "War between the States." But civil war also occurred within states, especially within border states, for numerous individuals went against their state. While Robert E. Lee resigned from the Union army to go with his state, into the Confederacy, famous Kentucky warriors such as John Hunt Morgan, Simon Buckner, and Albert Sidney Johnston rejected their state to enter Confederate ranks. Among white soldiers in Missouri, Maryland, and Kentucky, almost one of every three sought to conquer their own state.

Borderites often opposed their fathers as well as their states. In Frankfort, Kentucky, an observer reported that almost every family is "divided in sentiment," a domestically "awful state of things." Many fathers "are strong Unionists and the sons are off *fighting* for the South."[15] Four of Henry Clay's grandsons wore Confederate gray and three Union blue. John J. Crittenden's sons included a Confederate and a Union general. Among warring Breckinridges, a Yankee brother imprisoned his Confederate sibling.

To prevent borderites from serving as Confederate troops or guerrillas, Union troops had to guard borderland winnings. Forty thousand Union soldiers patrolled West Virginia alone. Thus while the borderite majority had voluntarily moved from neutrality to unionism, the dissenting minority had to be coerced into involuntary submission.

According to a favorite antebellum American theory, whenever a liberating army appeared inside a tyrant's coerced domain, the tyrant's subjects would rise up against the despot. The Civil War age called such revolution-inviting invaders "filibusterers." The term confuses latter-day readers, who use "filibusterer" to denote obstructionists who seek to talk a legislative measure to death. In the 1850s, "filibusterers" instead denoted organized private swashbuckling crews who inspired tyranny's victims to free themselves. Usually, these filibusterers encouraged Latin American revolutions. Famous 1850s filibusterers included Narciso Lopez and John Quitman, who unsuccessfully sought a Cuban revolution, and William Walker, who provoked a briefly successful Nicaragua uprising and died before an even more successful firing squad.

The most notorious antebellum filibusterer sought an insurrection at home. In 1859, New England's John Brown and his private troops seized the U.S. arsenal in western Virginia's Harpers Ferry. Brown then invited black slaves to seize their liberty. Scarce a slave volunteered for freedom, partly because few slaves inhabited this mountainous white belt area. The question swiftly became not whether the filibusterer could liberate blacks but which white would imprison him. Robert E. Lee, commanding the U.S. Marines, seized the honor.

The filibusterer phenomenon, albeit with public rather than private troops, resurfaced during the Civil War. Union armies scored monumental successes with filibustering tactics, encouraging especially southern blacks, but also southern whites, to rise against the Confederacy. In contrast, not one Confederate filibustering effort yielded uprisings against Federals' control of southern areas. Confederates were not worse filibusterers. Rather, Unionists possessed better targets. Many more black and white inhabitants of Confederate-held terrain wished to be liberated than did southern folk in Union-held terrain.

1862 became the big year for Confederates to try to liberate alleged southern victims of Yankee coercion. Confederate president Jefferson Davis became the biggest southern dreamer about filibustering. After his armies marched inside Border South territory, Davis predicted, popular revolutions would make the Confederacy twelve, thirteen, or fourteen states strong. (Not even Davis dreamed of securing Delaware!) Davis instructed his commanders to penetrate Kentucky and Maryland, then announce that they entered as liberators. Generals should beseech borderland Southerners to rise up and free the motherland from Yankee tyrants.[16]

In September 1862, Robert E. Lee tested Davis's chimera in Maryland. Lee harbored less hope of filibustering success. While the Virginia general wished to "afford the people . . . an opportunity of liberating themselves" from the "foreign yoke," he did not anticipate any "general rising of the people in our behalf."[17]

He anticipated correctly. As Lee headed up to Frederick, then to Harpers Ferry, then to the Antietam battlefield, his aide called on Marylanders "to rise at once in arms, and strike for liberty and right."[18] But western Maryland contained few slaveholders and no end of Unionists. Most pro-Confederate Marylanders lived southward, near the Chesapeake Bay, with George McClellan's federal army separating them from the liberator. More misguided still, Lee sought a popular revolution in John Brown's old locale. Just as there had been too few slaves to sustain the antislavery revolutionary, so there were too few masters to mass behind a slaveholders' army. A hundred or so western Marylanders, not many thousands, joined Lee the liberator.

A month later, Braxton Bragg tried to liberate Kentucky. Word had come back from Kentucky's great Confederate raider, Lexington's John Hunt Morgan, that the Bluegrass was ripe for filibustering. Kentucky's delegates to the Confederate Congress seconded Morgan's opinion. They urged Davis to advance into Kentucky and secure "the large proportion of the young men [who] will at once join our army."[19]

In September 1862, General Bragg raced from Tennessee toward Louisville with 30,000 troops. Rebels brought wagonloads of rifles, to arm whites who rose up for liberty. "Kentuckians!" the liberator proclaimed, "I have entered your state with the Confederate Army of the West and offer you the opportunity to free yourself from the tyranny of a despotic ruler." Bragg showed his liberating priorities by suddenly veering from his path toward undefended, extremely important Louisville, to celebrate filibustering in the state capital, otherwise unimportant Frankfort. Here in an elaborate ceremony on October 4, he installed Richard Hawes as the supposed official governor of Kentucky. Then he called on Kentuckians to rally behind their liberating governor.

Bragg's rally for liberty spared Louisville. Union general Don Carlos Buell had charged up from Tennessee, chasing the rebel general. When Bragg veered off to Frankfort to play inaugurate-the-governor, Buell won the race to Louisville. Braxton Bragg settled for joining forces with Confederate general Kirby Smith, who used his 10,000 men to capture Lexington.

Smith and Bragg together commanded 40,000 men. Don Carlos Buell, marching down on them from Louisville, commanded almost 60,000 Union troops. The numbers weighed against the Confederates unless filibustering triumphed. If tens of thousands of Kentuckians thrilled to the Bragg-Smith liberators and the Richard Hawes inaugural, Kentucky might be captured.

This time the borderland crisis occurred in an area seemingly ripe for filibustering. The drama took place not in the Baltimore of April 19, 1861, with 1 percent slaves, or in the antislavery-inclined St. Louis environs, where Nathaniel Lyon had effortlessly reduced "Fort" Jackson, or in the Harpers Ferry area, where John Brown had found scarcely a slave nor Robert E. Lee many slaveholders. Bragg and Smith had instead pierced the heavily enslaved Bluegrass region. Woodford County, lying on Kirby Smith's path between Lexington and Frankfort, contained 52 percent slaves, the highest percentage in Kentucky and the third highest in the Border South.

But John Hunt Morgan had badly miscalculated his home terrain's pro-Confederate potential. Braxton Bragg needed tens of thousands of recruits. Instead, several hundred Kentuckians straggled forth before portions of Bragg's and Buell's armies almost accidentally ran into each other at Perryville on October 8, 1862. There occurred Kentucky's most famous Civil War battle.

This indecisive encounter was no major battle by Robert E. Lee's standards, with fewer than 5,000 casualties on each side. But for Confederate filibustering, the stalemate at Perryville was the decisive combat. The thwarted Bragg drew back to Tennessee with the wagonloads of rifles mostly still in their packing cases. Bragg's retreat resembled Lee's scrambles back to Virginia, first from West Virginia and then from Maryland. Jefferson Davis's dream of adding the Border South to the Confederacy was as dead as the corpses littering the field at Perryville.

Filibustering fantasies remained alive only on the Union side by 1863. Lincoln long dreamed of arousing eastern Tennesseeans to revolt against the Confederacy. Unlike Davis, Lincoln eyed realistic filibustering targets, for in November 1861 eastern Tennesseeans rose *before* filibusterers were supposed to arrive. Alas, no Union filibusterers appeared, and Confederates wreaked retribution.

Eastern Tennessee fell into frightful guerrilla disorder until late 1863, when Union armies at last arrived in the Tennessee mountains. Then the people again rose up, awarding their liberators with almost 30,000 Union soldiers. After that filibustering victory, the Union possessed the Upper

South's largest white belts, from Delaware through Maryland, West Virginia, Kentucky, and Missouri and on down to eastern Tennessee. The consequences profoundly undercut the Confederate war effort.[20]

5

Civil War troop numbers, while notoriously inaccurate, suffice to show that southern white anti-Confederates seriously compromised Confederate military manpower.[21] Of the approximately 3,000,000 Civil War troops, about 900,000, almost all white, fought for the Confederacy. While almost 37 percent of slave state whites lived in the borderland, the Border South supplied only around 10 percent of the Confederacy's soldiers. If the border states had contributed 37 percent instead of 10 percent of Confederate fighting personnel, rebel ranks would have increased by another 250,000 men.

Instead, 200,000 border whites joined the Union army, compared to but 90,000 borderites in the Confederate army. Another 100,000 Middle South whites enlisted in Union ranks. Those 300,000 southern white Unionist sharpshooters replaced every Union fatality in the first two years of the war. The Confederacy's 1861–62 replacements, in contrast, ate deeply into the dwindling remainder of rebel white noncombatants. The Confederacy had to adopt a controversial draft of white men a year before the Union faced the necessity.

The border's pro-Union allegiances crippled the Confederacy even more seriously in the economic realm. While the Border South contained an impressive 37 percent of Slave South whites, it harbored a more impressive 50 percent of southern urbanization and industrialization. In 1860, the three largest Border South cities, Baltimore, St. Louis, and Louisville, contained more inhabitants than the fourteen largest Confederate cities. By gaining the border, the rebel nation would have doubled its factory capacity and bridged its most crippling industrial gap: the capacity to make and repair ships and railroads.

Baltimore makes the point all by itself, for railroads had created this city's wild growth almost all by themselves.[22] Flour processing and shipbuilding had helped fuel the city's 1840–60 boom. The Baltimore and Ohio Railroad, however, had primarily elevated Baltimore into the heady status of America's third largest metropolis in 1860, behind only greater New York (including

Brooklyn) and Philadelphia. (Baltimore was 25 percent larger than New Orleans, the Confederacy's biggest city.) Other Atlantic Coast urban centers—New York, Boston, Philadelphia—skimmed more profits from railroad trade and from railroad financing. But Baltimore developed more extensive factories to fashion railroad tracks, trestles, bridges, cars, and locomotives. Baltimore needed more such infrastructure than its Atlantic Coast rivals, for the city had to conquer more miles and tougher geographic obstacles, particularly the western Virginia mountains, to create its railway to the West.

Baltimore's railroad industries especially thrived in the Baltimore and Ohio Railroad shops around Mount Clare. In this sooty city within a city, the South's densest center of employment, the Baltimore and Ohio Railroad manufactured parts for stations, tracks, and bridges hundreds of miles west. Baltimore's specialized shops fashioned car wheels, car axles, car bodies, spark catchers, trestles, tracks, especially locomotives. The Baltimore and Ohio also became the prime customer for shops that turned out advanced factory tools. Denmead and Murray and Hazelhurst, for example, supplied castings for Abbott's rolling mill, which supplied plates for the Monumental Locomotive Works, which used engines crafted by Bartlett-Hayward. Between 1848 and 1852, interlocking Baltimore and Ohio shops built not only 200 locomotives but also sixty bridges to span western Virginia rivers and mountains. Other Baltimore shops fashioned steamships, railroad stations, and engine houses.

The Confederacy desperately needed this beehive of tools and skills for crafting iron behemoths. Alone in the South, Baltimore had the capital, expertise, and tooling to remake the southern rails as fast as they wore out (or were blown up). So too, alone in the South, Baltimore had the resources to create ironclad vessels up to Yankee standards. Instead, this pivotal slaveholding city boosted the Union's towering advantage.

The city became the Civil War hospital for Yankee railroads. Outside the Mount Clare shops, millions of pounds of iron railroad debris were piled as high as the factories, ready to be melted into iron sheets again, then refashioned to remake the latest exploded railroad bridge or ripped-up railroad track or expired locomotive. The Baltimore and Ohio bridge at Harpers Ferry, for example, five times demolished by guerrilla warriors, was five times operative again within a few weeks. Because of Baltimore's shops, the Baltimore and Ohio constantly functioned as the main east-west supply line for Union armies.

In contrast, under the crushing Civil War tasks of moving gigantic quantities of food, troops, and military equipment, Confederate railroads succumbed faster than Confederate troops. By midwar, an aid to the Confederacy's western commander lamented that "locomotives had not been repaired for six months, and many of them lay disabled." The colonel knew "not one place in the South where a driving-wheel can be made, and not one where a whole locomotive can be constructed."[23]

The colonel erred. Such a place thrived in the South. It just was not in the Confederacy. Without Baltimore to serve as Confederate railroad hospital, rebel generals increasingly could not move men and supplies swiftly from theater to theater. Nor could Lower South farms sufficiently feed troops who fought in the Middle South. Nor could the Confederacy compete with Union ironclads. (Baltimore shops plated the *Monitor* rather than the *Merrimack/Virginia!*)

Just as Baltimore, with its 212,418 inhabitants, dominated the Border South's eastern trade, so the border's second largest city, St. Louis, with 160,773 residents, mastered the western borderland's commerce. This metropolis of the Upper Mississippi contained four times more people than the Confederacy's second largest city, Richmond. But once again, not so much numbers of urbanites as the nature of their industrial output compromised the Confederacy. While Richmond contained the Tredegar Iron Works, the Confederacy's greatest source of finished iron, St. Louis factories transformed finished iron into paralyzing warships. Would-be conquerors of western rivers needed ironclad, steam-driven vessels. St. Louis gave the Union that gift, and no Confederate city could match it.

In August 1861, James B. Eads, owner of a St. Louis ship construction business, agreed to construct seven ironclad gunboats, designed by a naval architect named Samuel Pook. Pook's design and Eads's construction yielded a weird craft that looked like a turtle ("Pook's Turtles" they were dubbed). These flat-bottomed, paddle-wheel-driven vessels, perfect for shallow interior southern rivers, carried thirteen guns poking through a turtle-like shell of 2.5-inch iron armor. Pook's Turtles cost $89,000 each. Eight hundred St. Louis construction workers, laboring in nearly all the city's large machine shops and foundries, crafted the necessary twenty-one steam engines and thirty-five steam boilers in a few months in late 1861. The St. Louis firm of Harrison, Chouteau, and Valle rolled most of the armor plating. The resulting gunboats exemplified how the South's most advanced cities helped fashion a more advanced Union military machine.[24]

Still, the Border South's greatest boon to the Union involved not troop strength, not economic strength, but strategic position. This border contribution initially became obvious in that first Civil War crisis, over Washington, D.C. Had Maryland seceded, the District of Columbia would have been at the Confederates' mercy. Lincoln and his government would have had to flee beyond Maryland terrain, to sanctuary in Philadelphia or New York. So too, if the Border South had been passionately pro-Confederate, Jefferson Davis's nation would have sprawled up to the Ohio River, one of the world's most natural barriers to defend. South of the Ohio, the West Virginia mountains, a natural area for guerrilla warfare, would have been equally difficult for the Federals to subdue if most residents had been zealous Confederates. The Union had enough trouble pacifying the guerrilla-prone area when only a fraction of West Virginians swore allegiance to the Confederacy. After subduing the Ohio River environs and West Virginia mountains, Union armies would have had to conquer the entire Border South tier of states, just to reach the strategic position where they in fact began the Civil War.

Instead, Maryland ultimately gave Union soldiers a safe avenue toward protecting the president in Washington. The Ohio River became an unhindered highway for the Union's western troops. The West Virginia mountain passes and rivers provided an only somewhat troubled Union route toward Virginia's Shenandoah Valley, breadbasket for Robert E. Lee's Virginia army. The Baltimore and Ohio Railroad became a fine supply line for the Union's western invaders. The invaders enjoyed sanctuary inside the upper third of the South, as they prepared to subdue the lower two-thirds of slave labor states. Their invasion began not on the Pennsylvania-Ohio borders but below Maryland's boundary, inside Virginia, and below Kentucky's boundary, inside Tennessee. By compromising the Confederacy's manpower, economy, and especially strategic position, the borderland's unionism climactically yielded an early military turning point, one that gave the Federals an enormous headstart on their eventual anaconda strategy before the worst Civil War fighting had even begun.

The Jackpot 5

C ould the Union have secured a turning
point as early as the *ninth* month of the
Civil War?! The initial Civil War stalemate,
after all, supposedly lasted for several interminable years. That myth, based
on a misleading stress on the eastern theater of war, flourished long before
the present appetite for visual images. But Civil War photographs have
strengthened the misconception. Most photographers snapped pictures in
the East. For more than three years, as that photographic record reveals, the
Confederacy's and Union's eastern armies fought indecisively between
Richmond and Washington.

In the western theater, however, the war took an early decisive turn, one
that ultimately turned around the eastern theater. Film could seldom capture the western breakthrough, not with most photographers clicking shut-
ters hundreds of miles eastward. Nor could a critical cause of the turning
point be photographed, for no skin deep picture could expose the hearts
and minds of borderland whites. Words alone can demonstrate that the
Union's western armies exploited the borderland's home-front attitudes at a

pivotal military point of contact. By taking brilliant advantage of all the ways southern white anti-Confederates weakened the Confederacy, a previously underrated Union general, Ulysses S. Grant, captured two previously underappreciated rebel forts, Tennessee's Forts Henry and Donelson, and proceeded to collect an early military jackpot.[1]

1

Initially, Grant secured not a jackpot but a (then-assumed) lesser prize. In September 1861, first Confederate and subsequently Union generals captured Kentucky's gateways to the western Confederacy. The first violator of Kentucky's neutrality, the Confederates' Leonidas Polk, seized the (then-thought) first prize. Polk secured Columbus, Kentucky's highest bluff over the preeminent Mississippi River. Two weeks later, Confederates added the supposed second prize, Bowling Green, Kentucky's predominant railroad crossing. There, tracks between Louisville and Nashville crossed tracks between Memphis and Louisville.

Grant entered Kentucky a critical two days after Leonidas Polk, claiming that he came to repulse the invader rather than to violate Kentucky's neutrality. Grant settled for the supposed third-best Kentucky headquarters, Paducah and nearby Smithland. At these two Kentucky locales, the northward-flowing Tennessee and Cumberland Rivers join the Ohio River (which a few miles further, flows into the Mississippi River). From Paducah and Smithland, with ironclad river gunboats at his disposal, Grant controlled Kentucky's so-called twin rivers section. The Tennessee and Cumberland run like twins, almost parallel to each other and seldom more than a dozen miles apart, throughout their Kentucky journey up toward Paducah/Smithland and their separate mergers with the Ohio.

Prior to their twinned travel northward, the widely separated streams of the Tennessee and Cumberland more resemble a divorced couple. The Cumberland, pride of northern Tennessee, arises east of Nashville. It flows past that capital city and continues westward before it swerves north, to parallel the Tennessee River. In contrast, the Tennessee, pride of southern Tennessee, arises east of Knoxville. It flows westward, past Knoxville, Chat-

The Theater Commanders

Confederate General Albert Sidney Johnston. Courtesy of the U. S. Army Military History Institute.

Union General Henry Halleck. Courtesy of the U. S. Army Military History Institute.

tanooga, and northern Alabama before it turns northward, dozens of miles south of its belated twin's northward swerve.

In the summer of 1861, Confederates began twin fortifications about eleven miles apart in northwestern Tennessee, slightly north of the spot where the rivers become twins and slightly south of the Kentucky border. Between Paducah and northern Alabama, Fort Henry alone guarded the Tennessee River. Between Smithland and Nashville, Fort Donelson alone guarded the Cumberland.

These defensive installations remained half developed, for Confederates expected a Union attack elsewhere. Gideon Pillow, the most important Tennessee general during the forts' preparation stages, saw "no present danger on [the] Tennessee River—nothing of military importance to be gained by ascending [the] Tennessee River."[2] Since Tennessee's senior general saw slim importance in his state's sketchy Tennessee River fort, Kentucky's senior Confederate general saw scant reason to dispatch scarce troops from the Bluegrass. Albert Sidney Johnston, back home in Kentucky after long years of military service elsewhere, presided as overall commander of Confederates' western theater of war.[3] Soon after settling back in his ancestral state, Johnston realized that he possessed too few troops to guard all Kentucky's gates to the Confederacy. The western commander begged the Confederacy's commander in chief, his friend President Jefferson Davis, to send Easterners to save the West. Davis answered that he had no Easterners to send. Johnston would have to guess where the Union would assault the rebels' western heartland.

The Kentuckian guessed Bowling Green, where he established his command post. In Louisville, straight up the Louisville and Nashville Railroad from Bowling Green, Don Carlos Buell prepared a 50,000 man Union army. Buell intended, Johnston conceived, to press down on Bowling Green, capture the vital railroad crossing, then march down on Nashville. Johnston trained around 40,000 troops to block Buell in Bowling Green.

As for Ulysses S. Grant's approximately 15,000 man Union army, the Paducah/Smithland position offered two options. Grant could steam down the rivers of first importance, the Ohio and then the Mississippi, or up the rivers of second importance, the Tennessee and Cumberland. Johnston guessed that Grant would go first class. So the Kentuckian allotted around 20,000 troops to Leonidas Polk, guarding the bluff at Columbus, Kentucky, above the Mississippi River. Johnston sent only a few thousand leftover troops to Forts Henry and Donelson, in case Grant would again settle for twin river conquests.

By leaving Tennessee's twin river forts exposed to Grant, Johnston committed a crucial error. Ironically, one of the Civil War era's highest virtues, loyalty to one's state, furthered Johnston's mistake. This Kentuckian loved his ancestral terrain and thought of it as southern. In his Bowling Green base of operations, most inhabitants, atypically pro-Confederate Kentuckians, told Johnston that Kentucky would come up southern unless Johnston deserted it. Why would a native son desert Kentucky, when the home state guarded railroad and river gates to Tennessee? Why indeed would a Kentuckian postpone the perfection of his state's defenses for even a day, just to visit two Tennessee forts that Tennesseans called militarily of no present consequence? "The Government of the United States," Johnston privately explained in October 1861, "fully appreciating the vast resources . . . of Kentucky, will make its greatest efforts here. . . . If we could wrest this rich fringe from his grasp, the war could be . . . speedily decided upon our own terms."[4]

Yet Johnston's biggest problem was not his Kentucky cultural conditioning but his paltry share of Kentucky's resources. By the end of the Civil War, about 25,000 of Kentucky's white men of fighting age fought for the Confederacy, 50,000 for the Union, and 187,000 for neither side.[5] Those figures placed Kentucky last among southern states in percentage of whites who fought for the Confederacy and first in percentage of whites who fought for no one.

In early 1862, Kentucky's normal slackness in pro-Confederate (or pro-Union) commitment reached abnormal proportions, at the worst moment for Sidney Johnston and the Confederacy. Ahead loomed Kentucky slaveholders' most important military confrontation. Yet only two of Sidney Johnston's thirty-five infantry regiments (less than 6 percent) came from the state he was defending. Ulysses S. Grant commanded as many Kentucky infantry regiments, Leonidas Polk only half as many, and Don Carlos Buell fourteen times more, while at least 75 percent of Kentucky's white men of fighting age sat out this fight.[6] By choosing to concentrate troops in two Kentucky positions rather than in two Tennessee forts, Johnston chose his poison like a true-blue Kentuckian. But no healthy choices existed, not after so many Kentuckians opposed or ignored the Confederacy's pivotal stand in Kentucky.

The more Grant and a dozen other Union strategists studied Sidney Johnston's deployment of troops, the more the twin river forts attracted them. With help from steam-driven naval vessels, Grant's 15,000 troops could travel southward from Paducah and Smithland, up river and down continent, to reduce the twin river forts. After the easy conquests, Grant could move on the Tennessee and Cumberland Rivers unopposed, then land below Sidney Johnston at Bowling Green and/or Leonidas Polk at Columbus. After Don Carlos Buell brought 50,000 men down from Louisville, Confederates would be flattened between the two Union armies.

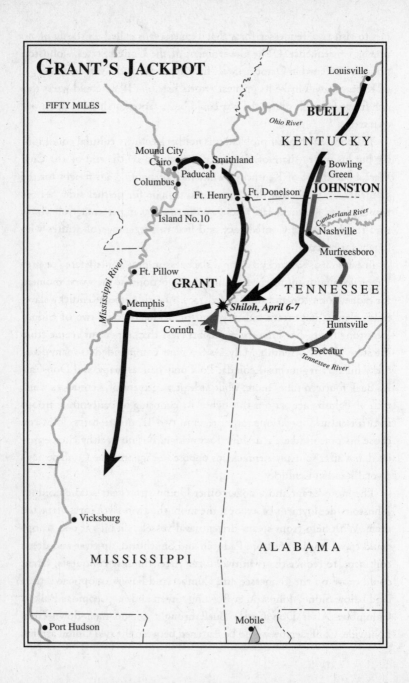

GRANT'S JACKPOT

FIFTY MILES

Louisville

BUELL

Ohio River

KENTUCKY

Mound City
Cairo   Smithland
         Paducah   Bowling
Columbus   Green
              Ft. Henry   Ft. Donelson   JOHNSTON

Island No.10   *Cumberland River*
                              Nashville

Ft. Pillow   Murfreesboro

GRANT   TENNESSEE

Memphis   Shiloh, April 6-7
                                    Huntsville
         Corinth
                                    Decatur
Mississippi River   *Tennessee River*

Vicksburg

                              ALABAMA

MISSISSIPPI

Port Hudson   Mobile

Here Grant glimpsed the mother of all "turning" tactics.[7] This favorite Civil War battlefield strategy called for a surprise attack on the weak point of a troop deployment (usually a flank). If the attackers broke through or around the defenders' line, the victors should turn, to wither the losers from behind (hence "turning the flank"). The victims would be trapped between front and rear fire.

Turning tactics resembled, but also differed from, siege tactics. Both sought to avoid headlong charges against rifles. Both moved *around* rather than *through* defenders. But the siege strategy called for continuing to move around and around, never charging, instead forcing defenders to charge or suffer strangling encirclement. In contrast, the turning strategy called for an offensive charge after defenders' weak point had been exposed.

Most often, turning tactics triumphed when heavier battalions outflanked undermanned lines. But to score an upset, an undermanned army could mass a high percentage of its troops against a low percentage of the stronger army's soldiers. As always in the Civil War, the stronger side would win, if it was sufficiently stronger and if its leader maximally capitalized on the strength. The wily fox, however, could outmaneuver a sleepy lion.

Grant, a wily lion, faced in Sidney Johnston a fox asleep to the danger. The Union general would apply the "turning" strategy, usually reserved for single battlefields, to an entire theater of war. Grant would attack Johnston's weak spot, the twin river forts, then turn behind Johnston's strongholds, Bowling Green and Columbus, thus providing the anvil for Don Carlos Buell's hammer. Or to put it the critical way, turning/sieging tactics, when applied to the stretched-out Johnston's most undermanned position, would take maximum advantage of what Kentucky's slack version of southernness had *not* given to poor Sidney Johnston.

Grant usually thought on a smaller scale. He was a field general, plotting the picky details to achieve the limited objective of conquering two forts. But the larger tactic of turning Johnston's whole theater of war occupied the background of his thought and the foreground of his superior, Henry Halleck's, mentality. Halleck, however, mulled over competing grand strategies. To concentrate on the twin river forts, Grant first had to persuade Halleck.

Preparation would fortify persuasion. If Grant's army collected more resources, the twin rivers strategy would seem more auspicious. In the fall of

1861, Grant embraced the perfect moment to stockpile war material. On both Union and Confederate sides, men brooded over the lesson of the first real Civil War battle, the affair at Bull Run on July 21, 1861. Union spectators had flocked to that northern Virginia battlefield, carrying picnic baskets. They had expected to watch a little bloodshed, enjoy a little snack, and cheer the home team when the rebels retreated. Instead, after much bloodshed, the Confederates' charge sent Union troops reeling in panicky retreat, almost trampling the picnickers. Then came the customary result of Civil War charges: not a surrender but a pause. Exhausted winners had too little left to pursue exhausted losers.

After Bull Run, picnickers and newspaper readers suspected that a Civil War surrender would not come easily, swiftly, or almost bloodlessly. Yet few soldiers had the equipment or training for lengthy combat. As generals and their suppliers scurried to prepare for an unexpected longer nightmare, most guns remained eerily silent throughout that fall and early winter of 1861–62.

During this ideal quiet time for Civil War preparation, Grant and his colleague Buell camped in ideal Kentucky sanctuaries to exploit Border South attitudes. While Grant in his Paducah/Smithland safe harbor stood a third of the way into the Slave South, Buell in his Louisville refuge could safely stride almost as far southward before facing Albert Sidney Johnston's guns. While Buell up in northern Kentucky recruited many more Kentuckians, Grant down in southwestern Kentucky added Kentucky and Missouri regiments. While Grant benefited from St. Louis's manufacture of Pook's Turtles, those steam-driven ironclads perfect for a watery invasion up the Tennessee and Cumberland Rivers, Buell benefited from Louisville's bulging warehouses, ripe to equip a landed push down the Louisville and Nashville Railroad. Border South Unionism added not only men and equipment but also transportation to Buell's and Grant's advantages. Thanks to the Baltimore and Ohio Railroad and the Ohio River, Yankee troops and equipment flowed effortlessly to Louisville, Paducah, and Smithland.

Kentuckians contributed most to the Union's interval of preparation by what they did *not* do, namely, disrupt either Grant's or Buell's sanctuary to receive supplies. Federal soldiers sat quietly in Paducah, Smithland, and Louisville, loading up to conquer slave states below, and almost no Kentucky guerrillas bothered them as they fattened. By lacking the zeal to harass

Yankees who would subdue slaveholders, Kentuckians vindicated what more zealous prewar Southerners had long worried about: The most northern third of the South might become fatally indifferent to Lower South proslavery preoccupations.

In late January 1862, Grant, now brimming with Border South and northern resources as well as with an idea, begged Henry Halleck for permission to attack the Tennessee River's Fort Henry. Flag Officer Andrew H. Foote, Grant's naval partner in the Paducah/Smithland preparations, also beseeched Halleck to focus on Fort Henry. Halleck liked and trusted the older, ultra-cautious, and teetotaling naval officer more than the brash, young (and occasionally inebriated) Grant. But Old Brains, as contemporaries called Halleck, still wanted to think about competing grand strategies. He told Grant and Foote to wait. The partners insisted on action. Simultaneously, President Lincoln demanded that Old Brains stop thinking and start attacking.

Halleck and many other Union strategists had for weeks considered the twin rivers probably the best place to attack. So Grant and Foote were pressuring their superior toward Old Brains' own widely accepted idea. On January 30, 1862, Halleck sent Grant permission to assault Fort Henry. When the telegram arrived, Grant's soldiers cheered. Their leader, tongue in cheek, ordered them to hush, lest they alert Leonidas Polk in Columbus.

2

Grant and Flag Officer Foote planned a coordinated army and navy surprise attack on Fort Henry. With his 15,000 soldiers, Grant would ride Foote's transports southward from Paducah, up the Tennessee River to landing points close to the fort. Then the army would march around and behind, to assault the sorry installation from its nonriver sides. At the hour when Grant expected to launch his land-based fireworks, Foote's "Western Flotilla" would assault from the river. This first Civil War siege might swiftly yield surrender. Then on to besiege Donelson.

But nature can delay the swiftest general. On invasion eve, February 5, 1862, rains came down torrentially. The next day, at the appointed high noon hour for the naval/infantry rendezvous, Grant's 15,000 men, unbeknown to Andrew Foote, struggled knee deep in mud, hours from Fort Henry. So when Foote's Western Flotilla attacked, its gunboats struck alone.

Yet the rains helped the navy as much as the downpour delayed the army. The Tennessee River rose on February 6, carrying federal keels above the triggers for Confederate "Polar Bears" (torpedoes fastened to the river bottom). The rising river also flooded out Fort Henry's lower section. With Polar Bears hibernating and only half a fort operative, the Union's four Pook's Turtles and three timberclads, lined with thick oak planks, reduced Fort Henry in eighty minutes. Never would the border's contribution to the Union gunboat advantage be more overwhelming. Indeed, Foote's St. Louis-built gunboats overwhelmed Fort Henry too swiftly, for Grant's mud-soaked infantry slogged in 120 minutes too late to complete the siege. So Fort Henry's evacuees escaped to Fort Donelson.

The Union navy celebrated by sending Lieutenant Commander Seth L. Phelps and three timberclads up the Tennessee River on a joyride of destruction, all the way to northern Alabama.[8] Phelps's mischief makers burned a critical railroad bridge, captured an important semi-ironclad steamboat and two smaller steamers, influenced the rebels to destroy three other steamers, and prepared to torch the vital Florence/Tuscumbia bridge over the Tennessee River. But before Union sailors could strike the match, Cotton South gentlemen begged Phelps for mercy. Would their unopposed conqueror spare their economic lifeline, spare their wives and daughters?

Phelps complied. The defeated gentry's contriteness encouraged him. Cheers for Union invaders, cascading from the river banks, moved him. By playing the merciful victor, he would appease the enemy, end the war, and achieve reunion. His was the chivalry of the pre–Bull Run days, when leaders such as Winfield Scott prayed that a little bloodshed would suffice. Phelps's nation would have to transcend his soft war mercy, even though his holiday breeze up the Tennessee River seemed to demonstrate that hard war could be mercifully avoided.

Henry Halleck, delighted to control the Tennessee River, ordered Grant to forget for a moment about attacking the Cumberland River and Fort Donelson. But Grant meant to claim the second fort before Confederates could regroup. Once Union soldiers possessed Fort Donelson, Nashville

The Fate of the Gunboats

Pook's Turtles' triumph at Fort Henry.   Courtesy of the U. S. Naval Academy,
Beverley R. Robinson Collection.

The deterring snow and cannon at Fort Donelson.   Courtesy of Eastern
National, Fort Washington, Pennsylvania, photograph by James P. Bagsby.

would be theirs too. Then Johnston in Bowling Green would be pinned between Buell in Louisville and Grant in Tennessee's capital city.

Once again, Grant demanded that Halleck let him loose for a kill. Once again, Old Brains reluctantly complied. For the first and not the last time, the impatient Grant had cut short the Civil War's customary pauses between attacks. Fort Henry's conqueror meant to own Fort Donelson in a day and Nashville in another.

3

The conquests took slightly longer. Fort Donelson, though no Gilbraltar, was hardly as pathetic as Fort Henry. Donelson had been built not down on a flood plain but up on a 100-foot hill. Compared to Fort Henry, the higher facility also sported more finished walls, twice the heavy guns, and six times more defenders. Albert Sidney Johnston, suddenly aware of mortal peril, had sent 15,000 of his Bowling Green troops to fortify the approximately 5,000 at Fort Donelson (most of them evacuees from Fort Henry). Although Johnston rushed many men to Fort Donelson, he probably only hoped to delay the fort's demise until his other Bowling Green troops could retreat to Nashville. So hints his cryptic, defeatist orders to his commander of Fort Donelson's reinforcements: "If you lose the fort, bring your troops to Nashville if possible." [9]

Grant marched his 15,000 troops the eleven miles from Fort Henry to Fort Donelson on a balmy February 12, a week after his soggy advance on Fort Henry. The sun-drenched paraders conceived that their mission had become a cakewalk. They sang. They danced. They shucked heavy northern clothing. Some military bureaucrat, they chortled, must have confused the Sunny South with the North Pole.

The discarded winter wear reemphasized the critical point. The Union's larger share of Border South resources killed not one Confederate soldier, unless Union soldiers utilized their advantage. After the first indecisive day of fighting at Fort Donelson, Grant's men learned that lesson the painful way. On the night of February 13, 1862, the soldiers could scarcely believe they had discarded warm clothing on their romp from Fort Henry. Down from inky skies came icy rain, then hail, then three inches of snow, then a howling wind, making the 12° temperature feel like -12°.

When the sun at last hovered over an icy terrain, the half-frozen troops caught a warming sight. Andrew Foote's Western Flotilla steamed into view, ready to celebrate St. Valentine's Day. The sailors meant to light the leaden skies with fireworks, as they had at Fort Henry. Maybe they could even beat their record by reducing Fort Donelson in less than eighty minutes.

This St. Valentine's Day, however, would be no day for record triumphs, at least not for young romantics aboard Foote's gunboats. The overconfident naval captain ordered his semi-repaired ironclads and timberclads too close to Fort Donelson. The consequence, like the infantry's discarded clothing, showed that superior resources win wars only when the superiority is properly deployed. As Foote commanded from the pilot house of the ironclad *St. Louis*, a Confederate ball ripped the ship's iron plate. One iron scrap sliced Foote's leg, another his arm. His wounded craft spun downstream, back toward Smithland, with other punctured iron turtles spinning alongside, until sailors could tie up the stricken vessels along the shore.

Only one sight cheered the appalled Union soldiers. The navy had convoyed 10,000 land reinforcements before it steamed too close to enemy fire. At Donelson for the first time, Grant possessed a numerical advantage, approximately 25,000 to 20,000 Confederates. That five to four margin, far slimmer than the two to one advantage customarily required for successful sieges, hardly necessitated the panic inside Fort Donelson, especially not on a day when Confederates had won an encouraging naval victory.

But rebels huddled inside the besieged fort exaggerated Grant's manpower and feared that Foote's river monsters would quickly return. (The pierced turtles would indeed have returned, but not quickly!) Confederates also believed that Buell's 50,000 would march down to complete an overwhelming siege, if necessary. Here, Johnston's men exaggerated their mortal danger not at all. Buell and Grant together had the two to one manpower advantage to strangle the rebels in Fort Donelson, assuming that the Union generals used their advantage skillfully. Winds screeched, the cold numbed, and underequipped Confederates had no warm clothes to throw away.

It seemed time to remember that Sidney Johnston had *not* ordered a fight to the death. It also seemed time to take to heart Johnston's command: "If you lose the fort, bring your troops to Nashville if possible." During a council of war on that evening after St. Valentine's Day, disputatious Confederate generals in Fort Donelson at last agreed to ambush Grant's right flank at dawn. Assaulters who broke through Grant's siege would turn away from Fort Donelson, toward safer and warmer days in Nashville.

When dawn came and hopeful escapees slammed into the Federals' flank, Confederates enjoyed one unexpected advantage. Grant, expecting no assault, had ridden away on horseback to consult the battered Foote aboard one of the flotilla's wounded turtles. As Grant, dismayed by the damage aboard ship, stepped back on land, a horseman raced up with more dismaying news. The rebel surprise attack (until this instant a surprise to Grant) had driven Grant's right flank back a mile.

While Grant galloped toward imagined catastrophe, General Lewis Wallace of Indiana partly repaired the siege. Grant had told subordinates to stay put until he returned. Wallace in the center, hearing the thunder on the right, instead moved his troops over and slowed the rebel advance.

Before hearing about Wallace's salutary insubordination, Grant found his former West Point cadet commander, General Charles Ferguson Smith, sitting under a tree, staying put as ordered. The ex-student ordered his ex-commander to be up and charging: "You must take Fort Donelson." The subordinate dutifully replied, "I will do it."[10] General Smith did his part. He menaced his troops with his sword, demanding that the youths cease retreating. His soldiers turned around and attacked. The Confederates fell back, wavered, consulted, and then slipped back into Fort Donelson.

After Grant found Smith and Smith's men found their nerve and the rebels found themselves trapped again in freezing Fort Donelson, only one question remained: Which general and his troops could flee before surrender on the morrow? That night and early morning, Virginia's General John B. Floyd, Tennessee's General Gideon Pillow, and some 2,500 rebels escaped by water, while Nathan Bedford Forrest and around 700 cavalrymen escaped by land. Kentucky's General Simon Buckner now alone commanded Fort Donelson's approximately 14,000 trapped rebels. It was all ending symbolically right: a Kentuckian who commanded too few Kentuckians surrendering to an army too well prepared inside Kentucky.

Early on February 16, Buckner asked Grant to negotiate terms of surrender. The Confederate expected gentlemen's terms, soft war appeasements, Seth Phelps-style generosity. Grant, however, did not share Phelps's attitude, especially after Charles F. Smith advised his ex-cadet that only unconditional surrender would suffice. Grant sent a terse message to Buckner, refusing to negotiate. The trapped rebel had no choice but to capitulate. As news of the triumph spread to the East, a jubilant press hung a hero's nickname on the winner. U.S. Grant had become Unconditional Surrender Grant, an American icon on his way to Paul Bunyan's stature.

4

Simon Buckner unconditionally surrendered not only the second crucial Confederate fort in ten days but also some 14,000 troops, 3,000 horses, 17 heavy guns, and 20,000 stands of arms. Yet Grant's payoff only began with two forts and their contents. Sidney Johnston now saw what Grant and Halleck had foreseen: Confederates must abandon their strong points after the Union controlled their weak point. Grant could menace Johnston from below and Buell could crunch down from above. Sidney Johnston in Nashville, like his men in Donelson, could only think about escaping a death trap.

Before Grant secured Fort Donelson, Johnston had pulled out of southern Kentucky and thus out of the only pro-Confederate part of this pivotal state and out of all control over Kentucky's strategic railroads to middle and western Tennessee. After Grant conquered Fort Donelson, Johnston kept on going past Nashville and thus out of the Confederacy's largest powder mill, the western Confederacy's best supply depot, and the Slave South's most elegant, most populated, most prosperous capital city, save only for Richmond. Several days later, Johnston pulled out of Clarksville, Tennessee, and thus out of the best Confederate iron mining region and second-best iron-finishing area, runner-up only to Richmond's iron factories. Meanwhile Leonidas Polk abandoned Columbus and thus Kentucky's power over the Mississippi. Having fought not a single other battle or lost a single other man after Grant captured their allegedly unimportant twin river forts, western Confederate armies were gone from Kentucky, gone from central Tennessee, gone from western Tennessee, fleeing over a Tennessee River bridge beyond Seth Phelps's late joyride, only able to regroup below the Middle South, at Corinth, Mississippi.

Since the Federals had now penetrated two-thirds of the Confederate heartland, an enthusiast might argue that the Union had almost won the Civil War in the West, before the worst fighting had even begun. That argument would exaggerate Grant's Henry-Donelson jackpot, large as it was. The soldiers who had conquered the twin-river forts would have to survive Sidney Johnston's brutal counterattack at Shiloh, Tennessee, in April 1862. There, Federals would suffer some 10,000 casualties and Grant would be almost pushed into his coveted Tennessee River before Buell would come to his rescue.[11] Thereafter, the twin river victors would have to spend fifteen months in brutal combat, before winning the siege at Vicksburg (July 4, 1863), then fifteen months of killing struggles prior to winning the siege of Atlanta (September 1, 1864). Only then would the war for the West (and thus the East) be almost won, and hardly before the horrendous killing commenced.

Still, the Henry-Donelson triumph did move Union forces well along toward achieving their eventual design for Civil War victory, before the worst fighting had even begun. According to that anaconda design, the Union would use multiple encirclements to cut the huge Confederate land mass down to size and slow the darting Robert E. Lee down to a crawl. Two landed rings, one within and one without the Virginia theater of war, would supplement the Winfield Scott-envisioned watery ring around the eastern Confederacy. The advantage of a triple anaconda: a thrice-encircled Lee would be ripe to conquer, even though little of the Trans-Mississippi South or the Lower South would have to be touched. The disadvantage: Union forces would have to subdue and retain the entire Mississippi Valley from the Ohio River to the Gulf of Mexico, in order to sever the Confederacy's east from its west, then subdue and retain the entire lower edge of the Middle South, from the Mississippi River to the Atlantic Ocean, in order to cut the Confederacy's north from its south. Two extended scissors to finalize three extended sieges—so extravagant a plan might cost more, especially in manpower, than even Northerners could afford, without big contributions from Southerners.

After the Union's early breakthrough at Henry/Donelson, southern contributions began to make the extravagant look affordable. Grant had penetrated a third of the way into the South, to a safe Border South starting place (Paducah), without losing a soldier. He had then moved another third of the way into the South, to occupy a hornet's nest of a Middle South launching pad (Shiloh!), with the loss of only 1,500 men. Having gained a gigantic head start on what became the triple siege strategy, the Union could move on to tighten those watery and landed anacondas around and inside Lee's theater of war, with white and increasingly black southern anti-Confederates bearing a saving part of the cost. "Fort Donelson was not only a beginning," concluded the great Civil War historian Bruce Catton. "It was one of the most decisive engagements of the entire war, and out of it came the slow, inexorable progression that led to Appomattox."[12]

5

With his Donelson-Henry jackpot, Grant served first notice of his military genius. But even geniuses need resources. Grant started deep in the Border South and moved almost effortlessly far into the Middle South because this war pitted the free labor states *plus* one-third of the slave labor states against but two-thirds of the slave labor states. If, instead, the Civil War had pitted free labor states against *all* slave labor states, all passionately committed to the Confederacy, men and materials could never have been sped to Buell and Grant via the Ohio River and the Baltimore and Ohio Railroad. St. Louis would never have supplied Pook's Turtles. Kentucky would never have given Don Carlos Buell an avenue toward Sidney Johnston or Grant a sanctuary in Paducah. Nor would Missouri and Kentucky have helped give Grant and Buell a manpower advantage over Johnston, forcing the Confederate chief to defend too many places with too few troops.

Instead, a zealously Confederate Kentucky could have given Johnston not a pathetic 6 percent of his infantry regiments but more like 50 percent— enough additional troops to fortify the twin river forts no less than Columbus and Bowling Green. With Southerners massed to defend their top as well as their bottom tier of states, Grant would have met his first implacable opposition on the southern edge of the North, not on the northern edge of the Lower South. Paducah, Smithland, Henry, Donelson, Shiloh, Vicksburg, Atlanta, three circles around Bobby Lee—those targets would have been unimaginable for many months, likely several years.

Civil War historians often highlight the Border South's decision for the Union in the early chapters of their narratives. If all southern states had seceded, judiciously writes James McPherson, "the South might well have won its independence. . . . The strategic importance of the rivers, railroads and mountains of the border states (including West Virginia) can hardly be exaggerated."[13] Allan Nevins concurs: "Strategically, the North held the entrances to the Shenandoah Valley, the Cumberland and Tennessee Rivers, and the Lower Mississippi. . . . Far different would have been the situation had the Confederacy rounded out its domains by seizing Kentucky, Missouri, and western Virginia. The balance then would have swayed against the Union."[14] Yet these two historians, like many Civil War buffs, forget their earlier observations about the Border South when they sum up why the Confederacy lost the war.

Abraham Lincoln never forgot. He always believed that if he lost the borderland's manpower, economic power, and militarily strategic location, he would lose the war. "I think to lose Kentucky is nearly the same as to lose the whole game," he wrote at the moment most Kentuckians moved from neutrality to greater annoyance at the Confederacy. "Kentucky gone, we cannot hold Missouri, nor as I think, Maryland. These all against us, and the job on our hands is too large for us. We would as well consent to separation at once, including the surrender of this capitol."[15] Only after he felt more secure that southern white anti-Confederates would compromise the Confederacy did Lincoln move on to secure the second southern contribution to the ultimate triple siege strategy: black anti-Confederates.

part three

Southern Black
Anti-Confederates

The Delay 6

Southern white and black anti-Confederates both contributed to the Union's eventual triple encirclement of Robert E. Lee. But the two contributions emerged from different southern regions, at different times, with a different initial reception, and with different results. Southern white anti-Confederates, mostly residing in the white belt South, especially helped conquer the Confederate heartland during the first two years of the war, with northern whites' thanks. In contrast, southern black anti-Confederates, mostly residing in the black belt South, especially helped retain the Confederate heartland during the last two years of the war, after overcoming whites' rejection of black troops. By preserving the Mississippi Valley as Union terrain, the Federals' disproportionately black army of occupation freed the disproportionately white army of conquest to move on, toward cornering Lee.

Anti-Confederate blacks' belated role demanded collaboration between Abraham Lincoln and runaway slaves. The ultimate Great Emancipator long shunned such a partnership. More than is now realized, the 1861–62 Lincoln

Abraham Lincoln, Weary Emancipator

The toll of Lincoln's journey, not only from exhausting war to almost victory, but also from determined delaying on emancipating to determined enforcement of the Emancipation Proclamation.   Courtesy of the Meserve-Kunhardt Collection, photograph by Alexander Gardner on February 5, 1865.

sought to avert federally imposed abolition on states, just as the 1863–65 Lincoln, also more than is now realized, resourcefully enforced antislavery inside southern states. Because of the gulf between the early and late presidential actions on imposing emancipation over states' objections, Lincoln's eventual black collaborators first had to push a procrastinator toward a zealot's mission. An appreciation of blacks' initial agency must begin with an understanding of Lincoln's initial heavy-handed resistance to any black role.

1

In 1860, Republicans elected Lincoln to liberate the white majoritarian republic immediately from the Slave Power's minority control, not to liberate slaves immediately inside sovereign states.[1] Lincoln, like most Republicans, hoped that containment of the Slave Power would someday lead to slavery's extinction. But that eventual liberation would have to come incrementally, after some vague process somehow resulting from containment.

During the secession crisis, Lincoln hewed to his mandate, as we have seen. He rejected minority ultimatums for extensions of slavery. He renounced the minority's secession from majoritarian government. But he endorsed a proposed unamendable Thirteenth Amendment to the U.S. Constitution, forever barring the federal government from menacing slavery inside the contained South.

As early wartime president, Lincoln never deviated from his prewar priorities: anything to secure white majoritarian Union, except caving in to minority dictation, but no coercive federal liberation of blacks in southern states, unless federal imposition became militarily necessary to save the Union. Lincoln clarified his priorities in his famous August 1862 public letter to Horace Greeley, editor of the New York Tribune. Despite my "oft-expressed *personal* wish that all men every where could be free," Lincoln explained, my "*official* duty . . . *is* to save the Union, and is *not* either to save or to destroy slavery. If I could save the Union without freeing *any* slave I would do it, and if I could save it by freeing *all* the slaves I would do it."[2]

Lincoln here hardly opposed emancipation in the spirit of a proslavery intransigent. This theoretical antislavery man would be pleased if his moral preference for abolition would serve military necessity. But for two years, the president saw slim prospect of that morally pleasant eventuality. Throughout 1861–62, Lincoln believed that by rejecting both federally imposed abolition and black troops, he would best save the Union. The president was a soft war zealot. Months after most Republicans repudiated soft war tactics, he believed that hard war, seeking to crush the rebels and to confiscate their slaves, would interminably lengthen the combat. But a softer reprimand, with no imposed emancipation, might lure Confederates back to the Union. While Lincoln soon boosted his first call for a mere 75,000 volunteers, he long hoped that merely (white) volunteers would win a short, soft war.

Lincoln's soft war theory stemmed not from airy abstraction but from pragmatic observation, throughout his first presidential baptism by fire. During the secession crisis, this shrewd political calculator had seen that Unionists held a huge Southwide majority, that the Middle South majority had been reluctant Confederates, that secessionists possibly lacked the requisite two-thirds majority even in South Carolina, and that secessionism fed on his alleged menace to slavery. Lincoln thus persistently believed, until belief became impossible, that after ex-Unionists credited his rejection of federally imposed abolition, they would return to an enslaved Union.

By remaining nonmenacing on slavery inside southern states, Lincoln also sought white men's support inside the Union. Northern Democrats opposed emancipation but relished the Union. Border slaveholders, having bet that Lincoln would not menace slavery, would remain in the Union if the president remained a nonemancipator. Furthermore, according to a favorite Lincoln (erroneous) theory, rebels considered their war unwinnable without the Border South. So Confederates would allegedly return after the borderland decided to remain.

During his first presidential year, the future Great Emancipator quashed every proposal to inject blacks into a war between whites. After his secretary of war, Simon Cameron, suggested federal use of black troops, Lincoln dispatched the discredited politician to be minister to Russia. When Union generals John Charles Frémont and David Hunter proclaimed disloyal masters' slaves freed in Missouri, South Carolina, Georgia, and Florida, Lincoln canceled these emancipation proclamations. When slave runaways dashed inside Union army lines, Lincoln's chief western general,

Henry Halleck, issued General Orders #3 (November 20, 1861), barring future fugitives from his invading army's lines and expelling present fugitives from his army's camps.[3]

While Lincoln's famous repudiation of Frémont and Hunter secured headlines, his silent concurrence in Halleck's underappreciated General Orders #3 deserved equal notoriety. Halleck's western troops, under Grant's command, would imminently penetrate that Confederate heartland. If Grant's soldiers barred black fugitives from army lines, slave runaways would be trapped between the Union's pointed bayonets and the Confederacy's angry captors. Thus could a relentlessly enforced General Orders #3 become a prime Lincoln administration weapon to keep the war a lily-white crusade.

2

Union infantrymen might have relentlessly enforced General Orders #3 if Confederates had also barred blacks' entrance into *their* lines.[4] Instead, Henry Halleck's all-white invaders faced biracial defenders. Slaves supplied rebel armies with occasional gunmen and many laborers.

Posterity thinks of Civil War armies as the soldiers' rather than the laborers' province. The Union's growing need for black soldiers now appears to be the rock that shattered an all-white army. But while Union recruiters' quest for black troops became important, that impulse came late in this story. Earlier, the Confederacy's use of black military laborers, and the Union's need to share that boon, helped runaway slaves weaken Halleck's (and indirectly Lincoln's) bar to fugitives.

Civil War armies needed workers as badly as sharpshooters. These lumbering military organizations became the industrial era's first super-giants. Before a mid-nineteenth-century army could flourish, railroads, ships, cannon, forts, breastworks, and trenches had to be built and repaired; axemen had to fell trees and carpenters had to saw logs; teamsters had to drag supplies and stevedores had to unload them; cooks had to prepare food and laundresses had to wash clothes; ambulance attendants had to cart off the wounded and hospital attendants had to comfort the ravaged. Home-front laborers also aided soldiers. New industries arose to supply troops with bullets, powder, and rifles. Old industries expanded to supply soldiers' food, clothes, and shoes. Confederates' need for labor made slave labor indispensable. No society could function, proslavery theorists had insisted, unless every level of the social hierarchy knew its place, did its job. In war even more than in peace, lofty whites faced doom unless lowly blacks labored resourcefully.

According to proslavery theory, masters' paternalism secured resourceful labor from family friends, not coerced work from terrorized serviles. The Civil War tested that theory. Never was willing labor more necessary. Never was coerced labor more problematic. Lashing masters and slashing patrolmen were often off fighting, leaving women or slaves themselves to master the home front. In the battle zone, white soldiers could not keep one eye on Yankee sharpshooters, another on black laborers. Proslavery theory had better match reality. Otherwise, disaster awaited a labor-deprived Confederacy.

During the Civil War's relatively quiet first year, slavery tolerably well passed its paternalistic test. Thousands of slaves labored inside army camps and fortifications. More thousands manned new munitions factories. Blacks comprised over half the toilers at Richmond's Tredegar Iron Works and over three in four at Selma, Alabama's, naval ordnance plant.[5] In the fields, slave millions produced a record cotton crop, even with many masters away. A few blacks donated cash to the Confederate cause. Two Mobile slaves bought $400 in Confederate bonds. One New Orleans slave subscribed for $200. A weeping elderly hackman offered his life savings, $100.[6]

When mutilated masters returned from the bloodbath, some slaves raged as well as wept. "Dey brung" Massa Billy home, one South Carolina slave grieved to a contemporary, "with he jaw split open . . . He teeth all shine through he cheek. . . . I be happy iffen I could kill me jes' one Yankee. I hated dem 'cause dey hurt my white people."[7] In more celebrated votes for *their* white people, some blacks hid whites' silver from Yankees. A North Carolina slave protected $15,000. A South Carolina slave sewed family valuables into his mattress.[8]

So-called body servants disproportionately served as treasure savers. Some body servants also served masters in the combat zone, especially during the Civil War's earlier, softer stage. Valets, acting as if army tents were

Masters' Big Tent valet. In this priceless photograph, the formally-attired black body servant stands behind the rough and ready infantrymen of the 5th Georgia. Courtesy of Joseph Canole, Jr.

Master's co-killer. Another priceless photograph, this time of a master and his armed ally. Andrew Chandler, 44th Mississippi Regiment, and his body servant, Silas Chandler. Courtesy of Andrew Chandler Battaile.

Big Houses, ministered to their lords' every need, even pulling on their titans' socks and shoes.[9] Soldiers' needs transcended footwear. Stories cascaded around the South (and still do) of servants who devotedly carted wounded masters to the hospital or hauled corpses back home.

Some servants even shot down masters' would-be killers. Southern laws barred blacks from firing weapons. Back home, however, trusted body servants on deer hunts had been crack shots. Family friends who bagged deer could also slay Yankees. According to a northern eyewitness, Virginia blacks with "rifles, muskets, sabers, bowie-knives, dirks, etc., . . . were seen riding on horses and mules, . . . promiscuously mixed up with all the Rebel horde."[10]

That word *promiscuously*, just what a Yankee would use, lends credibility to this report of black Confederate soldiers. Later in the war, after Yankees invited black troops to gun down rebels, northern whites segregated the allegedly inferior race in its own companies. Northerners, as the saying went, furthered the black race but shunned black individuals, while Southerners enslaved the race and embraced the individual. When black and white Confederates soldiered side by side, Yankee segregationists saw only the "promiscuous."

According to a currently politically correct theory, blacks hated slavery and seized all chances to undermine their masters. Most blacks indeed did flee from masters when Union armies appeared in the neighborhood. Body servants, the source of most black riflemen early in the war, did become less prevalent in Confederate camps after the war turned harder. Whites did have to force most Confederate blacks to work. But a small fraction of slaves served their masters inside the Confederate army. Halleck's soldiers hardly cheered because only occasional black Confederates pulled triggers. Lincoln's invaders suffered much anxiety because thousands of slaves built Confederate forts and earthworks. Anxious privates found much relief when many more of the Confederacy's indispensable black workers sprinted for Union lines.

Henry Halleck, however, barred masters' deserters from the lines. Enforcing Halleck's General Orders #3 meant shoving runaways back toward Confederate lines, to dig more trenches that would enable more white Confederates (and the occasional black sniper) to kill more faithful enforcers of Henry Halleck's command. Why not instead ignore General Orders #3 and welcome Confederate workers to Union lines?

Fortunately for troops who wished to ignore that critical order, an alternative word rose to power a half year before Henry Halleck scribbled his command. Wartime has its own words for its own laws. A law of war holds that enemy property, when used in combat, can be confiscated as "*contraband of war.*" The confiscators can then use the contraband property to kill the former property owner. Nothing could be more "contraband" than a Confederate property that had worked for the Confederate army and escaped to the Union army, begging to labor against former property holders.

The portentous word emerged in the first month of the war, at a Virginia locale rich in Civil War ironies.[11] Fortress Monroe guarded the Chesapeake Bay, close to the mouth of the James River. Near this spot where black contrabands first begged Union soldiers for freedom, whites had first shoved Africans onto North American soil. Here during the 1830s, Robert E. Lee had supervised the building of a federal fortress, with its white-columned commandant's residence bearing the look of a southern plantation mansion. Here during the 1860s, no Confederate would command Fortress Monroe. Instead, Jefferson Davis would be jailed inside the fortress for two postwar years, with his chief Yankee jailer luxuriating inside Lee's former Big House away from home.

On May 23, 1861, three slaves fled to this Union toehold in Confederate Virginia. They had been ordered, the fugitives claimed, to build a Confederate battery. Instead, they begged Fortress Monroe's commander, Benjamin F. Butler, to let them build Union installations. This same "Beast Ben" Butler had presided over an earlier historic first. After the Baltimore Riot of April 19, 1861, the Massachusetts general had secured Annapolis. His troops, Butler had claimed to Maryland's governor, came not to attack slavery but to quiet "apprehensions . . . of an insurrection of the negro population."[12]

Having initiated in Maryland an anti-insurrectionary policy (one that federal generals would forever support), Butler initiated at Fortress Monroe a profugitive policy (one that would ultimately devastate slavery). The Massachusetts general distinguished between insurrectionists' violent murdering and fugitives' nonviolent fleeing. Why send three peaceable Confederate military laborers back to help cripple Union soldiers when the runaways wished to help cripple their masters?

A day later, a representative of the slaveowner answered that Butler, as a federal official, must enforce the federal Fugitive Slave Law. Butler offered to enforce the law if the owner would obey every federal law. The owner preferred Confederate laws. Butler kept the property and hired it to work for wages.

Butler claimed first use of the word that summed up his policy. A northern journalist also laid claim. No matter. Whoever first uttered the three syllables, *contraband* blazed like a match thrown in bone-dry kindling. Words that designated a certain people as negroes, slaves, or property sometimes vanished into the smoke-filled Civil War air. When the new word replaced old ones, intractable puzzles disappeared. Serviles, having fled from slaving for one army to working for the other, sometimes were not called negroes, subject to northern distaste for colored folk. Fugitives sometimes were not called slaves, subject to Yankees' shudder at turning a war for Union into a war for emancipation. Runaways sometimes were not called property, subject to capitalist skittishness about governmental seizure of possessions. They were now often called *contraband*, subject to laws of war. They were now often considered akin to rifles seized from slain rebels, then used to gun down other rebels. The contraband might be returned, but only after the war, when the laws of peace resumed. Butler gave rebels a receipt that a court might honor, once war ended.

Ben Butler's first three contrabands erected a bakery. The next three dozen built breastworks to protect soldiers in neighboring Hampton. While Butler's troops cherished the protection, they preferred that others heave materials into place, under the torrid Virginia sun. So the contraband threw up embankments, collected wages for willing labor, and earned Butler's, and the nation's, pleased attention.

Two months later, the July 1861 Battle of Bull Run, with its rout of Union troops and picnickers, attracted the nation's angry preoccupation. Confederates' use of black laborers and snipers offered a superb scapegoat. "Slave-built batteries," reported the *Chicago Tribune*, "repulsed the finest army ever organized on the American Continent. . . . General McDowell threads his way through roads and defiles obstructed by Negroes, and plunges into a honey comb of batteries erected by Negroes."[13] Butler's breastworks and McDowell's retreat provoked Congress to pass the First

Confiscation Act (August 8, 1861). It forfeited rebel masters' claim to slaves who had helped the Confederate army. The law also barred the Union army from returning a fugitive slave to a disloyal master who had used the slave for disloyal purposes.[14]

This first wartime revision of the 1850 Fugitive Slave Law, like the word *contraband*, sidestepped trouble. The First Confiscation Act nowhere *permanently* forfeited disloyal slaveowners' claim to a fugitive. The omission, like Butler's receipts, implied that the forfeit might terminate after the war. Nor could the perhaps temporary forfeiture of a fugitive happen to a loyal master, nor to a disloyal master who had used his fugitive slave for nonmilitary purposes.

Once a fugitive slave reached Union lines and claimed that a disloyal master had used him for disloyal purposes, the pursuing slaveowner had to enter Union army lines, locate the slave, and convince an army officer that the contraband lied. It was not a promising recourse. But loyal masters demanded it. Lincoln, anxious to retain loyal Southerners, sometimes ordered generals to supply it.[15] So slaves ran inside army lines, masters ran after runaways, and generals ran into a labyrinth. Army officers often had to waste hours, days, trying to find the allegedly lying contraband, then trying to ascertain whether master or slave was fibbing.

The morass marked the oddest chapter yet in the history of the federal nonbureaucracy. In the 1850 Fugitive Slave Law, Congress had stepped gingerly around the national prejudice against federal bureaucrats. One-case commissioners had been authorized, sustained by one-case posses, to return a slave, then disappear from federal duty. The disappearances had left no police force to deter fugitives from passing over the Slave South's border to the free labor North.

Now the army gave the federal government a law-enforcing bureaucracy and loyal slaveholders a federal police. The First Confiscation Act clearly implied (and President Lincoln periodically insisted) that Union soldiers must return fugitives who had dashed inside army lines, assuming that the master had remained loyal and that the slave had never furthered the rebellion. Yet if the master had been disloyal or the slave used for disloyal purposes, the army, by enforcing the law, would strengthen its enemy. So soldiers as law enforcers *had* to discover who lied. Such tangled investigations, however, dimmed troops' focus on winning the war.

Thus, soldiers wanted out of supplying the federal government's long-missing civil law enforcers. The commander in chief sympathized, despite his wish to placate loyal masters. His government could only shed the bureaucratic role by expelling slaves from camp and allowing no more to enter. By barring fugitives from their lines, generals could get back to building an army and one-case commissioners could get back to judging when a fugitive should be returned. Hence Henry Halleck's pivotal General Orders #3 of November 1861, making his army off limits for slave runaways.

Halleck reaffirmed General Orders #3 two months later, as Ulysses S. Grant was marching on Forts Henry and Donelson. Halleck warned his invaders that they must keep fugitives outside army lines. It "does not belong to the military," Halleck insisted, "to decide upon the relation of master and man."[16] To General Halleck and his president, blacks remained not contraband but blacks. Even if slaves served Confederate armies, everyone inside Union lines must be white.

But the Union commander in chief and his western commander could not alone dictate the relation of master and man in the combat zone. A stream of decisions contradicting General Orders #3 came from the bottom instead of from the top, beginning with lowly blacks. Slaves' flight toward Union lines could force Union privates to see the contrabands' value as military laborers. That perception in the field could force Congress toward further fugitive slave law revisions, which could force the commander in chief to reconsider fugitives' military utility. A few, then a few more slave runaways thus could exert leverage all the way to the top of the Union ruling establishment, indirectly impelling federal interventions that could sap masters' deterrence to further fugitives.

Prewar masters' deterrence to runaways had featured neighborhood patrols. "Slavery could not exist a day or an hour anywhere," to repeat Illinois Senator Stephen A. Douglas's prescient pre–Civil War point, unless "local police" power augmented slaveholder power. As the American Revolutionary War experience had demonstrated, invading armies could wipe out patrols and encourage slaves to escape. When British armies had marched through the South, around 10 percent of plantation slaves had fled their masters. Now Grant's army, by demolishing southern police power, could

The Runaways

Escaping slaves. This spectacular photograph shows slaves escaping, with their possessions loaded on an oxcart. Courtesy of The Civil War Library and Museum, Philadelphia, Pennsylvania.

Escaped slaves. An equally arresting photograph of runaways, now freedmen, dressed in whatever garb could be found. Courtesy of the Library of Congress, photograph by Mathew Brady.

similarly abolish masters' deterrence in the combat zone, *if* privates ignored General Orders #3 and gave fugitives sanctuary.

No such possibilities troubled the Lower South's many uninvaded black belts. There, slave runaways remained at prewar slight levels. There, slaves' barn-burning, work-shirking, tool-breaking defiance somewhat increased during the Civil War, with white males away and plantation mistresses sometimes uncomfortable disciplinarians.[17] Such slave resistance could drive slaveholders wild. But only by massively running away could slaves help shatter the regime. Only Union invasion brought mass desertions. As an ex-slave in largely uninvaded Texas exclaimed, "the War didn't change nothin'. Sometimes you didn't knowed it was goin' on. It was the endin' of it that made the difference."[18]

Invasion made the difference for slave runaways, so long as the invaders displayed Benjamin F. Butler's attitudes rather than Henry Halleck's. With the right resistance, slaves could turn white soldiers' attitudes Butler's way. Insurrection was the wrong resistance. Northern generals (including Butler) promised to clasp hands with southern generals if a race war between southern blacks and whites replaced a sectional war between Union and Confederate whites. U.S. general George McClellan, for example, promised West Virginians (May 27, 1861) that we will, "with an iron hand, crush any . . . insurrection."[19] That same month, Ulysses S. Grant wrote that a northern army would "go south to suppress a negro insurrection . . . with the purest of motives."[20] That federal intrusion would have provided quite the ending to the Civil War: Lee, Grant, and McClellan united to conquor black revolutionaries!

Civil War slaves preferred to divide and conquer the enslaving race. With war already dividing whites, blacks had only to make themselves indispensable to masters' would-be conquerors. Nonviolent flight, followed by work for Union armies, offered slaves their leverage over Union soldiers, thus over Congress, and thus over the commander in chief. Civil War slaves almost never tried insurrection.[21] They tried flight whenever Union armies marched nearby.

No matter how close Union armies marched, successful flight required wariness, especially when Union invaders, bearing General Orders #3, first entered the Mississippi River Valley. Whenever runaways approached Halleck's soldiers, the stakes were excruciating. If privates disobeyed General

Halleck, safety for fugitives was at hand. If privates enforced Halleck's order, runaways faced Confederate sharpshooters, ordered to kill black fugitives. Slaves were sometimes forced to view runaways' corpses. At one
"sickening" scene, reported a Memphis slave, two black fugitives' "bodies
hung at the roadside . . . until the blue flies literally swarmed around them
and the stench was fearful."[22]

Yankees as well as slaves hated the stench. Northern soldiers who barred
fugitives from Union lines felt "pained to think," as one exclaimed, "that I
should have been the cause of this brutal chastisement." Another soldier reported that a black teenager broke from the woods, screaming "Massa, I
wants to go with you." The soldier answered that "I am not permitted to
do it." And then the "light went out of the poor fellow's eyes."[23]

But poor fellows kept coming back at Union soldiers, and a few more
came, and a few more came. All begged for protection from the army's enemy. All begged to help protect whites from Confederates. All forced white
privates to see that blacks were hardly violent insurrectionists. Instead, nonviolent runaways could help swing the balance of Civil War power, assuming
Union privates (and ultimately their president) would forget General Orders
#3 and give sanctuary to laborers who sought to liberate themselves.

3

William Lloyd Garrison's followers believed that runaways *had* to be given
sanctuary. Grant's western troops, however, usually came not from Garrison's stronghold, the relatively less racist New England, but from antiaboli-
tionism's bastion, the highly racist Midwest. Most Midwesterners came
South convinced that Jehovah had made blacks to be inferior, docile,
servile. Then antiabolitionists encountered a hardly servile runaway.

The invaders thus repeated prewar Yankee racists' experience. In the 1850s,
antiabolitionist citizens had winced at their obligation, under the Fugitive
Slave Law, to help reenslave runaways. In the early 1860s, antiabolitionist privates squirmed under their orders to shove a freedom seeker toward perpetual
servitude. "It seemed cruel," muttered a soldier who had just enforced General Orders #3, "to turn our backs on these, our only [southern] friends."[24]

Contraband building military barricades. In this excellent example of why whites
valued contrabands as military laborers, ex-slaves are building a high fence,
to protect a captured, strategically crucial railroad near Alexandria, Virginia (and
Washington D. C.) from Confederate saboteurs.   Courtesy of the National Archives.

Contraband reburying corpses. Another revealing photograph, showing another reason why whites valued black military laborers: to perform especially unpleasant tasks, this time reburying corpses after the slaughtering at Cold Harbor, Virginia. Courtesy of the U. S. Army Military History Institute.

By shoving helpful friends back toward helping the enemy, the Union army came to seem incompetent as well as cruel. After Grant's men penetrated the Confederate heartland, Southerners deployed guerrilla raids, train burnings, and bushwacking murders. Every tree might hide a Confederate sniper. Out of every dark night might ride a murderous cavalryman. To federal soldiers who suffered this guerrilla danger, the old soft war theory looked absurd. Rebels hardly turned tail and marched back into the Union because Mr. Lincoln let them keep their slaves and General Halleck refused to give their fugitives sanctuary.

By barring black runaways from sanctuary in Union army lines, General Orders #3 banned white troops' best shields against guerrillas. A fugitive often knew where rebels hid and where they would strike. After being debriefed, black spies cut down trees that protected Confederate snipers and threw up earthworks that stymied Confederate guerrillas. Or would white privates prefer to perform such exhausting military labor themselves? "One hour's digging in Louisiana clay under a Louisiana sun," answered one private, "and we are forever pledged to do all we can to fill up our ranks with the despised and long-neglected race."[25]

In August 1862, a Union private in Tennessee scribbled in his diary that "contrabands (a new name for the negro slaves) are building forts around here and felling trees across the roads to keep the enemy from surprising us. . . . If a *culled man* will dig trenches and chop timber and even fight the enemy, he is just the fellow we want."[26] As such attitudes swelled in the ranks, field generals reported that General Orders #3 was becoming unenforceable. "I deem it prejudicial to the harmony and discipline of the troops," wrote one of Don Carlos Buell's generals, "to require them to perform what they all consider an obnoxious duty."[27]

Some generals also considered General Orders #3 obnoxious. General O. M. Mitchel wrote from Alabama in May 1862 that "negroes are our only friends, and in two instances I owe my own safety to their faithfulness." Without faithful "guards among the slaves on the plantations bordering the river from Bridgeport to Florence," we must "abandon the line of railway." Then "Northern Alabama falls back into the hands of the enemy."[28] A Union colonel in Nashville exclaimed that "if I want to find out anything hereabouts, I hunt up a Negro." Or as Benjamin F. Butler declared, "whoever else might be excluded from headquarters, no Negro should ever be."[29]

Among Lincoln's generals, George McClellan especially wished to exclude blacks from white men's war. Yet McClellan conceded that his "most reliable information . . . comes from fugitive slaves."[30] His compatriot in the Virginia theater, General Abner Doubleday, ordered that no fugitive be excluded from lines. Their "valuable information . . . cannot be obtained from any other source," reported Doubleday's assistant. They know "all the roads, paths, and fords, . . . and they make excellent guides."[31]

On August 9, 1862, McClellan ordered protection for blacks who entered tents such as Abner Doubleday's. Slaves "have always understood,"

McClellan noted, that after the U.S. military service accepted them "in any capacity, they could never be reclaimed by their former holders." McClellan promised black informants "permanent military protection against any compulsory return to a condition of servitude."[32]

Permanent freedom represented quite a commitment from the army's most notorious foe of a war for emancipation. With McClellan, of all people, deviating from the spirit of General Orders #3, could any order barring fugitives fit a disorderly guerrilla war? The orderly McClellan thought he found an answer. He accepted contraband spies but banned contraband laborers.

U.S. Senator Zachariah Chandler of Michigan ridiculed McClellan's distinction. Black military laborers no less than black spies, argued Chandler, saved white lives. Chandler claimed that of his state's 4,000 casualties in McClellan's army, 2,500 had operated only "*the Spade*. McClellan will not make Negroes to dig ditches, cut down timber & do hard work, but will force my brave boys to do this menial work and die doing it." As if answering Chandler, a Union private from Tennessee explained why "a good many soldiers" would rather wield a spade than befriend a fugitive: Racist warriors remained "bitterly opposed to having 'niggers' take any hand in the war."[33]

Grant and Sherman believed that foot soldiers had no right to decide who would take a hand in the war. After Henry Halleck laid down General Orders #3, subordinates must follow headquarters' policy. So Grant and Sherman, among other generals, reiterated that their troops must stop blacks at the picket lines. Their privates continued to halt some, let others through. By mid-1862, a fugitive in the Mississippi Valley might or might not receive army sanctuary. The uncertainty deterred some would-be fugitives and demanded courage from all runaways.

But General Orders #3 was fraying in the face of fugitives' need for sanctuary, generals' need for labor and information, and soldiers' need to protect themselves. In mid-1862, Tennessee's Gideon Pillow reported that his 400 slaves had all departed. Ben Butler estimated that 10,000 runaways had escaped in lower Louisiana. On a march through northern Alabama in May 1862, Joseph Keilor marveled at hundreds of fugitives, "bearing their bedding, clothing, and other effects on their heads and backs, . . . shouting and singing a medley of songs of freedom. . . . We marched for a good part of the day between almost continuous lines of them."[34]

Such defiance of General Orders #3 enlarged the generals' problems. At first, when Halleck had snapped army gates shut against fugitives, male runaways had usually taken their desperate chances alone, without their wives and children. But as enforcement of General Orders #3 loosened, black dependents more often accompanied black males.[35] While women and children usually performed no military labor, they ate up military rations. Field generals increasingly howled at Lincoln, asking what they should do with the hungry fugitives that Halleck's fraying General Orders #3 had not deterred.

The question demonstrated that black fugitives and white soldiers had begun an irreversible transformation of the countryside. Washington authorities had only two options. The nation's civil and military commanders could ignore the unstoppable and thus do nothing to hasten incremental emancipation. Or the ruling establishment could turn the runaways' dashes for army sanctuary into a rush toward antislavery.

4

Congress, deciding first, hoped for an antislavery rush, yet conceded its inability to speed ahead unless the president concurred. Previously, in its 1861 First Confiscation Act, Congress had freed only disloyal masters' military laborers. Now, in its July 17, 1862, Militia and Second Confiscation Acts, the Republican congressional majority proclaimed the freedom of *all* slaves in disloyal areas.[36]

That seemingly gigantic leap from *some* to *all* could make no practical difference in numbers of slaves freed. Not congressional linguistics but slaves' flight to freedom had become the practical mode of liberation. The army's policy toward runaways had become the federal instrument to hasten or inhibit flight toward liberty. The issue about army policy had changed since the First Confiscation Act. No longer did the question involve whether all, some, or none of the fugitives within army lines should be delivered back to slaveholders. Ever since General Orders #3, the question had been whether runaways should be admitted to army lines at all. On that question, Congress's sweeping emancipation proclamation of July 17 had no impact. The army (and especially its commander in chief) had to decide whether nonmilitary folk who ventured inside military installations interfered with military efficiency, whether black slaves or white family members were the nonmilitary intruders.

Because of the army's (and its commander in chief's) jurisdiction over military efficiency in military camps, the president could undermine the constitutionality no less than the practicality of congressionally declared emancipation. Short of an antislavery constitutional amendment, only military necessity could make federal emancipation constitutional. If the army's commander denied that the July 17 congressional emancipation served military necessity, the Supreme Court would likely strike down the congressional intrusion.

In its July 17 legislation, Congress implicitly conceded that the commander in chief must dominate an emancipation based on military necessity. Despite its theoretical proclamation of a sweeping emancipation, Congress begged for yet another, more practical emancipation proclamation, this time by the president. The Militia and the Second Confiscation Acts invited Lincoln to declare that he intended to free slaves in rebel-held territories, sixty days after the declaration. To enforce the declaration inside rebel-held territory, Congress authorized the president to receive "persons of African descent" into army lines and to enlist the contraband "into the service of the United States, for the purpose of constructing entrenchments, or performing camp service, or any labor, or any military or naval service for which they may be found competent."

Assuming the commander in chief found blacks competent for military service, and assuming he wished to accept the congressional invitation to issue emancipation proclamations, he could transform an exclusively white men's war for Union into a war also fought by blacks, also for black men's freedom. In addition, by ordering his army to administer his transforming decree, he could reverse American bureaucratic history. Gone would be the pre-*Prigg versus Pennsylvania* days, when state administrators had assumed the federal government's task of returning fugitives. Also gone would be the post-1850 days, when one-case commissioners had substituted for vanished state bureaucrats. Gone too would be the General Orders #3 era, when Henry Halleck ordered his soldiers to vanish from enforcing the fugitive law. Into America's federal bureaucratic vacuum, the widest in the Western World, would march Mr. Lincoln's soldiers. These administrators would give the runaways sanctuary and thereby accelerate a revolution already under way in Union-occupied Confederate territory.

Lincoln feared accelerated revolution. He continued to hope that a softer policy on emancipation would soften slaveholders' resistance to reunion. He continued to worry that a presidential commitment to federally imposed emancipation would weaken the Border South's attachment to the Union. If he gained southern black anti-Confederates at the cost of losing southern white anti-Confederates, he might commit military suicide. Lincoln also cocked his keen political eye on the fall midterm congressional elections of 1862. If he gained black nonvoters at the expense of losing white voters, he might commit political suicide.

Political and military survival, Lincoln believed on July 17, 1862, required a presidential stall on responding to the congressional invitation to issue an emancipation proclamation. A little delay might enable the Republican Party to consolidate its hold over the federal government, and the federal government to consolidate its hold over the Border South. A season of indecision on emancipation proclamations would also allow time for a final and definitive test of whether a soft policy on emancipation could induce rebels' voluntary return to a Union that protected slavery.

On one aspect of the fugitive slave/army question, Lincoln ended his delays. In his executive order of July 22, he authorized his army to employ fugitives as military laborers.[37] Still, unemployable black men, women, and children packed army camps. What to do with this hungry black surplus? The stalling president did not decide. His subordinates' decisions yielded a chaos of conflicting orders. Grant and Sherman employed black male laborers but barred other blacks from army lines (a revised version of General Orders #3). Commanders in South Carolina, Kansas, and Louisiana recruited black soldiers from excess laborers (a revolutionary repudiation of General Orders #3). Higher army and War Department authorities sanctioned 5,000 South Carolina black troops but repudiated the Kansas privates and waffled on the Louisiana soldiers. As for the highest authority, the commander in chief privately declared that "he was not prepared to go to the length of enlisting Negroes as soldiers."[38]

Lincoln was equally unprepared to end the chaos of military orders until he tested yet another option. Your hard war authorization of a coercive emancipation proclamation, he told Congress on that potentially fateful July 17, should have added soft war inducements to Confederates to avoid emancipation. The president preferred to give rebels "something to lose by persisting" in the war, "something to save by desisting," and time to reconsider whether persisting in disunion would best save slavery.[39] To underline the gains of coming back to the Union, Lincoln meant to offer rebels exemption from any emancipation proclamation, if they voluntarily returned before an announced deadline.

Lincoln also begged Congress to offer a sweetheart deal if voluntarily returning rebels or Border South states would voluntarily emancipate their slaves. The president based his voluntary plan on the sine qua non of slaveholders' position: that only states, and never the federal government, could impose abolition. The federal government's role must be restricted to financing abolition, to induce a state voluntarily to liberate itself. Lincoln also hoped that the federal government would purchase a Latin American oasis and provide free tickets to it, to induce freedmen voluntarily to deport themselves.[40] Lincoln wanted all this induced voluntary change to occur gradually, over perhaps thirty-seven years.

In a now forgotten but revealing addendum, the president also asked Congress to provide an avenue for an emancipated state to travel back to slavery. A reenslaving state, Lincoln proposed, need only return the federal government's previous emancipating payments, if it wished to reverse abolition.[41] As Lincoln had reason to know, that explicit permission to resurrect slavery could become lethal. His own emancipated Illinois had staged a referendum on repealing abolition in 1824. The convulsive proposal to reinstitute slavery in Illinois had garnered an ominous 42 percent of the popular vote. So too in the late 1850s, southern California had clamored to secede from free labor California and enter the Union as a slave state.[42] By going out of his way to permit another chapter in *that* history, Lincoln indicated his total commitment to states' exclusive power to decide on their own labor institutions.

Lincoln's reenslavement option made the choice between presidential and congressional emancipation the more stark. The president hoped Congress would offer a federal bribe to induce rebels to return voluntarily and to induce voluntary, perhaps temporary, state abolition. Congress hoped the president would deploy the army to protect and perhaps arm the contraband and thereby coercively shatter slavery forever. The president, with his jurisdiction over military power, temporarily had the upper hand. Congress, however, could soon force his hand. Lincoln could not forever stonewall against a Congress controlled by his own Republican Party, any more than Republican congressmen could forever stonewall against their soldier-constituents' opinion of fugitives. By inducing a favorable response first from soldiers, then from Republicans in Congress, the contraband had exerted much more pressure on the White House than fugitives alone could have mustered. In the face of that pressure from below, the man at the top had to prove that his voluntary inducements could work as well as or better than congressional coercive emancipation. And the proof had to come fast.

5

Lincoln knew that white Southerners rejected voluntary emancipation in part because they feared free blacks. So he invited free black leaders to the White House on August 14, 1862. His guests hoped to persuade the president to let their people into his army. He instead told them to take their folk out of his country. All men, the president reminded his guests, aspire "to enjoy equality with the best." In "this broad continent, . . . not a single man of your race is made the equal of a single man of ours." Thus "for the sake of your race you should sacrifice something of your present comfort" in the United States, to lead your people toward temporary discomfort in Latin America. There, blacks could become "as grand . . . as the white people." His guests' preference for present comfort over future grandeur, he scolded them in the nadir of Lincoln sentences, spread "an extremely selfish view of the case."[43]

When black leaders reported the White House definition of selfishness, black folk retorted that their right to enjoy America equaled that of the selfish President.[44] Border South congressmen also fired back rejections of the president's emancipation bribes. In three 1862 conferences, they told Lincoln that he would never procure the $300–$400 per slave that he had in mind, that they would never accept so low a price, and that his financial inducements would never convince blacks to leave. Your plan, claimed U.S. Senator Lazarus Whitehead Powell of Kentucky, is "full of arsenic, sugar coated."[45]

Lincoln answered that borderland calculators poisoned themselves. "The institution in your states," he accurately predicted, "will be extinguished by mere friction and abrasion . . . of the war. It will be gone, and you will have nothing valuable in lieu of it." If borderites instead pocketed some $300–$400 in federal bonds per slave, they would enrich the Union as well as themselves. Confederates allegedly would repudiate disunion, once they knew that the borderland had emancipated itself and thus would never join a slaveholders' nation.[46]

Border South and Deep South Unionists thanked Mr. Lincoln for his voluntarism on emancipation by demanding coercive presidential efforts to return fugitive slaves. An exasperated president replied, in one of his splendid figures of speech, that slaveholders must stop moaning about runaways, "for broken eggs cannot be mended." Especially Lower South slaveholders must fast seek reunion before all their eggs became "past mending." He had tried "to hold . . . within bounds" military pressures for accepting fugitives into army camps. He could not promise slaveholders much more "time to help themselves."[47]

On September 13, 1863, the president knew his time for stalling was expiring. The congressional hard war, coercive emancipation authorizations were two months old. Lincoln's soft war, voluntary emancipation experiments were a bust. Still, the stymied president publicly complained that an emancipation proclamation from the White House "might do little good." Since "I cannot even enforce the Constitution in the rebel States," my decree could be a command without compulsion. So futile a gesture would be as pathetic as a "Pope's bull against the comet," decreeing that fire must stop streaking across the heavens.

Lincoln conceded that a purely paper decree might symbolically "help us in Europe" and in some northern quarters. More "unquestionably," a presidential battle cry of freedom would "weaken the rebels by drawing off their slaves." But the president wondered what we could then do "with the blacks. If we were to arm them," he exclaimed in another nadir-of-Lincoln sentences, their "arms" might soon "be in the hands of the rebels." He feared that we could never "feed and care for such a multitude." He worried that after his army departed conquered terrain, masters would reduce blacks "to slavery again." Moreover, Border South soldiers wielded "fifty thousand bayonets in the Union armies." An emancipation proclamation might drive those bayonet wielders "over to the rebels." The president treasured one certainty: Delay helps. "Every day increases" border men's "Union feeling."[48]

On September 22, 1862, Lincoln proclaimed 100 days of further delay. In his Preliminary Emancipation Proclamation, he announced that he would issue a final emancipation proclamation, freeing slaves (in rebel-held areas only) on January 1, 1863. The Second Confiscation Act had invited an immediate presidential emancipation proclamation, to become effective sixty days after July 17. Instead, Lincoln's Preliminary and Final Emancipation Proclamations stretched sixty days after July 17 into 169 days.

Lincoln's Preliminary Emancipation Proclamation announced that a hard war for federally imposed emancipation in rebel-held areas would begin on the first day of the new year. It also announced soft conditions for a slavery-preserving reunion before the old year expired. The Final Emancipation Proclamation, declared the Preliminary Emancipation Proclamation, would impose abolition only in areas *not* under Union control on January 1. To come back under Union control in time, a secessionist state need not repudiate slavery. Disunionists need not repeal disunion. Secessionists need not reconvene state secession conventions or replicate the two-thirds popular majority that had secured disunion. A simple majority in a Confederate state need only participate in elections for U.S. congressmen before the January 1 deadline. Unless "strong countervailing testimony" indicated that election participants still favored disunion, the president would consider the "state and the people thereof . . . not then in rebellion" and not subject to the Final Emancipation Proclamation.[49]

By offering a last-minute choice between suffering abolition in an emancipating war or voting for congressmen in an enslaved Union, the president would at last shock the southern majority into recognizing that he hardly menaced slavery. His nonmenacing offer would sweep away difficulties for a rebellion-repudiating southern majority: the difficulty of rallying two-thirds majorities and state conventions; the difficulty of completing elaborate constitutional procedures in 100 days; the difficulty of dishonorably apologizing for past mistakes. Instead, by the honorable act of conducting a U.S. congressional election, a simple majority of any Confederate state could pretend that secession never happened.

As he would subsequently prove after he issued the Final Emancipation Proclamation, Lincoln did not rest content with a Pope's bull against comets. Rather, he used special bureaucrats to seek to transform words into action. From mid-October to mid-November 1862, he sent personal envoys to Louisiana, Tennessee, and Arkansas. His envoys bore tidings of an even softer landing into a slavery-protecting Union than the Preliminary Emancipation Proclamation had offered. If citizens desired "to avoid the unsatisfactory" terms of the Final Emancipation Proclamation "and to have peace again on the old terms" (i.e., with slavery intact), they should rally "the largest number of the people possible" to vote in an "election of members of the Congress of the United States," while still following "forms of law as far as convenient."[50]

Follow "forms of law as far as convenient"! Procure "the largest number of people possible"! (Now not even a simple majority need vote before January 1.) This apostle of white men's majoritarian law would now play loose with legal forms and majoritarian requirements. This future Great Emancipator would also possibly doom three Confederate states' blacks to perpetual slavery in order to lure the states' whites back to a supposedly majoritarian Union.

With his commitment to last-minute work against coercive emancipation, Lincoln showed again how much the fugitives and their new Republican congressional allies were up against in pushing this theoretical emancipationist toward forcible abolition. Lincoln's anti-emancipationist commissioners to Louisiana, Tennessee, and Arkansas also demonstrated that more than short-term political motives detained the future Great Emancipator from his destiny. Cynics call Lincoln only a crafty politician, delaying forced emancipation until after the elections of fall 1862. But Lincoln's commissioners worked hardest after the elections. Lincoln aimed to win not just the 1862 elections but also the war (which was the best way to sweep elections long after 1862); and avoidance of federally imposed emancipation still seemed to him the wisest military course.

Lincoln's envoys, however, could arrange only two localized Louisiana elections. The exasperated president had only one soft war whimper left. In his December 1, 1862, Annual Message to Congress, the president suggested an antislavery constitutional amendment. For the next thirty-eight years, Lincoln proposed, a noncoercive federal government should offer compensation if a state voluntarily freed its slaves (the money to be returned if the state later reestablished slavery). Federal coffers should also finance voluntary colonization of freedmen.

"*We* cannot escape history," he told congressmen. Only "in *giving* freedom to the *slave*" can "we *assure* freedom to the *free*—honorable alike in what we give, and what we preserve."[51] It was a magnificent line, Lincolnian rhetoric at its most sublime. Yet the words decorated a bribe that states need not accept for thirty-eight years (and an emancipation that states who took the bribe could later repudiate). Nor did states that scorned the bribe ever have to emancipate. Nor would this Congress have passed any antislavery amendment, much less in a month, as Secretary of the Treasury Salmon P. Chase warned the president.[52]

Yet a week before the December 1 annual message, Lincoln's friend David B. Davis found the president's "whole soul . . . absorbed in his plan of remunerative emancipation. . . . He thinks that if Congress don't fail him that the problem is solved." As the historian David Donald suggests, Lincoln may have hoped that with the emancipation amendment as bait, his three commissioners to Tennessee, Louisiana, and Arkansas could better lure once-reluctant Confederates back to the Union.[53]

Lincoln's ally Orville Browning found the right word for the president's December 1 proposal and his commissioner scheme: "hallucination." Lincoln, usually the shrewdest of political realists, obviously needed one final lesson in the realities. Congressmen provided the instruction. They showed as little interest in the president's latest constitutional amendment as blacks had shown in deportation and as borderites had shown in the offer of $400 per slave and as Louisiana, Tennessee, and Arkansas had shown in voting for U.S. congressmen.

Lincoln's failed 1862 experiments yielded one major success. Failure cleared the president's head. The negative reception of his December 1 annual message finalized the failure. No longer could Lincoln believe in the efficacy of soft war weapons—his initial call for 75,000 volunteers to win the war in three months; Winfield Scott's conception that a watery anaconda might largely avoid a land war; the presidential belief that avoiding emancipation could bring rebels back; Seth Phelps's prayer that if he spared the Florence, Alabama, bridge, the war would be over. None of this shackled war for the Union would suffice.

Only a very hard war could save the Union. Lincoln knew that the manpower demands of that war would be exorbitant. Fugitive slaves offered massive manpower. Military necessity now demanded that the stalemate with Congress end, that federally imposed emancipation begin. The president now believed, with a convert's fanaticism, that saving the white men's Union demanded rallying slaves against slaveholders.

6

Long after the Final Emancipation Proclamation of January 1, 1863, after the ensuing collaboration between fugitives and the army had fatally compromised slavery, the commander in chief would famously say that he had not moved events. Rather, events had moved him. He was right, but only about 1862. If Lincoln had been assassinated on December 31, 1862, he would have gone down in history as neither a dominating president nor as a Great Emancipator. His miscalculation that a once-majority of southern Unionists could (or would want to) topple a once-minority of southern disunionists, his misperception that the Lower and Middle Souths would trot back into the Union if Border South states forever rejected secession, his half-year stall on using Congress's July 17 emancipation authorizations, his army's General Orders #3, his putdown of blacks' potential soldiering ability and their hopes for equality inside the United States, his procedures for abolitionizing states to reestablish slavery, his last-minute willingness to exempt 1,000,000 slaves from emancipation, his long-standing willingness to free all whites from the Slave Power even if all blacks remained enslaved—all these 1862 soft war wanderings, if unmitigated by the hard war zeal that Lincoln subsequently deployed, would have left a more debateable claim to greatness.

Coercive emancipation's great movers in 1862 had finally galvanized the voluntarist. The initial movers, the ones who set all Lincoln's other movers in motion, were fugitive slaves, whose escape from their masters taught increasing numbers of white Yankees that blacks could help win this war. Whites who caught the slaves' lessons included Union privates, who increasingly treasured the contrabands as spies and as military laborers; congressional Republicans, who raged at the inanity of failing to use the rebels' runaway property to destroy the Confederacy; some of Halleck's own generals, who saw General Orders #3 as detrimental to operations in the field; and all the ultraradicals and ultraconservatives, whites and blacks, rebels and Unionists, who could only agree that Lincoln's soft war, voluntary alternatives would not suffice. From that tidal wave of pressure stepped clear a coercive emancipator who was worth the wait, who would now move events as decisively as events had moved him, and who would make January 1, 1863, the biggest turning point in Civil War history.

The Collaboration 7

The year 1863 brought increasing collaboration between Union soldiers and fugitive slaves. Swiftly disappearing was runaways' 1862 bane: General Orders #3, with its closure of Union army lines against black escapees. Fast emerging was slaveholders' 1863–65 bane: the army's determined courting of determined fugitives. Wherever the army invaded, perils of running away declined, as did fugitives' wariness about flight. The new order began on the first day of the new year, when Lincoln announced a new partnership with anti-Confederate blacks.

1

By becoming slaves' partner, the former procrastinator had not turned himself totally inside out. Throughout the 1850s, Lincoln had called slavery wrong. He had prayed for its ultimate extinction. He had stonewalled against its expansion. Throughout 1861–62, he had hoped that federal financing would induce states to emancipate. He had had to be shoved harder than congressional Republicans toward forcing abolition on states. But he had told those shoving that if he became convinced that saving the Union for white men necessitated federal emancipation of black men, he would not have to be pushed toward antislavery, his personal preference.

After he proclaimed imposed abolition a military necessity, Lincoln continued to offer rebels enticingly soft landings back into the Union. After December 31, 1862, the soft landings could not include repudiation of the Emancipation Proclamation or reenslavement of any black who had been freed by military necessity. Yet as the historian William Harris has demonstrated, the post-1862 Lincoln always favored compensation for slaveholders and gradual emancipation, if a slower, gentler abolition would hasten rebels' return.[1] As late as February 3, 1865, in his Hampton Roads (Virginia) Conference with three rebel leaders, Lincoln perhaps told Confederate Vice President Alexander Stephens that a five-year delay on emancipation might be acceptable if rebel states immediately returned to the Union.[2] Two days later, Lincoln suggested rewarding slaveholders with $100 per slave, if "all resistance" to federal authority ended by April 1 and all states adopted emancipation by July 1.[3]

Late in the war, when the president pondered whether black freedmen should vote, the problem of how to lure southern whites toward reunion remained important. Lincoln personally preferred making voters of "some of the colored people," particularly "the very intelligent, and especially those who have fought gallantly in our ranks."[4] But he provided rebel states the opportunity to override his personal preference on black voting, just as he had previously invited states to reject his personal preference on black freedom and lately perhaps invited Stephens to save five more years of slavery.

Such recurring invitations aside, the president's change on January 1, 1863, remained large—from federal financing of voluntary, possibly temporary emancipation to federal imposition of coerced, assuredly permanent antislavery. Lincoln made the change larger by leaping from last-minute desperation for salvaging the old voluntarism to first-minute gusto for beginning the new imposition. No Republican had more feared that if the federal government forced federal emancipation on states, more whites would depart the Union. Thus Lincoln immediately sought compensating gains from blacks. The resulting newly aggressive emancipator fulfilled every prayer of the contraband who had helped push the commander in chief toward a war-winning collaboration.

2

On the first day of 1863, Lincoln's Final Emancipation Proclamation seemed newly aggressive not because it declared that slaves in designated rebel-held areas "henceforward shall be free," certainly not because it left slavery in nondesignated areas untouched, not even because it promised that the Union's "military and naval authorities" would "recognize and maintain the freedom" of those emancipated in the designated areas. The Preliminary Emancipation Proclamation had pledged these provisions. The final statement actually emancipated fewer slaves than the preliminary version had promised. By erasing rebel-held portions of Tennessee from his designation of areas to be emancipated, Lincoln implicitly exempted the very Confederate locale where his army exerted most authority.[5]

But in a much more startling erasure, the president scrubbed from the Preliminary Emancipation Proclamation its soft war temporizing, including its endorsement of colonization for freedmen and its exemption from emancipation when a rebel state's majority voted in a U.S. congressional election. Even more startling, the president's final proclamation added to the preliminary document the entire hard war arsenal that Congress had authorized on July 17, 1862, including and especially the declaration that fugitive slaves and other blacks would "be received into the armed services of the United States."

Despite these transforming erasures and additions, the historical literature has robbed Lincoln's breakthrough of its power. We hear, for example, that the Final Emancipation Proclamation reads like a "bill of lading," indicating its proclaimer's icy attitude toward his creation.[6] Lincoln supposedly trumpeted no battle cry for freedom, for when committed, the man's rhetorical flourishes soared.

Yet like all great wordsmiths, Lincoln fitted language to the occasion. This occasion demanded not a charismatic plea for new authority but a remorseless deployment of military power already possessed. I proclaim emancipation, the president announced, "by virtue of the power in me vested as Commander-in-Chief of the Army and Navy of the United States, in time of actual armed rebellion." The commander's language reads not like an entrepreneur's bill for past services but like a warrior's brandishing of a new weapon.

The proclamation has also been accused of emancipating slaves in rebel-held areas, where Lincoln lacked power to administer anything, while barring emancipation from Union-held areas, where the president possessed power to administer everything. That argument ignores the fact that in rebel-held areas, Lincoln presided over the only powerful federal bureaucracy he anywhere commanded: a conquering army, perfect to smooth the fugitives' road toward liberating themselves. That army, also omnipresent in Union-held border areas, could there also forge an emancipating collaboration with fugitive slaves.

The proclamation's antislavery power glistened in Lincoln's private letter, written eight days after the Final Emancipation Proclamation. The president had received intimations that Confederate "officers of high rank . . . desire the restoration of peace" on the old slavery basis. Ten days earlier, the soft war president would have cherished the news. Now, the hard war commander in chief dismissed the tidings. "I struggled nearly a year and a half to get along without touching the 'institution,'" Lincoln wrote. "When finally I conditionally determined to touch it, I gave a hundred days fair notice." I allowed rebels over three months to become again "good citizens of the United States" and thereby turn emancipation "wholly aside." Since Confederates instead "chose to disregard" my warning, my proclamation became "a military necessity." After "being made," the proclamation "must stand," for "broken eggs can not be mended" (that figure of speech again!). To come back into the Union, slave states must now approve at least "gradual emancipation." That new requirement enlarged the purpose of the war and the condition for ending it, if the president could control such matters.[7]

A controlling commander in chief could not tolerate soldiers' resistance to his commands, like the late resistance to General Orders #3. Troops would probably not resist his new order to welcome fugitives into Union lines (privates, after all, had already half killed General Orders #3). But white warriors might resist his new command to enlist blacks as soldiers. Back in July 1862, Lincoln had authorized the army to use black runaways only as military laborers. That distinction between black laboring and black soldiering fit whites' racial prejudices. By removing the distinction, Lincoln defied whites' customary declaration that "we don't want to fight side and side with the nigger. We think we are too superior a race for that."[8] Such racists also considered blacks too inferior—too cowering in the presence of masters—to kill courageously.

Lincoln's problem: how to add supposed inferiors to his army while still catering to supposed superiors' racial prejudice. A conception of how to pull off the trick had been bubbling on the surface of Union thought for months. Lincoln skimmed off the tactic and used his skillful wordsmanship (supposedly absent from the Proclamation) to craft a magic word, one that could slip the thorny black troop concept smoothly down white racists' scratchy throats. "Blacks will be used in the Union army," the commander in chief announced in his Final Emancipation Proclamation, "to *garrison* forts, positions, and other places, and to man vessels" [emphasis mine].

That word *garrison* swiftly became as important as *contraband*. Previously, "contraband" had leached humanity from emancipation, turning abolition from freeing a black into using the enemy's property against the enemy. Now, "garrisoning" leached racial equality from black soldiering, relegating blacks to guarding behind the lines while whites strode to the front.

With "garrisoning," Lincoln also threw the conservative colonization idea around the radical soldier idea. The cunning camouflage led even so radical an abolitionist as Wendell Phillips to buy the idea without realizing the trick. Phillips noted that earlier the president had asked a black whether I may "colonize you among the sickly deserts or the vast jungles of South America." Now, Lincoln requested that a black "let me colonize you in the forts of the Union, and put rifles in your hands!"[9] Phillips here missed the irony, soothing to racial reactionaries: Rifle-bearing blacks would be colonized in enclaves, whether in garrisons or on ships, almost as separated from supposed superiors as if the supposed inferiors had left for Latin American steambaths.

The garrison concept furthermore turned blacks' supposed elevation from laborer to soldier into a continued menial role. Back in August 1862,

Governor Samuel Kirkwood of Iowa had written about "*sixty men on 'extra duty*' as teamsters, etc. whose place could just as well be filled with *niggers.*" If the army used black contraband for "making roads, chopping wood, policing camps," white soldiers would be released to take "*Richmond or any other rebel city.*" As for "negroes fighting," the governor declared that he would have no "regret if . . . a part of the *dead* are niggers."[10] With the garrison vocabulary and concept, Lincoln played into that low-minded cynicism, while still toying with Phillips's high-minded joy. An awesome politician, growing toward the peak of his talent, now hastened the American emancipation pace.

In a brief note written thirteen days after the proclamation, Lincoln clarified why a previous malingerer had suddenly sped ahead. "The proclamation has been issued," Lincoln wrote, for "we were not succeeding—at best, were progressing slowly—without it." Now that "we bear all the disadvantage of it, . . . we must also take some benefit from it." He would reap benefits by designating some positions we now hold to "be *garrisoned* by colored troops," whether "in whole or in part." Garrisoning by blacks would free whites "now necessary at those places, to be employed elsewhere" [emphasis mine].[11]

Other racial discriminations in the Union's use of black soldiers also eased whites' racial objections. Black privates received $7/month and whites $13 (until Congress equalized the pay in 1864). Blacks served solely in segregated units, under solely white commissioned officers (until late in the war, when over 100 blacks, starting with an almost white mulatto, won commissions, usually as noncommanding chaplains). In addition to a disproportionate amount of soldiering behind the lines, blacks endured a disproportionate amount of nasty "fatigue duty." Often, they guarded unhealthy contraband labor camps. Facing more exposures to epidemics and less to bullets than white troops, black soldiers suffered less from battle fatalities and more from fatal diseases.[12]

Blacks often agitated against these discriminations. Agitators eventually secured those nine dozen black commissioned officers and equal pay for privates. But while southern anti-Confederate blacks resourcefully protested, they also served. Their service in second-class roles inspired more white acceptance of the garrison philosophy, which inspired more soldiers to beckon more slaves from Confederate lines, which inspired more potential fugitives to dare flight. In late March 1863, the president waxed ecstatic about the new collaboration. "The colored population," he wrote, "is the great *available* and yet *unavailed* of, force for restoring the Union. The bare sight of fifty thousand armed, and drilled black soldiers on the banks of the Mississippi, would end the rebellion at once."[13]

3

To entice 50,000 black soldiers (or as it turned out, 178,000), the president molded his army into the world's most powerful antislavery bureaucracy. When the commander in chief issued antislavery orders, the command to step lively to the president's new tune went straight down an enforcing military hierarchy. Thus Henry Halleck, now the army's general in chief, alerted his leading subordinate, Ulysses S. Grant, to the commander in chief's changed outlook. The government means "to withdraw from the enemy as much productive labor as possible," Halleck wrote Grant on March 31, 1863, "and to employ those so withdrawn, to the best possible advantage against the enemy." Since every laboring black frees a white Confederate to fight against us, "every slave withdrawn from the enemy, is equivalent to a white man put *hors de combat*." The Union will use southern blacks "for the defense of forts, depôts, etc., . . . to hold points on the Mississippi during the sickly season," and to serve "as laborers, teamsters, cooks, etc."

Many of your officers, Halleck warned Grant, reportedly "discourage the negroes from coming under our protection" and "by ill treatment, force them to return to their masters." The commander in chief has spun 180° on these matters, Halleck wrote, and his army must spin accordingly. "The character of the war has much changed," leaving "no possible hope of a reconciliation with the rebels." So the government "has adopted a policy, and we must cheerfully and faithfully carry out that policy."[14]

Grant faithfully complied. In February 1863, in a watered-down version of General Orders #3, he had ordered unemployable blacks barred from his lines. In April 1863, he instead ordered subordinates "to encourage all negroes

Contraband Enticers

Benjamin F. Butler, who welcomed and put the first contraband to work at Fortress Monroe, Virginia and may have first used the soothing word. Courtesy of the U. S. Army Military History Institute.

Lorenzo Thomas, Lincoln's right hand man in enforcing the (hardly unenforceable) Emancipation Proclamation. Courtesy of the U. S. Army Military History Institute.

to come within our lines," to "afford all facilities for the completion" of black regiments, even to remove "prejudices against them." Our commander is now an emancipator, Grant concluded, and we must thus zealously emancipate, for soldiers must "carry out a policy which they would not inaugurate, in the same good faith and with the same zeal as if it were of their choosing."[15]

To ensure that soldiers carried out emancipation, Lincoln sent Adjutant-General Lorenzo Thomas to the Mississippi Valley in April 1863. The special presidential envoy bore instructions to insist on the new policy and to prepare a blueprint for federal use of fugitives. Our president, Lorenzo

Thomas told the troops in widely reported addresses, is "slow in coming to a determination." But "once he puts his foot down, . . . he is not going to take it up. He has put his foot down." He will not tolerate soldiers who bar fugitives. Runaways are to "be received with open arms; they are to be fed and clothed; they are to be armed."[16]

Lorenzo Thomas's insistences showed again that Lincoln issued no papal bulls against comets. While the president's sketchy civil bureaucracy could no more secure emancipation than extinguish comets, this innovative head bureaucrat reached beyond civil bureaucrats to find his army law enforcers. The president also reached beyond normal army bureaucrats to send Thomas, his own envoy, to ensure that his willpower galvanized his soldiers. But what a difference a half year had made in his charges to special envoys. In late 1862, he had sent special representatives to Arkansas, Louisiana, and Tennessee to seek a reunion based on perpetual slavery. He now sent Lorenzo Thomas to demand that his army hasten emancipation.

After inspecting the Tennessee-Mississippi front and the runaways now flooding Union lines, special envoy Thomas sent back to Washington his blueprint for the new Mississippi Valley order. Ex-slaves, wrote Lorenzo Thomas, "must be settled in rear of our lines as our armies advance, . . . in position to make their own living." Most of the "men should be employed with our armies as laborers and teamsters," with some "induced" and others "conscripted" to be "soldiers." Still other males, "with the women and children," should be "placed on the abandoned plantations to till the ground," with "competent [white] men . . . as overseers. . . . The negro Regiments could give protection to these plantations, and also operate effectively against the guerrillas." They could additionally "garrison positions" already conquered, so that "additional [white] regiments could be sent to the front."[17]

Lincoln endorsed Lorenzo Thomas's overall plan, not least because its key parts had previously succeeded. Contraband agricultural experiments had produced bountiful harvests in the South Carolina sea islands in 1861–62. There Confederate masters' escape from the Union navy, followed by slaves' employment as paid contraband, had enriched the Union with bumper cotton crops.[18] So too, the garrison part of Thomas's plan had succeeded in Louisiana in 1862. There Ben Butler had chosen the first black troops enlisted in the Civil War, the *Confederates'* Louisiana Native Guards, to be among the first enlisted into the Union army. Butler employed the troops for garrison duty in "unhealthy positions" and for "fatigue duty, such as making roads, building bridges, and draining marshes."[19]

In May 1863, Lincoln appointed Lorenzo Thomas to head the new War Department Bureau of Colored Troops, charged with carrying out the scheme. Thomas returned to the western theater of war, this time bearing presidential orders to entice fugitive slaves, to establish contraband labor camps, and to perfect blacks' defenses of garrisons. With that special bureaucratic establishment augmenting the normal administrative hierarchy, Lincoln pointed his army toward enforcing his (allegedly unenforceable) Emancipation Proclamation.

Or to be more precise, Lincoln's western army moved beyond the emancipation authorized in the Final Emancipation Proclamation. That proclamation, in continued hopes of luring loyal Tennesseeans back into the Union, had implicitly exempted all of Tennessee, including its rebel-controlled areas, from the presidential grant of freedom. To bypass the exemption, cunning Union officials offered Tennessee slaves not immediate freedom in exchange for running away but eventual freedom in exchange for good military service. In Tennessee, Lincoln's men also offered slave soldiers' masters a voucher for postwar compensation, akin to Benjamin Butler's receipts for contrabands, in exchange for putting up with the ruse. The result: 20,130 Tennessee blacks, although supposedly exempt from the Emancipation Proclamation, fought in the Union army.

Thus did the president replace southern antifugitive patrols with an extended northern liberty line. Before the war, only Border South fugitives could enjoy help from a nearby Yankee liberator. Now the army brought helpful Northerners down to the Middle South, sometimes down to the Lower South. Lincoln's extended liberty line still hardly offered freedom on a silver platter. Black fugitives could be captured and frightfully punished if they failed to reach welcoming soldiers. Especially in Mississippi Valley combat zones, filthy soldier uniforms often prevented runaways from knowing whether distant troops were rebels or Federals. But the white collaborator in the White House had lowered the danger, and black collaborators in the field became more daring. Without that black response, the Emancipation Proclamation would have indeed been a papal bull against comets. With the contrabands' surge toward their new allies, the newly Great Emancipator had co-achieved an expanding wave of freedom.

4

The Thomas labor system featured wages for new freedmen. Sometimes army personnel presided over contraband labor camps and paid the wages. Sometimes the military leased abandoned plantations to capitalists, often Northerners, charged with paying and protecting the contraband. Outside contraband camps, some masters in invaded areas also paid their slaves to labor, fearing that blacks would abscond otherwise.[20]

To protect wage laborers and to garrison conquered forts, Thomas massively recruited black soldiers. His biggest problem was no longer white troops, who now helped him attract fugitives, but runaways' frequent preference for work as civilian wage earners. For many an ex-slave, that glorious new role beat fatigue or garrison duty in the army, under often unpleasant white officers. Still, Thomas cajoled the fugitives, and when pleading failed, he conscripted them. Thomas and his subordinates raised 21,000 black troops in the Mississippi Valley by the end of 1863, 56,000 by the end of 1864, and 76,000 by the end of the war, or 41 percent of Union black troops.[21] Mississippi Valley black troops added a final payoff to Grant's Henry-Donelson jackpot. They also provided the final proof that by substituting aggressive enticement of fugitives for the fugitive-inhibiting General Orders #3, and by using the army bureaucracy to ensure that troops followed his transformation, Lincoln had forged a partnership with slaves that could be lethal to slaveholders.

Lincoln's new partners wanted to prove they could be lethal in front line combat, not on back line fatigue duty. Occasionally, they received their chance. Their most famous opportunity occurred at Fort Wagner, guarding the harbor of Charleston, South Carolina, on July 18, 1863. Their famous leader was Colonel Robert Gould Shaw, white commander of the all-black (except for the all-white commissioned officers) 54th Massachusetts Infantry.[22] Shaw implored his commanding general to let his 630 blacks lead the assault on Fort Wagner. When this colonel begged, generals listened.

Shaw had been educated at Harvard and enriched by one of Massachusetts' premier families. At Fort Wagner, he commanded a superior company of northern free blacks, including one of Frederick Douglass's sons. His recruiters comprised the northern abolitionist elite, including Douglass. These credentials aside, Shaw's division commander, Major General Truman Seymour, cynically gave blacks first chance to be killed. We will "put those d—d niggers from Massachusetts in the advance," chortled Seymour, for "we may as well get rid of them one time as another."[23]

Shaw led his blacks down a three-quarter-mile narrow spit of sand, over a four-foot water-logged ditch, and up Fort Wagner's elevated main wall. Civil War offensive tactics were never worse. Rebel defenders, protected inside the fort, gunned down unprotected chargers. Miraculously, Shaw and a few blacks jumped the ditch and climbed the wall. There, swaying in the darkness atop the parapet, with no idea where to leap down on Confederates who pointed bayoneted rifles at them, miracles ended for the Boston Brahmin and his troops. A shot pierced the commander's heart. He pitched into the fort, falling "*foeward*," wrote the poet James Russell Lowell, "as fits a man."* Many of Shaw's troops also lay slaughtered. On the morrow, Confederates tumbled Shaw's corpse into a grave outside the walls, supposedly sneering words to the effect of "we have buried him with his niggers."

Such alleged sneers generate legends. In our time, Robert Gould Shaw's legend marches on, encased in the Shaw Memorial sculpture above Boston Common and illustrated in the movie *Glory*. In his own time, Shaw's story helped destroy the myth of a black race allegedly too docile to fight. The thought of Shaw's expired heart, forever entombed with courageous blacks, led many a Yankee to recant former opinions that the allegedly inferior race would never make good soldiers.

Still, the wildly exceptional Shaw incident distorts posterity's image of Civil War black troops. Whites rarely allowed black regiments to lead charges. Most black companies contained southern ex-slaves, not northern free blacks. Most recently freed black soldiers patrolled out west, back of the lines. Few sported Harvard-educated heirs as officers. The more typical,

---

* The probably unnecessary emphasis is mine. Lowell's wonderful word invention is fittingly inscribed on the Shaw Memorial. For more on that sculpture, see pp. 135–38.

if less famous, black proof of manhood in battle occurred at Milliken's Bend, a month before Robert Gould Shaw shared blacks' glory.

The town of Milliken's Bend thrived twenty miles up the Mississippi River from Vicksburg. Beneath the town, a Unionist camp guarded the river bend. In mid-May 1863, Ulysses S. Grant stripped the Milliken's Bend camp of all but 160 whites, seeking to concentrate men on the siege of Vicksburg. To replace white warriors, 1,250 newly enlisted blacks garrisoned the camp. On the steaming night of June 6, 1863, four rebel regiments surprised black guards. The black novices, soldiers for only sixteen days, fumbled with their guns, fell back, stood firm, and flashed their bayonets. The blacks' white captain called the ensuing bayonet brawl "a horrible fight, the worst I was ever engaged in—not even excepting Shiloh."[24] In one ironic tableau, a Union black and a Confederate white lay slain, arms locked like brothers, each with the other's bayonet planted in his belly.[25]

At last, a Union ship reinforced the unyielding blacks, and the rebels retreated. Black soldiers, declared an astounded Confederate battle report, resisted us "with considerable obstinacy, while the white or true Yankee portion ran like whipped curs." One Confederate master suffered the best proof of black obstinacy. His slave captured him "and brought him into camp with great gusto." As a Wisconsin cavalry officer described the lesson many Northerners learned from Fort Wagner and Milliken's Bend (and from the battle for Port Hudson, Louisiana, where black troops futilely charged and their bodies were left to rot under the blazing sun), "I never believed in niggers before, but by Jasus, they are hell for fighting."[26]

5

By the end of 1863, Mississippi Valley masters winced that blacks had become hell in running away. Slave flight had been a trickle when no Union army was present and like a thin stream when General Orders #3 half prevailed; it became akin to a roaring river when Lincoln's troops welcomed blacks. The new situation especially attracted kindly masters' favorites, the "family-raised negroes." The same lament echoed again and again: "Those I *trusted most* deceived me most!" Runaways included my "favorite of all the negroes I ever owned—he was more like a good friend than a servant to me!" My trusted black "is a great rascal acting in this manner. . . . He is an ungrateful and hypocritical wretch." And "they left without a goodby."[27] With those wails, would-be paternalists conceded that coercive patrols outside the gates, more than paternalist affection inside the estate, had kept slaves at "home."

Posterity can never know how many allegedly ungrateful wretches ran away. Guesses hover around 500,000 successful Civil War fugitives, or one in eight slaves. The 12.5 percentage seems approximately right, for most Lower South neighborhoods never experienced the sine qua non of massive runaways: an invading army that substituted an encouraging Yankee gateway for deterring local patrols. The 500,000 number also seems remotely right, for after Federals scrapped General Orders #3, slaves' flights became extremely heavy in invaded areas.[28]

The capacity of some federal invaders to encourage heavy streams of runaways resembled the capacity of some federal coercion to encourage the Unionist wall of Border South states. Without Union troops in black belt neighborhoods, few slaves dared escape, just as without federal intimidators in white belt neighborhoods, secessionists might have intimidated the majority of Missouri and West Virginia Unionists. But in both cases, Union armies did no more than allow potentially anti-Confederate Southerners, black and white, to express their preferences. Because most slaves preferred freedom and most white borderites preferred the Union, Lincoln's legions cleared the way for hundreds of thousands of enthusiastic Union soldiers. That infusion of eager Union recruits would have been unthinkable if these Southerners had been forced at the point of bayonets to suppress their anti-Confederate disloyalty.

Because of so many Southerners' unionist preferences, Lincoln's soldiers became the most successful Civil War filibusterers. When Yankees pounded an area, urging slaves to flee from tyrants, the number of blacks who responded far exceeded the number of southern whites who joined Braxton Bragg's Confederate filibustering effort, on his way to Perryville, or Robert E. Lee's, on the way to Antietam Creek. Even federal filibusterers' large yield of eastern Tennessee whites paled in comparison to Mississippi Valley blacks' response to liberators.

Thus did the collaboration of soldiers and runaways secure the fugitive slave road to emancipation. Nowhere else in the Americas did that road dominate the emancipation process. This phenomenon exposed an Achilles heel as vulnerable as any that ever crippled a ruling class inside its invaded domain. After Civil War blacks could "run off without danger of recapture," concluded William Tecumseh Sherman, nothing could "revive slavery." Or as Ulysses S. Grant exclaimed when he left the great river and pointed his troops eastward, "Slavery is already dead and cannot be resurrected."[29]

On the day Grant issued slavery's Mississippi Valley death certificate—August 30, 1863—slavery was also dying in the Border South. Border slavery's demise followed the script that pre–Civil War Southerners had foreseen. When agitating for fugitive slave laws or for enslaved Kansas, Southerners had worried that too slim a police force stood between fugitive-enticing Yankees and the South's northern hinterlands. When warning that Abraham Lincoln would menace slavery in the borderlands, disunionists had predicted that the president would enforce fugitive slave laws too little, spread patronage to antislavery whites too much, and abolish slavery in Washington, D.C.

Secessionists' predictions about a free labor District's disastrous consequences had paralleled earlier southern predictions about free soil Kansas's antislavery impact. Just as borderland Missouri, with under 10 percent of its people enslaved, would supposedly succumb to Kansas neighbors who welcomed fugitives, so enslaved Maryland, with half its blacks already free, would allegedly succumb to fugitive-welcoming Washington, D.C., neighbors. The predicted day of reckoning for southern Maryland slaveholders came on April 16, 1862, when Republican congressmen, despite some Lincoln objections, abolished slavery in the capital. Freedom's new terrain instantly became an antislavery magnet. The District needed military laborers. Contraband camps sprang up around the capital, with labor hungry commanders none too scrupulous about investigating whether black arrivals were freedmen or slaves. Slaves thus sneaked into the army and into freedom.[30]

In Maryland as in the Mississippi Valley, fugitives multiplied whenever Union soldiers penetrated a neighborhood.[31] Union soldiers became fixtures in many Maryland neighborhoods after the Baltimore riot of April 19, 1861. Troops' presence led to the familiar 1861–62 tale of Union armies and fugitives: masters running into Union lines after runaway slaves; the

Lincoln administration begging generals to help loyal slaveholders find escaped property; harassed generals having too little time to be helpful; some outraged privates finding helpfulness immoral; and then fugitives and soldiers drilling holes in army regulations against runaways. The upshot was early vindication of secessionists' prophecy that however hard Lincoln pretended (or honestly tried) to enforce the Fugitive Slave Law, soft enforcement would bring forth runaways.

Since Lincoln's Final Emancipation Proclamation exempted loyal areas, Border South slaves could not automatically free themselves by dashing inside Union army camps. But border slaveholders' reprieve from Lincoln's new emancipating regime frayed in later 1863, when army recruiting stations supplemented army camps. Recruiters who craved able-bodied black males often welcomed fugitive slaves who begged to enlist. So much for initial regulations that only freed blacks could be recruited.

As the army's appetite for black troops increased, the War Department's regulations relaxed. The department first allowed slaves of disloyal masters to volunteer, later slaves of loyal masters who consented (and received compensation), still later slaves of nonconsenting masters. Then in January 1865, Congress freed enlisted slaves' dependents. Thereafter, black husbands could liberate wives and children with successful dashes to recruiting stations.

Such dashes still required courage. The Union's recruiting agents sometimes rejected suspect or unhealthy blacks. Masters' agents sometimes intercepted runaways, and masters' retribution on runaways could be terrible. Grim retaliations could deter sprints toward recruiting stations. Furthermore, not every slave loved the army route to liberty (which could be a route to the grave).

By mid-1864 in many border places, roving recruiting squads bypassed these problems. Now slaves did not have to sneak past masters to recruiting stations. Instead, army recruiters, often themselves black, sneaked past masters to the slave quarters. When slaves fled from both masters *and* recruiters, roving recruiters sometimes kidnapped the escapees.

The debacle left border slaveholders three options. Some still futilely hounded the army for their runaways. More used wages to bribe slaves to stay. A few agitated for abolition, in hopes of currying political favor from Lincoln. Many nonslaveholding politicians also chose the latter strategy.

Another vindication of the secessionists' prophecy transpired: Lincoln did indeed hand patronage to border antislavery advocates, thereby encouraging state abolition laws.[32] So federal imposition of antislavery sometimes became unnecessary. Secessionists had predicted that too.

Lincoln deployed more federal patronage than even secessionists had envisioned. Here again, the army gave the commander in chief his allegedly missing antislavery weapons. The new troop recruiting business far outstripped that previously biggest federal business, the post office. The federal draft law of March 1863 established both a president-appointed board of enrollment and a provost marshal in each congressional district. Provost marshals appointed deputies who appointed assistants—appointments all controlled, directly or indirectly, by the commander in chief. To Lincoln, good politics as well as good patriotism demanded the appointment of border Republicans who sympathized with voluntary state emancipation.[33] He had, after all, always (wrongly) thought that if border states voluntarily gave up slavery, rebels would voluntarily give up the Confederacy.

In the borderlands, Maryland gave up the institution first. Before the war, half of Maryland's blacks had been freed. Washington, D.C., beckoned the other half after mid-1862. Army camps and army recruiters attracted and sometimes seized runaways with increasingly invasive procedures after mid-1863. Then in 1864, with the administration feeding patronage to white politicians of the "right" stripe, the staggering institution collapsed. In November 1864, Maryland became an exclusively free labor state. Missouri whites wiped out their last shred of slavery two months later.[34]

The most enslaved Border South state, Kentucky, and the least enslaved, Delaware, clung to their remnants until the postwar Thirteenth Amendment completed national antislavery (without their consent). Kentucky slavery survived the war, barely, because army recruiters more slowly received authorizations to go after unconsenting Kentuckians' slaves.[35] As the abolitionists' sneer continued to run, Lincoln hoped to have God on his side, but he *had* to have Kentucky whites.

Still, around 40 percent of Kentucky's able-bodied male slaves served in the Union army.[36] These 24,052 black Kentuckians ranked second in number (only barely) to Louisianans among Union southern black recruits. Kentucky's black soldiers freed not only themselves but also (after January

1865) their wives and children. Meanwhile, Delaware kept its handful of slaves, for the Union army never occupied this almost totally Unionist state. The seemingly odd holdout of Delaware, the least enslaved state, reemphasizes the critical point: An attracting army and cautious runaways together secured abolition, fugitive slave style, whether in the Mississippi Valley or in the borderlands.

What did *not* happen as borderland emancipation crept forward is deeply revealing, recalling what did *not* happen during Maryland's post-April 19 secession crisis and during Grant's preparations in Kentucky for his Henry-Donelson campaigns. Aside from western Missouri guerrillas, most borderland whites did not wage eternal irregular warfare against Union supposed invaders or drive unendingly for disunion, not even after Lincoln had become a very immediate menace to slavery. Before the Civil War, the Lower South's aggressive defenders had accused borderites not of rejecting slavery but of being soft in defending it, of not caring enough about what should be their highest priority. We will be nothing like slack, borderites had answered, if Yankees clearly besiege slavery.

The siege had come. Slackness had continued. Inertia had been fatal. Proslavery's uncompromising warriors had been right after all: A third of the South had too compromised a proslavery spirit to stand and deliver at the crisis of slavery's fate.

6

So which half of the collaboration, runaway slaves or Lincoln and his army, most freed the slaves? That abstruse controversy, unfortunately popular of late, deflects attention from the essential emancipating power: the indispensable collaboration.[37] Fugitive slaves could not have ended slavery without the army's intervention, any more than Lincoln's army could have forged a successful liberty line without the fugitives' intervention. White police power was too powerful and slave resisters too canny for mass flight to occur until chances of success brightened. So prewar fugitives had remained scarce when Northerners lived far away. Wartime fugitives continued to be scant when Yankee armies remained far off.

When Union troops first marched close, more blacks ran away, weakening General Orders #3. But the leaky barricade deterred other slaves. After black fugitives' pressure helped impel Lincoln to substitute the welcome mat for the barricade, many more runaways challenged the less formidable risks of escaping. So probing fugitives discovered that the federal invasion made flight less dangerous. Then more runaways weakened the invaders' enforcement of General Orders #3. Then more invaders became more inviting and more slaves more daring. Who freed the slaves, the army or the runaways? Let us first decide which came first, the chicken or the egg.

A more fruitful analysis could discern how the army/fugitive collaboration illuminates not only wartime emancipation but also black history before and after the war. Viewing prewar slavery from the vantage point of the Civil War, some slaves' paternalistic ties to masters seem obvious. Witness some blacks' willing participation in Confederate armies, whether as occasional sharpshooters or as customary laborers. The war, however, also shows (as it showed outraged paternalists) that paternalistic governance did not alone control most slaves, who did depart without saying goodbye. Intimidating force was mandatory, including police power beyond the plantation, to maintain slavery.

The war further demonstrated that when prewar Southerners demanded fugitive slave laws and Kansas-Nebraska Acts to bolster police deterrence of fugitives in borderland areas, they had good reason to seek protection. Wartime fugitives showed that most slaves were neither zombie-like Samboes nor butchering Nat Turners but wary Frederick Douglasses, probing nonviolently for openings that might allow a safe escape—and streaming through escape routes when safe passage seemed plausible.

Runaways' wartime gambles on dashes *from* the slave quarters also reemphasize the limitations of dwelling exclusively on prewar slaves' cultural creations *inside* the quarters. Slaves did not merely flee the cultural damage of slavery. They fled the very fact of slavery. Fugitives were very much agents in the way freedom came, not sole agents but crucial agents who found the way to deflect whites' history. Just as there could have been no prewar fugitive slave crises or wartime congressional laws on contraband without black runaways, so there could have been few southern black anti-

Confederates without the hundreds of thousands of runaways who bet their destiny and their people's future on flight.

After the flights came the final act of emancipation, again featuring collaboration between blacks and the commander in chief. The Thirteenth Amendment to the U.S. Constitution, abolishing slavery everywhere in the nation, passed Congress on January 31, 1865, under much pressure from Lincoln. Before the year expired, the necessary three-fourths of the states had ratified the amendment. Lincoln's lobbying for this antislavery climax contrasted with his agitation for two previously proposed Thirteenth Amendments. The president's endorsements had swung from forever prohibiting federal emancipation (March 4, 1861) to permitting federal financing of a state's emancipation (December 1, 1862) to empowering exclusively federal emancipation (January 1865). This moral progression would have led many an American politician to smug self-congratulation. Lincoln instead modestly, attractively, knew that lowly slaves had helped secure the victory.

The Thirteenth Amendment sealed the triumph. In most Deep South areas, the army had not invaded and few fugitives had freed themselves. In the Middle South, where military necessity had enabled more slaves to become contraband, postwar courts could rule that blacks must be reenslaved after the necessity evaporated. Only an antislavery constitutional amendment could guarantee the contraband permanent freedom and liberate the many Lower South slaves that no military necessity had touched.

U.S. constitutional amendments require overwhelming majorities: two-thirds of Congress plus three-fourths of the states. An antislavery amendment annihilated many states' basic social institution, in a nation where federal power had never reached so far before. The Thirteenth Amendment also gave freedom to blacks and confiscated property from whites, in a Union previously dedicated to protecting largely white freedom and property. That gigantic shift in whites' view of the world required wide and deep public conviction that such a revolutionary change was rightful.

Slaves' actions and Lincoln's leadership together forged the necessary sense of emancipation's fitness. Under the magnifying glass of war, slaves had undermined many white stereotypes. They had proved themselves to be neither docile nor uppity nor insurrectionist nor barbarian. They had struggled like men against their army's racial discriminations while still fighting like patriots against Confederates.[38] When protesting against their discriminatory wages, black soldiers had almost never declared that they would not fight until their paychecks equaled whites. Instead, protestors had usually refused to accept *any* payment for their soldiering, until their wages matched whites'. To that nonprovoking (and ultimately successful) style of nonviolent resistance, they had added useful services in ugly military duties, whether cleaning latrines or erecting dangerous fortifications or guarding disease-ridden labor camps or garrisoning exposed forts. When allowed to serve as front line warriors, whether at Fort Wagner or Port Hudson or Milliken's Bend or with Grant at Petersburg late in the war, they had courageously charged toward annihilation, undertrained and underarmed yet as committed as the average white. White soldiers, seeing fugitives' heroics, had bridled at imposing General Orders #3 on such freedom seekers. Other Yankees, reading of blacks' military exploits, believed that saviors of the Union hardly deserved postwar slavery.

A contrary black behavior would have undermined the Thirteenth Amendment. If slaves had risen in insurrection, or if black soldiers had refused to fight without equal pay or without black officers, or if freedmen had massively rejected unpleasant duties behind the lines, too many white Americans would probably have rejected the Thirteenth Amendment. Blacks seldom allowed that scenario to be tested. From their vulnerability under slavery, they had become experts on how to read whites. They understood that their Civil War prospects demanded going as far as but no farther than whites could approve. The nonviolent runaway and the cooperative soldier were just the roles to strike. Whites' acceptance of the Thirteenth Amendment rewarded blacks for their astutely nonthreatening agency in their own liberation.

7

To appreciate white collaborators' insistence on nonthreatening black agency, nothing compares to Augustus Saint-Gaudens's Robert Shaw Memorial (1897). The magnificent 11' x 14' bronze tableau was first permanently installed halfway up a hill overlooking the Boston Common. There

The Shaw Memorial

The Shaw Memorial as it appeared when first unveiled in Boston in 1897.
Courtesy of The Houghton Library, Harvard University, Cambridge, Massachusetts.

it still stands as centerpiece of arguably America's most aesthetically and symbolically powerful city block. The gems around Saint-Gaudens's statue, and the Shaw Memorial itself, gain force by reiterating a master theme in Yankee culture: the grave danger of empowering untrustworthy republicans, of any class or color.

Across Beacon Street from the Shaw Memorial, Charles Bulfinch's Masschusetts State House (1795) crowns the hill. Bulfinch's perfectly balanced home for republican government catches the essence of American Revolutionaries' antidote to vulnerable mobocracies: an aristocratic republic, checked and balanced against irresponsible demagogues and irrational mobs. Halfway between the Massachusetts State House and the Shaw Memorial, a bronze rendition of Horace Mann presides. The wealthy Mann, the leading pre–Civil War crusader for free schools for the masses, hoped that universal public education would civilize and Americanize lower-class whites (especially immigrants), thereby molding raw human material into responsible citizens. Halfway between the Boston Common and the Shaw Memorial, the Park Street Church stands. Here in 1829, William Lloyd Garrison first fulminated against unchecked slaveholders' unbalanced power.

The Shaw Memorial deserves to be at the center of these pleas for reliable republicans. Despite northern whites' apprehensions about impoverished or foreign or slaveholding members of their own race, empowering a supposed backward race roused extra forebodings. Saint-Gaudens eased misgivings by consigning his sculpture's tidy lines of black soldiers safely to the background, with a white angel drifting reassuringly above.

The sculptor also soothingly depicted the blacks as focused and resolved yet quiet, serene. The last five columns of men seem as nonviolent as soldiers striding toward a violent confrontation can be. Their peaceable canteens, knapsacks, and sleeping rolls bulge prominently. Their rifles rest lightly on shoulders and cupping hands. Up front marches not an armed black but a weaponless drummer boy. His beat seems stable, steady, alien from the wild pounding of an unnatural fanatic. He leads "dark outcasts," remarked William James, who seem "so true to nature that one can almost hear them breathing as they march."[39]

Their white commander's stance helps identify them as outcasts who surge against inhumanity.[40] Robert Gould Shaw, consuming the sculpture's foreground astride his huge horse, obscures two-fifths of his black soldiers as he directs the 54th Massachusetts Regiment toward Charleston and the suicidal charge at Fort Wagner. The white commander who hides 40 percent of his blacks hints at a white men's U.S. Constitution that counted each slave as three-fifths of a man.[41] At the same time, Shaw's posture, ramrod straight and still on his horse in contrast to the forward slant of the black marchers, underlines blacks' agency in moving a biracial collaboration toward recasting a black as fully a man. Yet not the black outcasts but Shaw has a weapon at the ready, his sword. The bronze tableau celebrates blacks as respectful, faithful, surging followers of the enlightened leadership that Bulfinch, Mann, Garrison, and Boston Brahmins such as Shaw would bestow on republics.

Saint-Gaudens here rejected two stereotypes and perpetuated another. He rejected the notion that Northerners love the race, Southerners love the individual. In this Northerner's bronze relief, one can discern twenty-one black faces, each unique. The sculptor also rejected Northerners' prewar image of potentially barbarous children who might rise in insurrection. But Saint-Gaudens perpetuated Northerners' stereotype of wartime blacks who obeyed liberators' every command. Saint-Gaudens's portrait of calmly obedient privates missed Civil War blacks' struggle against army orders that first excluded them and subsequently discriminated against them. But the sculpture caught the spirit of blacks' work within the white system, using resistance that whites could approve, nonviolently fleeing toward the white power structure without murder in their eyes, and then earning a nation's gratitude for unpleasant martial duties, effectively performed. With the Thirteenth Amendment, that image, combined with Lincoln's shrewd politicking, brought the collaboration between black and white liberators to climax.

8

From this Civil War collaboration, a biracial tradition evolved. In the alliance between Frederick Douglass, nonviolent runaway who raised troops for (and donated offspring to) the Massachusetts 54th, and Robert Gould Shaw, Brahmin officer and custodian of white traditions, lay the seeds of freedom marchers who a century later would assault segregation and disenfranchisement. Remove Shaw from his horse, discard his sword, sculpt him alongside black marchers who firmly grasp placards instead of lightly shouldering rifles, place Martin Luther King, Jr., beside the nonviolent drummer boy—there you have the twentieth-century version of the nineteenth-century collaboration.

Fugitive slaves of the 1860s and civil rights crusaders of the 1960s both understood that nonviolent resistance would best divide and conquer a racist American majority. If an exploited racial minority cannot prevail alone, a fraction of the exploiting race must help. Whether in Douglass's time or King's, black violence counterproductively fused white exploiters. Douglass's and King's nonviolent tactics instead divided the white establishment and secured white admirers and allies.

Blacks thereby outplayed the would-be master race in a minority's all-important divide-and-conquer game. In preCivil War times, such a slave victory had seemed remote, for slaveowners had played divide-and-conquer far more successfully. To deter slave insurrection, masters had bribed black informants to betray black rebels. Upper class titans had thus severed lower class brotherhoods and gained the knowledge to smother almost every black conspiracy before a white could be touched. So too, to protect themselves against the North's permanent white majority, prewar southern politicians had courted northern whites who disliked blacks and dreaded a civil war. The Slave Power had thus split the Yankees and secured national majorities for fugitive-inhibiting laws.

Then the Slave Power had overplayed its hand, in the counterproductive manner of slave insurrectionists, and had therefore united a majority that had to be divided. The Slave Power's escalating demands for minority legislation both repelled northern allies who had appeased the South and fueled Lincoln's anti–Slave Power rise to the presidency. Secessionists' revolt against the Union completed northern whites' fusion against the Slave Power and opened fissures within the Slave South. Lincoln pounced on opportunities to divide and conquer southern folk, just as runaways seized opportunities to divide and conquer white folk. The conquerors' collaboration yielded a harvest of black anti-Confederates that profoundly compromised the Confederacy.

The Harvest 8

The Union's harvest of southern black anti-Confederates widened its economic, home front, and especially manpower advantages. By garrisoning captured forts, guarding railroad tracks, and protecting contraband camps, black troops freed white troops to lend Grant's and Sherman's advancing armies overwhelming numerical superiority. Ex-slaves also contributed one-eighth of Grant's eastern armies during their final siege of Lee and much of Sherman's military labor during his climactic march through Georgia and the Carolinas.

1

Abolitionists had told the pre-1863 Lincoln that an emancipation proclamation would make one equal two. One slave emancipated would yield one worker lost to the Confederacy plus one worker gained for the Union. After January 1, 1863, Lincoln helped to achieve just this result. Something like

350,000 southern blacks added their labor to the Union army and navy (and subtracted that labor from Confederate enterprise). Of these men, some 200,000 worked for the military as unenlisted laborers. Another 150,000 enlisted as soldiers or sailors (with northern free blacks adding another 50,000).

More ex-slaves continued to work plantation soil. Now, not lashes but wages induced their labor. Now, not masters but masters' conquerors owned or leased their site of labor. By subtracting products from the rebels' degenerating economy and adding riches to Federals' booming enterprise, these fugitives from slavery truly made one equal two.

In the 1860s, a wild inflation in Confederate prices turned one-penny candy into a one-dollar treat. A savage depreciation in slave prices simultaneously drove a prime field hand's market value down ten times. As poverty spread, bread riots afflicted rebel cities and semistarvation depleted Robert E. Lee's army.[1]

Not so much blighted production as blocked transportation pitched the Confederate economy downward. While Winfield Scott's watery anaconda around the eastern Confederacy remained uncompleted until the war's last three months, even an incomplete trade stoppage damaged an already shaky Confederate economy. English sleek and low blockade runners could slip compact loads (such as 500,000 of the new rifles) past the Union navy. Cotton, however, was too bulky for these slim carriers to take much back to England. The amount of American cotton exported from 1862 to 1865 plummeted to 5 percent of the bales exported in 1858–60.[2]

The Lower South food crop became as unmovable as its cotton harvest. Southern railroads had not been built to carry tons of grain to 100,000 famished troops. Rails wore out. Expert Confederate repairmen did not abound (not with Baltimore's experts repairing the Union's railroads). Federal armies left twisted rails in their wake. Freight cars loaded with grain increasingly tilted off dilapidated tracks, leaving farmers' produce to molder beyond the grasp of hungry civilians and soldiers.

While failed transportation became the Confederate economy's enemy number one, fugitive slaves joined Union armies in placing a respectable second. When runaways deserted the fields, plantation production slipped toward zero. Masters sometimes responded with so-called refugeeing. This new variation on the word "refuge" denoted slaveholders' newest entrepreneurial requirement: to dispatch an endangered investment to a safe refuge, lest fugitive slaves disappear.

"Refugeeing" reveals as much about southern racial attitudes as "contraband" and "garrisoning" reveal about northern racial conceptions.[3] Refugeeing masters sometimes herded only able-bodied male adults toward safe havens, leaving women and children behind—just as in prewar times, economically pressed masters had sometimes sold wives, husbands, or children away from black families. Wartime refugeeing, like prewar slave sales, showed that planter paternalism, sometimes impressive in flush times, grew more tenuous in disruptive times.

Refugeeing proved to be not only disruptive for some slave families but also useless to save the eastern Confederacy's economy. Some masters prodded slaves only a short distance from the Virginia combat zone, often to North Carolina. These slaveholders helped feed Lee's army. To secure their safest refuge from the fugitive problem, however, many masters refugeed potential escapees far from the main fighting. Texas long offered the best distant haven. Since the Federals barely invaded the Lone Star state, slave labor there grew cotton and food with close to prewar efficiency. Since much of Texas remained virgin land, refugeeing Southerners could still find choice acres to buy. In 1862, as the U. S. Navy churned up the Mississippi and Grant's troop swarmed into the Mississippi Valley, black refugees, around 150,000 of them, choked the road to Texas.

Grant terminated the golden interlude of refugeeing, mid-1862 to mid-1863, by seizing Vicksburg. Thereafter, the Mississippi River severed the Confederacy, shutting the refugee pipeline and preventing Texas produce from reaching eastern Confederates. Refugeeing had helped make Texas the Confederacy's gardenland—and as irrelevant to Robert E. Lee as Siberia.

While Texas refugees and their products no longer bolstered the eastern Confederacy's economy, the Texas escape valve had at least prevented some fugitives from boosting the Union's economy. Wherever federal armed forces prevailed, whether in the South Carolina sea islands or in the Mississippi Valley, black runaways raised cotton, sugar, and grains for Union consumers. Lincoln and his generals had once worried about feeding nonlaborers if armies welcomed fugitives. Now the contraband grew food

Contraband Earning Agricultural Wages

Contraband as agricultural laborers. These ex-slaves, farming sweet potatoes in the lush South Carolina lowcountry, exemplify how some of the best southern soils helped nourish the Union economy.

Courtesy of the U. S. Army Military History Institute.

for a million ex-slaves, including the women and children that refugeeing masters had left behind. The contraband also helped supply cotton to New England and British manufacturers, food to Union troops, and sugar to northern consumers.[4]

This agricultural boon from southern blacks paralleled the manufacturing boon from border state whites. Just as Baltimore, Louisville, and St. Louis added the Slave South's richest industrial areas to booming Union production, so the Carolina coast and the Mississippi River delta contributed the slavocracy's richest plantation areas to soaring Union wealth. The impoverished Confederacy could not afford these gifts to the enemy, just as the undermanned Confederate army could not afford to lose the black military laborers now toiling for the Union. Economically, the new math was right: one lost fugitive did equal two Union gains.

2

The escaped blacks' second impact on home-front morale also doubled rebels' troubles. The Confederacy's first military draft law (April 1862) sparked its most debilitating home-front controversy. The law included the infamous "twenty nigger" exclusion, exempting from the military draft any white man who oversaw twenty or more slaves. The resulting disparaging motto, "rich men's war and poor men's fight," helped provoke draft dodging and desertions among slaveless Confederate whites.[5]

Until the last stages of the war, Gary Gallagher correctly argues, Confederate plebeians who fought against Yankees massively outnumbered rednecks who fought against a supposedly rich men's war. Still, tens of thousands of poorer Confederate whites did earlier resist military service. Draft dodgers, draft rioters, and army deserters especially abounded in the white belt areas of Lower South states, including Jones County in southeastern Mississippi (where Newton Knight and his unionist guerrillas ruled their self-styled "Kingdom of Jones"); Jackson County in northeastern Alabama (which in March 1864 seceded from the Confederacy, to rejoin the Union); and the Wiregrass region of southeastern Georgia, including the pine barrens and especially the Okefenokee Swamp. (An Alabama officer termed the Wiregrass a "Den for Tories and deserters from our Army.") As one Alabama redneck expressed class hatreds in such areas, planters ached "to git you . . . to fight for their infurnal negroes and after you do there fighting you may kiss there hine parts for o they care."[6]

Northerners suffered destructive draft riots too.[7] The larger Union army, however, could better tolerate draft resistance. Moreover, during the first year of Confederate draft upheaval, the Union's citizens faced no draft to resist. The Confederacy's earlier and more damaging turmoil over forcing whites to fight, while not nearly as destructive as blacks' and borderites' desertions or as widespread as Confederate whites' zeal to win, remained an important secondary cause of Confederate defeat.

Southern blacks helped provoke that division between Confederate whites. Just as without fugitive slaves, there would have been neither a prewar Fugitive Slave Law nor wartime emancipation via the contraband route, so without restless slaves, there would have been no need for a "twenty nigger" clause. Worse, Confederate soldiers had to guard against slave escapes from combat zones, even during battles against more numerous Yankees. Worse still, anti-Confederate blacks eased Northerners' need to draft whites. The Union drafted around the same number of white men, 200,000, as it enrolled black men. Without black troops, Lincoln's administration would have had to enlarge its draft of whites, increasing the northern home front's tension. By lessening antidraft trouble in the North and intensifying that trouble in the South, southern blacks showed again that one did equal two.

Black anti-Confederates exerted a still larger negative impact on the rebels' share of American military manpower. The free labor states started the Civil War with 61 percent of the U.S. population. The Border South raised the Union percentage to 75 percent. Confederate blacks' willingness to flee could boost Union supporters to 84.5 percent of American peoples. Many a culture has won a war when outnumbered three to two. Not many have survived a long war of attrition when outmanned seventeen to three, especially when the most successful military tactic (in this case, siege warfare) customarily required two to one numerical advantages.

By the end of the war, 178,000 blacks had joined the Union army. Another 18,000 had entered the Navy. Enlisted blacks from mid-1863 to 1865 outnumbered all Union fatalities in the period, matching enlisted southern whites' impact from mid-1861 to mid-1863. In 1864, Lincoln called a war without blacks' "help . . . more than we can bear," just as he had earlier called a war without borderites' aid "too much for us." "We can not spare the hundred and forty or fifty thousand [blacks] now serving us as soldiers, seamen and laborers," declared the president.[8] At the end of the war, Confederate blacks had the potential numbers to add 600,000 more troops to a Union black corps that at the moment of surrender outnumbered all Confederate whites in active service.

Black troops had no such importance (and scant numbers) during the six months between the Final Emancipation Proclamation and the conquest of Vicksburg (July 4, 1863). So long as Union forces only sought to hold the line against Lee in Virginia and complete the conquest of the Mississippi Valley, the federal army contained sufficient whites. But after Vicksburg fell, its satellite fort, Port Hudson, swiftly succumbed. Then Federals owned the Valley and the very nature of the Union war effort changed.

Union conquerors, having severed the Confederacy east from west, next sought to slice the rebels north from south. This new movement toward an eventual triple siege demanded a massive increase in troops. An army of occupation had to be kept in the Mississippi River Valley. An additional army of conquest had to march across the northern edge of the Lower South (with a dip down to the northern Georgia railroad center of Atlanta). The Union's would-be fashioners of a landed anaconda around the Virginia theater would need two to one troop advantages over the rebels for successful siege warfare; and the would-be encirclers of Robert E. Lee inside Virginia would need the same superiority. All these post-Vicksburg needs for far more Union troops made the siege of Vicksburg the greatest turning point since the Final Emancipation Proclamation, in the story of how southern blacks compromised the Confederacy.

3

Ulysses S. Grant, who loved to move quickly, found the reduction of Vicksburg exasperatingly slow, especially compared to his swift capture of Forts Henry and Donelson. Where the Ohio and Tennessee Rivers had sped Grant into the Confederate heartland, nature helped block the warrior from Vicksburg, towering over the Mississippi's eastern side. The bluff's height discouraged assault from below, while Mississippi River swamps crippled invasion from the north. The southeastern approach to Vicksburg offered drier land. But bogs north of the city and the river to the west stood between southeastern terra firma and northerly intruders.

First, Grant futilely experimented with slogging through the northeastern approach, oozing with wetlands and rebels. Then he equally futilely experimented with forcing the Mississippi to run as straight as the Ohio, with black contrabands often digging the canals. Finally, the exasperated commander decided to march down the saturated but less rebel infested western side of the river, to a point south of Vicksburg. He hoped that naval convoys could drift past the bluff's ominous cannon, then transport his marchers over to the dry southeastern approach to the city. He subsequently planned to move ever further from his supply lines, live off confis-

The Siege of Vicksburg

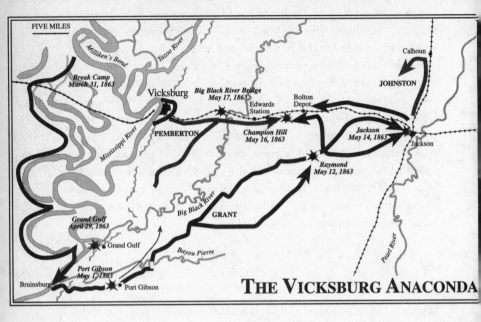

THE VICKSBURG ANACONDA

The Union's Vicksburg target. Courtesy of the U. S. Army Military History Institute.

Confederate cannon at Vicksburg, deterring Union attack from the river. Courtesy of *The Civil War Times Illustrated* Archives, Harrisburg, Pennsylvania.

The Union's sanctuary at Vicksburg for patient Union besiegers.
Courtesy of the Old Court House Museum, Vicksburg.

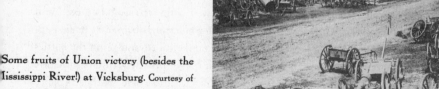

Some fruits of Union victory (besides the Mississippi River!) at Vicksburg. Courtesy of the *Civil War Illustrated Times* Archives.

cated food, march east to capture Jackson, Mississippi's capital, then back-track to lay a siege around Vicksburg.

Grant's plan initially appalled brilliant army strategists, including Sherman, later master of living off the land. Navy personnel also doubted that they could sneak past Vicksburg's hostile fire. The doubters erred. The convoys did slide by Vicksburg; Grant did hitch a ride to the river's eastern side after marching down the western side; the men did confiscate enough to eat; and their encirclement of Vicksburg did prove killing. Grant thus again proved that siege warfare provided the Union's best path to victory. On July 4, 1863, a Confederate army twice as large as the one Grant had captured at Fort Donelson unconditionally surrendered. Rebels handed over, Sherman gloated, "27,000 prisoners, 128 Field Guns and 100 siege pieces . . . beside the immense amount of ammunition, shot shells, horses, wagons, etc." Sherman correctly added that "the Capture of Donelson was as important a beginning as the Capture of Vicksburg [was] the End of the one Great Design."[9]

Both endpieces of the Union's Mississippi Valley design for severing the Confederacy showed that great victories require great strategists. Both triumphs also demonstrated that great generals need great resources. At Donelson and Vicksburg, Grant enjoyed better naval resources. To ensure better army resources at Vicksburg, the conqueror stripped previously conquered fortifications of whites, replacing them with newly enlisted blacks. It was in this campaign that black troops gained their first chance to prove themselves fighting *men*—not docile "boys"—at Milliken's Bend.

After Vicksburg, Lincoln knew that black garrisoning would have to spread past Milliken's Bend, to key Mississippi Valley locations that Grant would be departing. If all Union troops evacuated the western river forts, contraband camps, and railroads tracks, Confederate guerrillas would move into the vacuum. Then everything hard won in the west would be lost. Yet if Grant had to leave tens of thousands of white troops behind to retain conquered terrain, he would sacrifice vital numerical advantages in the battles ahead. One week after Vicksburg fell, New York City rioters violently protested against the draft of white men, in the worst civil disturbance Americans had ever endured. To add an army of occupation without weakening an army of invasion, the Union would have to draft still more white soldiers, at the risk of still more draft riots—unless black troops massively helped guard the Mississippi Valley.

To ensure that Grant grasped the garrisoning necessity, Lincoln wrote on August 9, 1863, reciting the now familiar arithmetic. The enticing and arming of fugitives, Lincoln explained, "works doubly, weakening the enemy and strengthening us. We were not fully ripe for it until the river was opened. Now, I think at least a hundred thousand [blacks] can, and ought to be rapidly organized along its shores, relieving all the white troops to serve elsewhere."[10]

Lincoln need not have written. Grant had sent blacks to garrison Milliken's Bend before Vicksburg fell. Immediately after Vicksburg surrendered (and before Lincoln's letter), Grant replaced white conquerors with black guards. I did not want "white men," the victor explained, "to do any work that can possibly be avoided during the hot months."[11]

Thereafter, exceptions abounded to western blacks' predominant garrison-style duty, for some black troops and many black military laborers joined advancing white troops. In all, black combat troops participated in forty-one major battles and 449 minor skirmishes. At the Battle of Nashville that almost finished off John Bell Hood, around 3,500 Union blacks fought (around 6 percent of George Thomas's troops). At the Siege of Petersburg that almost finished off Robert E. Lee, around 15,000 Union blacks fought (around 12.5 percent of the troops in Ulysses S. Grant's several Virginia armies).

Still, most black troops were western ex-slaves, and most new freedmen served behind the lines. Grant's black troops at Petersburg, for example, while far outnumbering all other black combat soldiers, were themselves outnumbered by the 18,299 blacks who garrisoned the Mississippi River forts in March 1865.[12] Meanwhile, blacks guards in other western military installations, contraband camps, and railroads outnumbered ex-slaves in the river forts.

William Tecumseh Sherman's infamous Spooner Letter (July 30, 1864) explained why "a large proportion of our fighting men" relished the consignment of a heavy proportion of black soldiers to the garrisons. White "Soldiers and Volunteers who are fighting," wrote Sherman, must not be placed "on a par with . . . the negro," who "is in a transition state and is not

Ex-slaves as Union Warriors

Contraband as artillerymen. Courtesy of the Chicago Historical Society.

Contraband as infantrymen. Courtesy of the Ohio Historical Society,
Columbus, Ohio.

Contraband as naval personnel. Courtesy of the U. S. Army Military History Institute.

the equal of the white man. . . . I prefer some negroes as pioneers, teamsters, cooks, and servants, others gradually to experiment in the art of the Soldier, beginning with the duties of local garrison."[13]

Garrison-type duties involved nasty work, whether patrolmen guarded forts or railroads or contraband camps. It also could be boring and therefore dangerous work. Black guards had to remain especially alert, for Confederate ambushers especially aspired to kill ex-slaves who aimed guns at ex-masters. The rebels' most savage revenge occurred in April 1864 at Tennessee's Fort Pillow, guarding the Mississippi River above Memphis. There Nathan Bedford Forrest's Confederate guerrillas slaughtered hundreds of blacks (and some whites) while the victims attempted to surrender. This and other Forrest sprees, together with raids by dozens of other rebel irregular warriors, made an army of occupation mandatory. As the most important recent revision of Civil War military history emphasizes, smothering guerrilla resistance after the major battles became almost as important to a Union victory as the battles themselves. That fresh viewpoint underlines the importance of humble garrisoning.

A comparison of the Civil War and the American Revolutionary War also highlights the significance of black garrisoning. When seeking to sub-due American rebels, the British induced almost as high as a percentage of southern slaves to run away as occurred in the Civil War. Lord Dunmore and a few other royal officials wished to turn the runaways into a black loy-alist army. But the proposal yielded only a few hundred black troops. Most British strategists wished slaves to do no more than flee from their masters. Some cynical Brits found their own use for fleeing slaves. Redcoats some-times sold the confiscated property for cash to British West Indies masters.

A different Civil War military strategy impelled a different use of fugi-tives. Redcoats fought as premodern, preindustrial filibusterers. They in-vaded areas, called upon Tories to rise up, then moved on. Besides using fewer troops (and thus fewer fugitive slaves) to guard behind advancing troops, Britain's preindustrial age army needed fewer military laborers than did industrial age armies. Redcoats used some fugitives in these latter-day roles (especially in the Savannah and Charleston garrisons) and a few run-aways as officers' servants (much like body servants in the Confederates' Bull Run army). But to King George's army, a fugitive slave remained pri-marily just property confiscated from the enemy. To the Union, a runaway became also one vital guard or laborer gained for the back lines, ensuring overwhelming combat forces for invaders who marched forward.

Black troops' behind-the-scene Civil War importance, after advancing armies claimed center stage, resembled black runaways' importance, when Congresses enacted fugitive slave laws. Just as black runaways provoked congressional deliberations as much as if they had served inside the legisla-tive halls, so blacks in the Union's western army of occupation strength-ened eastern armies as much as if they had swapped assignments with whites in the army of conquest. The total number of Union troops under-taking necessary assignments, not the skin color in any particular locale, created the Federals' decisive plurality in late-war eastern battles. The mili-tary importance of those large pluralities dominates the story of western soldiers' first (and worst) setback on their march eastward.

4

Upon leaving the Mississippi River Valley, Federals plotted first to liberate east Tennessee Unionists in Knoxville/Chattanooga and to shut down those railroad crossings.[14] Then they would turn south, to besiege Atlanta's railroad center. Robert E. Lee would be doomed in the Virginia theater, Jefferson Davis sensed, if the Union could create a landed anaconda to shut off supply lines between that theater and the Lower South. Thus Confederates had to stop the Federals between Chattanooga and Atlanta. So Davis ordered a critical portion of Lee's Virginia army, General James Longstreet and some 15,000 troops, to ride trains toward Georgia. Longstreet's assignment: to reinforce the Confederate army then massing some ten miles south of Chattanooga, near Chickamauga Creek. Longstreet's reinforcement gave Confederates a rare advantage: more troops on a key battlefield.

At Chickamauga, the rebels proved that they would have been harder to defeat if no anti-Confederate Southerners had swelled Union armies toward their usual pluralities (and had instead brought Confederate armies closer to parity). On September 19, 1863, Union and Confederate armies probed for each others' weaknesses in dense woods. The next day, the Federals' maneuvers accidentally left a momentary gap in their right flank. James Longstreet's Confederates poured through the opening. Union soldiers, in danger of being turned and trapped, scrambled back toward Chattanooga. Federal General George Thomas, thereafter known as the "Rock of Chickamauga," held firm long enough to protect the retreat and avert total disaster.

Having failed to trap Union invaders at Chickamauga, rebels surrounded Chattanooga. The encirclement turned the tables. This time, Confederates laid the siege and the Federals endured it. This time, rebels enjoyed a splendid topographical opportunity to teach haughty Yankees that Southerners could besiege too, if given half a chance. Chattanooga (and the Union army) backed up against a sweeping curve in the Tennessee River. Along both sides of the town, high swells of land, called Lookout Mountain and Missionary Ridge, ran southward toward the Chickamauga battlefield. A successful siege of Chattanooga needed only to control the Tennessee River, fortify the heights, and run a sufficiently thick line of troops across the valley and over to the river.

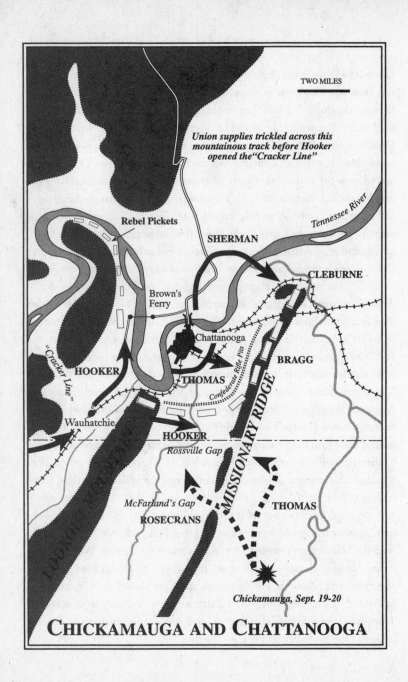

TWO MILES

Union supplies trickled across this mountainous track before Hooker opened the "Cracker Line"

Rebel Pickets

SHERMAN

CLEBURNE

Tennessee River

Brown's Ferry

Chattanooga

"Cracker Line"

HOOKER

BRAGG

THOMAS

Confederate Rifle Pits

Wauhatchie

HOOKER

Rossville Gap

McFarland's Gap

ROSECRANS

MISSIONARY RIDGE

THOMAS

LOOKOUT MOUNTAIN

Chickamauga, Sept. 19-20

CHICKAMAUGA AND CHATTANOOGA

Even these undemanding requirements demanded more than the Confederacy could muster. The rebel navy lacked sufficient gunboats to dominate the river, and the rebel army lacked enough troops to fortify the siege all the way to the river. Behind the thinning of the siege near the river lay the impossibility of an undermanned Slave South attaining a two to one plurality, what with half its inhabitants favoring the enemy or favoring no one. It was like Sidney Johnston futilely trying to fortify all points in his Kentucky/Tennessee line of defense, when most Kentuckians barely cared or worse.

The weak point in the rebels' 1863 Chattanooga siege, as in Johnston's 1862 line of defense, was on the Tennessee River. This time, another General Smith, William "Baldy" rather than Charles Ferguson, starred in the western breakthrough. At Chattanooga, Baldy Smith noted the rebel siege's thinness near the river. Using Smith's findings, Union reinforcements cut through the Confederate siege at Brown's Ferry, on the Tennessee River west of Chattanooga, on the night of October 27.

The unopposed conquest, taking all of ten minutes, opened the so-called Cracker Line, enabling some (slim) rations to reach hungry Union troops. With the river under Union control, William T. Sherman and Joseph Hooker, armed with Baldy Smith's information, stormed into Chattanooga's environs with about 36,000 reinforcements. Meanwhile, those Confederate reinforcers at Chickamauga, James Longstreet's 15,000 stalwarts, pulled out to assault Knoxville. Longstreet thereby demonstrated again that the stretched-out Confederacy had too few troops to guard too many places, much less to lay a victorious siege.

The siege was in fact over. The brawl now pitted reinforced Federals down in the valley against depleted Confederates up on Lookout Mountain and atop Missionary Ridge. For that combat, the Union had regained its customary manpower advantage of almost two to one. The Federals' psychological advantage exceeded the customary. The giddy rise and unnerving fall of the rebels' fortunes had dangerously sapped Confederate troop morale. Before Chickamauga, the Confederates' Army of Tennessee had suffered draining defeats for almost two years, at Fort Henry, Fort Donelson, Shiloh, Perryville, and Vicksburg. Then angry losers had whipped their oppressors at Chickamauga and holed them up in Chattanooga, starving Federals so terribly that horses fell like flies.

The turnaround had been euphoric. How sweet to strangle Federals in a murderous, maybe war-ending siege, after righteous Yanks had captured 40,000 comrades by encircling Donelson and Vicksburg. How satisfying to pin Grant's men against that omnipresent Tennessee River, after Grant had barely escaped a bath in the river at Shiloh and George Thomas had barely protected the escape from Chickamauga.

And then how heartbreaking to watch Grant's men burst through the siege as effortlessly as if pricking some soap bubble, then romp into Chattanooga's valley with formidable numbers. Bitterly disappointed rebel troops in the Army of Tennessee fell to screaming at each other, raging at their generals, especially their head general, Braxton Bragg, and suspecting that nothing could beat the relentless foe. Meanwhile, federal rescuers, having cut through what had seemed like an alarming siege as if it were paper, swelled with pride; and the proud Yankees who had been rescued wished to prove themselves manly enough to have whipped the rebels, even without the Cracker Line.

Under these unusual circumstances, the usual advantage of protected Confederate riflemen over reckless Union chargers narrowed. When battlefield power became more even, superior field commanders became more critical. The Federals' William Tecumseh Sherman was not usually the inferior commander. But Sherman, brilliant at planning flanking movements, was no genius at plotting frontal assaults. In contrast, his adversary at Missionary Ridge, the Confederate's Patrick Cleburne, delivered a superb counterpunch.

In the Federals' first charge up Missionary Ridge in the Battle of Chattanooga, November 23–25, 1863, Sherman picked the wrong summit to conquer. Then he poorly designed an assault on the right target. As exposed Yankees struggled up Missionary Ridge, Cleburne rallied his dispirited troops. Rebels riddled Sherman's winded men with bullets, then charged down hill atop them. Never had Sherman tasted such defeat.

The next and pivotal assault on Missionary Ridge came not from Sherman or Joe Hooker on the flanks of the Union line, but from George Thomas in the center. Thomas's Chickamauga veterans planned not an end run around the rebels but a rush straight ahead. Union rushers would have to traverse a mile-long plain, the last 500 yards without a tree to shield

The "Miracle" at Missionary Ridge

This photograph of the forbidding terrain at Missionary Ridge, akin to the deterring Cemetery Ridge at Gettysburg, shows why the Union charge to victory seemed to be a miracle. Courtesy of the U. S. Army Military History Institute.

them, just to reach rebel rifle pits (an early version of twentieth-century foxholes), located about 300 dangerous yards short of Missionary Ridge. Subsequently, the Federals would have to dash to and then scramble up rugged, thickly vegetated heights, often by pulling themselves higher with their hands, despite a hail of bullets and cannonballs from protected Confederate positions halfway up and on top.

It was the typical prescription for Civil War disaster. Thomas's troops charge to and up Missionary Ridge would have to cover more treacherous ground than did the rebels' George Pickett on his famous suicidal charge through a valley of death and up Cemetery Ridge on the third day at Gettysburg. But at Chattanooga, the previous sieve of a siege had left defenders psychologically depleted, unless some rare Patrick Cleburne lent heart to the dispirited. As Thomas's men began a superhuman effort, not the charismatic Cleburne but the detested Braxton Bragg was the Confederate commander galloping along Missionary Ridge, trying to rally nervous rebels. Bragg, despised by his men for allegedly single-handedly squandering the glory of Chickamauga, could by now spur no more than his own horse toward greater effort. In contrast, Thomas's men's were spurred on by their mortification of having to flee from Chickamauga, plus their mortification of having to be rescued from the siege of Chattanooga.

Thomas's troops tore over the treeless plains toward rebel rifle pits. Upon reaching this first Confederate protected position, the Rock of Chickamauga's stalwarts found most of the rebel riflemen wildly retreating. The exulting assaulters kept right on going, to the steep ridge and up its forbidding heights, braving heavy enemy fire throughout their excruciating climb. Scrambling atop the summit, panting victors found panicky losers defying Bragg, fleeing back toward Chickamauga, even faster than frightened Federals had two months earlier lurched back toward Chattanooga.

Some astonished observers called the Federals' victorious charge the Miracle at Missionary Ridge. But the collapse of the Confederates' morale, after a seemingly golden siege had proved to be fool's gold, was no miracle. Nor was any miracle responsible for the deficiency of Confederate manpower to fortify the encirclement. The southern whites and blacks who expanded the Union army, and the unavailability of half the Slave South's population to augment the Confederate army, were a natural outcome of the very nature of Slave South society—and never more fatal than at the siege of Chattanooga.[15]

Chattanooga was arguably the Confederates' last chance (and surely their best chance) to stop the anaconda now closing in on Lee's theater of war from the west. The encounter was also arguably the most revealing of Civil War engagements. Never before or after was the importance of siege tactics and numerical advantages more obvious. Never again would rebels come close to numerical parity. Never again could they attempt a siege. Never again could Confederates stop Federals unless Federals stopped themselves.

The Union could still stop itself if its generals tried to run over rather than around rebel armies. Unless assaulters enjoyed unusually auspicious circumstances, as at Missionary Ridge, fewer men could prevail if the more numerous charged wildly at protected riflemen. But many more men could constantly turn the flank of many fewer men, driving the outmanned back in smaller and smaller circles. The slow siege was usually the winner, the reckless charge usually the disaster for Federals heading east and bearing two to one numerical advantages, not least because black troops guarded their rear.

5

William Tecumseh Sherman, off to besiege Atlanta after helping crack the rebels' siege of Chattanooga, disliked reckless charges (which was one reason he planned them rather poorly).[16] For a fabulous fighting man, this general grieved unusually graphically over "the horrid nature of this war," with its "piles of dead gentlemen & wounded & maimed" and its "mangled bodies . . . in every conceivable shape, without heads, legs."[17] Whenever possible, Sherman wanted to win by bloodless devastation rather than by bloody dismembering, by savaging the home front rather than by slaying the soldiers, especially his own soldiers.

His Atlanta campaign was a masterpiece of *not* brawling.[18] Only once did Sherman err, in his infamous charge at Kennesaw Mountain (June 27, 1864). He there lost 3,000 men; the Confederates, 500. Such losses could dissipate Sherman's two to one manpower advantage. But except for this mistake, Sherman constantly turned the flank of his main opponent, Joseph E. Johnston. Johnston gave ground grudgingly, always daring Sherman to charge again, always convinced that Sherman would lose if "he made . . . assaults on me."[19] Instead, Sherman relentlessly encircled Johnston's troops and Atlanta itself.

Jefferson Davis, exasperated by Johnston's retreats, replaced the cautious defender with the all-too-daring John Bell Hood, whose left arm had been savaged at Gettysburg and right leg had been amputated at Chickamauga. Although Hood's baleful eyes gave him the mournful look of a bloodhound, no Yankee bullet seemed capable of discouraging this giant of a man, not even the necessity of being strapped into the saddle. Once Davis

The Siege of Atlanta

Kennesaw Mountain and the folly of impatient Union chargers. Courtesy of the U. S. Army Military History Institute.

Some fruits of victory at the Atlanta railroad yard, a reward for patient Union besiegers.
Courtesy of the Library of Congress.

raised him to command, Hood ordered charge after charge at Sherman. Hood's attack, however, secured no relief from Sherman's siege and brought upon his men twice as many casualties as afflicted the Union's encircling army, already two times larger. Hood finally cut his way out of the siege, conceding Atlanta to Sherman (September 1, 1864).

Sherman first thought to chase Hood, who headed toward Mississippi. Then the victor at Atlanta had a better idea. He would dispatch some of his soldiers, led by George Thomas, to finish off Hood.[20] With the bulk of his troops, Sherman would turn *away* from Hood and move southeast toward the sea, toward Savannah, toward making the Deep South's "inhabitants feel that war & individual ruin are synonymous [sic]." He would "make Georgia howl."[21]

The general especially aspired to make Confederate *citizens* howl. "Uncle Billy," as his troops affectionately called Sherman, had found the soft phase of the war exasperating. Who ever heard of a war, he had exploded, where one side assumed the enemy "were *not* Enemies" and could be cajoled, not demoralized, into submission. He relished the hard phase of the war, in which the Confederate people were assumed to be enemies and their "negro property and personal property are fair subjects of conquest."[22] He has not come down in history as much of an "Uncle Billy," this conqueror who would rip the spirit from noncombatants. Yet his home-front devastation sustained his own weird version of softer war: a war that he sought to win without savaging all the arms and legs of all the John Bell Hoods.

Sherman's march to the Georgia seashore and back through the Carolinas was perfect for demoralizing property owners. The Union had so many more troops now that Confederates could only slightly delay Sherman. Meanwhile many Lower South blacks seized their first chance for freedom the fugitive way. As Sherman's troops strode toward Savannah, reported one of their generals, "we could see, on each side of our line of march, crowds of these people coming to us through roads and across the fields, bringing with them . . . horses, mules, cows, dogs, old family carriages." The blacks were allowed "to follow in rear of our column, and at times they were almost in numbers equal to the army they were following."[23]

Sherman, one might think, would have been delighted. Here marched the enemy's property away from the enemy. But of all Grant's generals,

Devastation at Columbia. This picture of the ashes in Columbia, South Carolina epitomizes how Sherman's men devastated not only the capital of secession but also civilians' zeal to continue.
Courtesy of the Leib Image Archives, East Berlin, Pennsylvania.

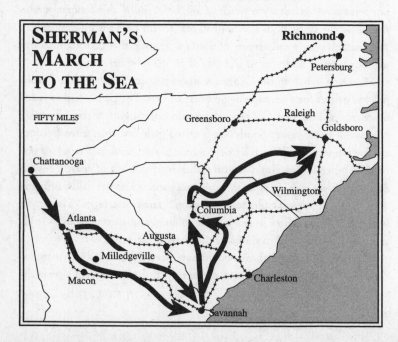

SHERMAN'S
MARCH
TO THE SEA

FIFTY MILES

Richmond

Petersburg

Greensboro

Raleigh

Goldsboro

Chattanooga

Wilmington

Atlanta

Columbia

Augusta

Milledgeville

Macon

Charleston

Savannah

Sherman had the most contempt for blacks. His antiblack comments could be piled higher than towering slaves: "But the nigger? Why, in God's name, can't sensible men let him alone." "I wont trust niggers to fight." "I like niggers *well enough* as niggers, but when fools & idiots try & make niggers better than ourselves I have an opinion."[24]

His opinion was that runaways wonderfully deprived the enemy of property and workers, usefully gave him heavy duty military laborers, but counterproductively clogged his army with other militarily useless (and hungry) blacks. The problem had dictated his approval of Henry Halleck's General Orders #3. Solutions seemed to him in short supply on his march toward Savannah. Make soldiers of black hordes? Instead, Sherman made laborers out of his one black regiment at Savannah, the 110th U.S. Colored Infantry.[25] Make black runaways into more laborers? Sherman relished the chance, with able-bodied males. But among black paraders who chanted freedom's songs, most were too young or too old or too weak or too sick or female.

His determination to rid his lines of black nonlaborers led to remarks obnoxious even by Sherman's standards. "My first duty," he wrote Halleck upon arrival at Savannah, "will be to clear the army of surplus negroes, mules, and horses."[26] Such provoking statements impelled the Lincoln administration to send Secretary of War Edwin Stanton down to Savannah to investigate. Stanton arranged to meet simultaneously with Sherman and twenty black leaders on January 12, 1865.

At the key moment of this key meeting, whites inquired how runaway slaves could support themselves instead of eating troops' rations. The blacks' spokesman answered that "the way we can best take care of ourselves is to have land, and turn it and till it by . . . the labor of the women and children and old men," while "the young men should enlist in the service of the Government, . . . in such manner as they may be wanted."

Sherman relished blacks' suggestion, for his own sake perhaps more than theirs. By sending militarily useless blacks off to till their own acres, he would remove his army's contraband impediments, dispatch Mr. Stanton back to Washington, and use black males the only way he considered helpful—as brute laborers. So three days after hearing the blacks' proposal, Sherman issued Special Field Orders #15, handing the contraband a swath of coastal farm land thirty miles wide, from Jacksonville, Florida, to

Charleston, South Carolina. By early April 1865, army administrators of Sherman's order had given 20,000 freedmen a farm, each averaging fifty acres.[27]

Here, Civil War racial reform reached its apogee. Land ownership could add liberation from economic bondage to liberation from masters' lashes. The Lincoln administration's mode of collaborating with blacks here also reached its climax. Once again, black fugitives pressed for what they wanted—this time, land as well as sanctuary. Once again, the thin federal civil bureaucracy could not handle the problem. Once again, the Lincoln administration used the army, its only thick administrative arm, to grant the request and thereby gain the black partners it needed to win the war.

Yet Special Field Orders #15 would also demonstrate the vulnerability of army-administered racial reform. In peacetime, the civil government could cancel army orders that rested only on war necessity. Worse, the army as a reforming bureaucracy would soon disappear, for nineteenth-century Americans hated standing armies as much as federal bureaucracies. After the soldiers headed home, too few federal officials would remain to protect the disadvantaged, despite the best efforts of the civilian substitute for the troops, the federal Freedmen's Bureau. The post-Reconstruction federal bureaucracy would resemble its meager form in the one-case-and-disappear commissioner era of the Fugitive Slave Law of 1850. Another century would pass before federal administrators could match William Tecumseh Sherman's reforming clout.

The effect of Special Field Orders #15 lasted barely a year, perhaps because Lincoln lived only another three months. Since Lincoln had hoped for a soft landing for rebels in the Union, perhaps he would have ordered blacks to return white Southerners' land. Or would an honor-bound commander in chief have honored his generals' pledge to blacks? At any rate, Lincoln's successor, the Tennesseean Andrew Johnson, thought reconstruction had gone dishonorably far when the army handed whites' property to blacks. The new president returned most of the Sherman-granted land to slaveholders when he pardoned them.

President Johnson's gutting of Special Field Orders #15, arguably the era's greatest tragedy, assuredly undid what might have become the era's greatest irony. If Sherman's transfer of masters' lands to ex-slaves had endured past its wartime rationale and grantor, the most racist of Lincoln's generals would have pushed postwar America a step beyond the achievement of the Great Emancipator. Other ironies, however, clung to slaves' generous (and disparaging) Uncle Billy. Sherman's boldest move of the war, for example, partially defeated his resolve to keep black troops in garrisons.

Weeks after Sherman divided his army and dispatched George Thomas to chase John Bell Hood, Thomas feared that his fraction of Sherman's white soldiers might not suffice to repulse the undaunted Hood, who had swerved from his retreat into Mississippi toward an invasion of Tennessee. Thomas thus called troops out of the garrisons, making no mention of skin color. Sherman's second in command then learned the racial lesson that the superior never fathomed. Before the Battle of Nashville (December 15–16, 1864), George Thomas had doubted blacks' potential as soldiers. After watching his 3,500 black troops battle at Nashville, and after observing "bodies of colored men . . . on the very works of the enemy," Thomas pronounced his doubts "settled; Negroes will fight."[28]

The still-doubting Sherman, having indirectly unlocked the garrisons' gates, equally ironically set the record for a frontline army's dependence on contraband. On his march back from the sea through Columbia, South Carolina (which he famously burned), to North Carolina (where he snipped off another of Lee's supply lines), Sherman found few Confederate soldiers to kill. But Uncle Billy found much rebel property to wreck. Sherman's wrecking crew needed laborers. Sherman loathed army recruiters of blacks in part because they filched his indispensable workers.

Sherman's march back from Savannah required especially immense amounts of labor. Rain poured down abnormally hard that early winter of 1865 in already soaking lowcountry Carolina. Confederates gloated that the Yankee raider would be stuck in swamps for months, as Grant and Sherman had been northeast of Vicksburg. This time, however, Yankee engineers and their contraband laborers routed nature. In a military happening far more remarkable than the siege of Atlanta, Sherman's black pioneers built so-called corduroy roads with timber, allowing wagons to roll above the muck. They also foraged for food, destroyed Confederates' property, and helped compromise the Confederacy so badly that Charleston collapsed when Sherman merely faked an approach to it. Sherman strode out of the goo in only a few weeks, with his contraband laborers ready to help twist up hundreds more miles of southern railroad tracks.

Sherman here resurrected 1862. Black males as military laborers, not as soldiers, had first wrung sanctuary from Union troops. But to secure the boon of blacks' heavy labor, the Union army had to solve a perpetual problem: where should the fugitives incapable of hauling the heavy loads live and labor? Sherman's answer, go cultivate your own soil, soared morally beyond Lorenzo Thomas's answer, go find a low-paying job in a disease-infested contraband camp.

Yet northern "fanatics," raged Sherman, call me no "Friend of the Negro." He called himself "the best kind of a friend to Sambo." Who, after all, has "conducted to safe places more Negroes?" And who, he could have added, has put more contraband to productive military labor or has given more freedmen more economic hope?[29] Who indeed—and who with less respect for the folk he redeemed?

6

While Sherman needed more laborers to cross a saturated swamp, Grant needed more soldiers to lay the climactic siege around Lee's Virginia army. Where Sherman remained stuck on his conception of contraband as largely fit for only menial labor, Grant moved past his conception of black soldiers as largely fit for only garrison duty. "The colored man," reasoned Grant, "has been accustomed all his life to lean on the white man, and if a good officer is placed over him, he will learn readily and make a good soldier."[30]

Sherman, in contrast, believed learning would never replace leaning, not among blacks that he considered underequipped with brainpower. Soldiers must "do many things without orders," explained Sherman. "Negroes are not equal to this."[31] But Grant's 15,000 black frontline troops proved as equal to soldiering as Sherman's many thousand contraband proved equal to swamp mucking. Twenty-two of Grant's black troops in Virginia won Congressional Medals of Honor, often for skillfully commanding after their white officers had caught a bullet.[32]

Grant treasured black learners, for his mode of fighting led many a body to catch a bullet. Unlike Sherman, Grant did not dwell graphically on piles of headless, legless corpses. The two generals occupied the right positions. Sherman was perfect for demoralizing the citizens, and Grant was perfect for directing the bloodletting. Grant became the army's supreme director when Lincoln appointed him general in chief (and the first American lieutenant general since George Washington). The commission, rendered on March 1, 1864, made Lieutenant General Grant not master of one army but coordinator of a dozen, all combining to strangle Robert E. Lee.

In the lieutenant general's climactic coordination, several Union armies would encircle Lee's troops inside the Virginia theater of war. Meanwhile, other federal fighting men would complete Winfield Scott's watery noose and the Grant-Sherman landed noose around that theater. Navy/army assaults would capture Mobile Bay, Charleston, and especially Wilmington, North Carolina, thus pinching off the few remaining Confederate supply lines to England. Simultaneously, Sherman would conquer Atlanta and North Carolina, snapping Lee's supply lines to the Lower South, while Phil Sheridan would conquer the Valley of Virginia, shutting Lee off from his nearby breadbasket.

Still, Grant did not always have a triple siege in mind or remorselessly seek those three circles around Lee, any more than he always had in mind turning behind Sidney Johnston's entire army in Henry/Donelson days. Day-to-day soldiering more often seeks immediate goals for the next day. Those goals can daily shift. Thus Grant one day tried to dynamite a hole in Lee's front rather than encircle it (the utterly unsuccessful crater strategy employed at Petersburg). Another day, he approved Sherman's movement *away* from encircling Lee (the supremely successful March to the Sea). But in 1864–65, the triple siege strategy always hovered in the background and moved ever more to the center of the lieutenant general's thinking; and posterity can see how thoroughly it finally overwhelmed Lee.

Yet in early 1864, the impatient Grant could not bear to wait for overwhelming anacondas. So he changed the unwritten Civil War rules. Under other people's understandings (but never really Grant's), armies had fought for several days, then usually paused for several weeks. Grant instead now pressed his generals in Virginia to fight continuously, never separating from

Lee, never allowing Confederates to rest. It was like going after Fort Donelson immediately after seizing Fort Henry, only this time Grant's war without pause would last for the duration.

This scheme to keep the pressure on Lee was fine, if carried out in Sherman's patient style. The imperative was to stress movement around the undermanned enemy's flank, avoiding unnecessary charges into earthworks and rifles. From May 5 to June 2, 1864, at the horrendous Virginia battles of the Wilderness, Spotsylvania, and North Anna, generals under Grant, while charging far more often than Lee, also spread wider around Lee's thinner lines. As the combination of flanking and charging drove Lee back, he suffered about 25,000 casualties, compared to the Federals' approximately 44,000. If that ratio continued, the undermanned Lee would slowly lose too many men, just as he was slowly losing too much territory.

Then Grant could abide the slowness no longer. Just as Sherman, for one of history's most notorious conductors of mass destruction, found killing remarkably distasteful, so Grant, for one of history's most masterful conductor of sieges, found siege warfare remarkably frustrating. He wanted victory, not next year but tomorrow. So on June 3 at Cold Harbor, he impatiently ordered appalling charges. Hundreds of his terrified men pinned their names and addresses to their lapels, so their bodies could be identified. On the eve of the battle, a soldier wrote on his diary page for the next day, "June 3. Cold Harbor. I was killed."[33]

And so he was. Six thousand Union chargers became casualties on June 3, compared to 1500 rebels. The assaulters suffered 3500 casualties in just one ghastly hour. If such demoralizing losses continued, Grant could lose the war, despite outnumbering Lee two to one. Or to put it another way, the Union's lieutenant general had found the way to throw away the potentially decisive numerical advantages that southern anti-Confederates had contributed to Yankee forces.

The loser learned his lesson. Cold Harbor became to Grant what Kennesaw Mountain had been to Sherman. The army's head general reluctantly resumed the slow way, the patient way, the siege way (with, Grant being Grant, a few impatient charges thrown in). Grant swung his armies wider than Lee's again and again, driving the rebels back to Petersburg, where the longest siege of the Civil War began in mid-June 1864.

The Strangulation of Virginia

Fortifications at Petersburg during the longest siege of the war. Courtesy of the U. S. Army Military History Institute.

Fatalities at Petersburg. Courtesy of the U. S. Army Military History Institute.

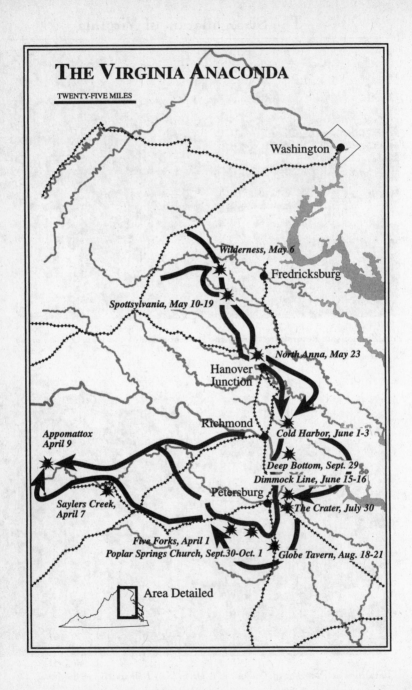

THE VIRGINIA ANACONDA

TWENTY-FIVE MILES

Washington

Wilderness, May 6

Fredricksburg

Spottsylvania, May 10-19

North Anna, May 23

Hanover
Junction

Richmond

Appomattox
April 9

Cold Harbor, June 1-3

Deep Bottom, Sept. 29

Dimmock Line, June 15-16

Petersburg

Saylers Creek,
April 7

The Crater, July 30

Five Forks, April 1

Poplar Springs Church, Sept.30-Oct. 1

Globe Tavern, Aug. 18-21

Area Detailed

As summer gave way to fall, then fall to winter, the wisdom of Grant's overall design became obvious. Lee was indeed encircled inside his theater of war, and the navy and army nooses outside that area tightened. By late January 1865, the Union had conquered Wilmington, North Carolina, Mobile Bay, and the Virginia Valley. Lee, three times surrounded, suffered killing desertions. His nondeserters half starved. Confederate whites could supply few replacements.

While much had compromised Lee in 1864, the year of developing sieges, the Union army's huge numerical advantage had been the worst of it—this and Grant/Sherman's *almost*-constant canniness about using sieges to turn numerical advantages into victories. Behind the Union's overwhelming numbers lay black troops, wherever they served, for their numbers exceeded Grant's plurality over Lee *plus* Sherman's over Johnston and Hood.

Worse, the Union army had many southern blacks left to harvest. In mid-March 1865, Sherman paused in Goldsboro, North Carolina, on his way from the sea to the Virginia theater. He could easily turn around to enter the many uninvaded portions of the Lower South. No Confederate army could block him. Hundreds of thousands of potential runaways would greet him. While Sherman would disdain using this additional contraband as troops, Grant would arm every able-bodied black male that his compatriot delivered. The Confederacy's last hope was to find countervailing manpower, beyond its whites' exhausted resources.

part four
Last Full Measure

The Last Best Hope 9

A southern section containing four of every ten Americans would not likely outlast the northern section in a long war of attrition, not with two of the South's four sympathizing more with the Union, not with few reinforcements from outside the white Confederates' ranks offsetting the many southern defectors. The American Revolutionary War had demonstrated the importance of offsetting reinforcements. Only a slightly lower percentage of southern slaves, to repeat, fled to their masters' enemy during the American Revolutionary War than during the Civil War. Yet the runaways of 1776–83, compared to those of 1861–65, did little to tilt the balance of military power. Revolutionary War fugitives exerted comparatively less leverage, partly because the preindustrial British army needed less military labor, partly because the British needed fewer black soldiers for their scant armies of occupation, but mostly because France came to the rescue of colonial Americans. American gains from French military power more than offset the loss of black labor power.

White Confederates sought equivalent counterbalancing reinforcements from Englishmen, from Northern Democrats, and finally in desperation, from their own slaves. They failed. The story of this failure, while seem-ingly tangential to the story of the southern house divided, indispensably helps explain why southern anti-Confederates much influenced the Civil War outcome.

Robert E. Lee would not have explained white Confederates' necessity for help from without by citing defections from within. He only complained about too few Confederate troops and too few reserves. But he would have agreed with another way to put the numbers game: Not even the most dazzling Confederate general could forever offset all Northerners and half the South-erners in a long war of attrition. The quest for allies to counter the Union's constantly more crushing numbers helped shape Lee's military strategy.

1

Lee deployed an offensive-minded defensive strategy. He charged those rifles sometimes, although his undermanned predicament arguably de-manded purely defensive tactics. Lee's most sustained offenses came in Sep-tember 1862, when he invaded the Border South, reaching Antietam Creek, Maryland, and in June–July 1863, when he invaded the North, reaching Gettysburg, Pennsylvania. On the third day of the Gettysburg battle, Vir-ginia's George Pickett and other Confederate leaders brought Lee's Attack and Maybe Die tactics to climax.[1] Pickett's Virginians led Confederate chargers over an open field, toward protected federal riflemen.

Disaster. Pickett's Charge lost 62 percent of Pickett's 5,000 troops. Two weeks later, at Fort Wagner, Robert Gould Shaw's black chargers suffered similar annihilation. Ten months later, at Cold Harbor, Ulysses S. Grant added his name to this roll call of blunderers. The consistent moral: Ex-cept under highly unusual circumstances, avoid headlong charges against protected riflemen, unless you have had enough of life.

Lee has suffered more than enough from critics because his attacks al-legedly bled the Lost Cause to death. Lee's men at Gettysburg, for example, numbered 43,000 *fewer* than the Federals' troops. Yet Lee lost 5,000 *more* men. Lee limped backward with only two-thirds of his Gettysburg army, while the Federals crawled forward with three-fourths of theirs.

In the seven most important battles in which Lee seized the offensive, he lost 19.2 percent of his assaulters, while the Federals lost 13.2 percent of their defenders. If Lee had suffered only the defenders' 13.2 percent casualties in those seven battles, he would have lost 25,000 fewer men: 25,000 extra losses for a Confederate army with under one soldier per two Union troops. That seems disastrous in a protracted war of attrition. A cannier tactician, Lee's detractors conclude, would have shunned the charge, monopolized the defensive, and whittled down the larger, not the smaller army.

Yet Lee had reason to mix offense with defense. Federal despair at subduing his offensive-defensive strategy forced the Union to tighten two anacondas around his Virginia theater, and to slip a third anaconda around him. That expensive Union strategy, requiring hundreds of thousands of extra men, puts Lee's 25,000 losses in perspective.

Lee feared worse losses than 25,000 if he incessantly retreated. He might wither southern morale, which for decades had feasted on honorable attacks on Yankee defamers. Endless slinking backward might also yield not reckless Union charges but cautious Union flanking tactics, leading to retreating rebels' eventual encirclement. Then Lee's army would have to charge after all, just to cut its way out of a starving siege. Lee furthermore saw no way to win a war of attrition if no outsiders compensated for white Confederates' troop shortfall. Aggressive victories, Lee hoped, might lure new supporters. But by cowering back, Confederate whites would surely go it alone, unaided, besieged, and demoralized.

2

Many Southerners, although not Lee, considered Englishmen their likely saviors.[2] In James Hammond's famous King Cotton outburst on the U.S. Senate floor in 1858, the South Carolinian explained why Britain would aid a slaveholders' nation. By allowing her best raw cotton supplier to fall, Hammond claimed, England would topple "and carry the whole civilized world with her." No earthly power dared "war on cotton. . . . Cotton is King."[3]

When rebels dared war against the Union, they sought to force Englishmen to worship King Cotton. During the Civil War's first year, almost all

Confederates refused to export cotton to England, hoping to pressure the British to side with their nation. Previous American embargoes had failed because too many Americans had defied the few federal law enforcers. The best example: President Thomas Jefferson's sieve of an embargo in 1808.

The Confederate embargo was no sieve, even though no government enforced it. Confederate citizens voluntarily supported the almost entirely nongovernmental sanction. Rebel stalwarts even staged huge patriotic bonfires, with their valuable cotton feeding the flames. This willingness to sacrifice reinforces Gary Gallagher's point: Confederate whites most often displayed passionate commitment. That usually productive passion, however, here yielded counterproductively inflated visions of King Cotton's power.

Ironically, southern producers had sapped that power themselves. The South's enormous 1857–60 crops had saddled English manufacturers with a glut of raw cotton that lasted until mid-1862. By then, other economic monarchs had tempered King Cotton's dominance. King Wheat and King Corn ruled more English account books after the British imported more northern grains in the early 1860s. Union and Confederate orders for ships, rifles, and troops' clothes also boosted England's defense industry. By 1863, the British could secure tolerable amounts of cotton from India, from Egypt, and from the newest southern ruling class: migrant capitalists from the North, who leased contraband labor camps and paid ex-slaves to grow southern cotton.

Even if England had not developed new sources of cotton, new need for grains, and new customers for war industries, cotton would not have presided over English deliberations. The British government's master attitude toward the American Civil War, exclaimed Foreign Secretary Lord John Russell, remains "for God's sake let us if possible keep out of it!"[4] Plunging into it, English rulers agreed, would once again fritter away power needed against European rulers. Twice during the previous century, Englishmen had poured resources down that bottomless pit, a land war in the New World. England had lost its greatest colony in the American Revolutionary War, then failed to recapture it in the War of 1812. "Never again" became English rulers' resolve. Their attitude resembled late-twentieth-century Americans' post-Vietnam repugnance for another land war in Asia.

Lord Palmerston served as British prime minister and as ultimate decision maker on any English inclination to intervene in the Civil War.

Palmerston summed up his unfaltering disinclination in his favorite boxing metaphor: "They who in quarrels interpose, will often get a bloody nose."[5] Palmerston feared more than a bloody nose, if he sent Englishmen to rescue Confederates. Retaliating Americans might seize Canada, especially in the winter, when ice would preclude dispatching British reinforcements.

English lords had scoffed at such possibilities back in the days when they dismissed American militiamen as ragtag yeomen. But now the Union possessed an industrial-age army. Moreover, where England had once ruled the waves, American ironclads might now challenge her navy. Why risk lives and Canada too against this New World colossus, when the United States had proved itself unconquerable in precolossus days? And why throw away English leverage over the European balance of power to achieve far less important (to England) leverage over the American balance of power?

Lord Palmerston, like almost all English leaders, saw insufficient reasons. True, English aristocratic republicans smugly chuckled when American braggarts' egalitarian republic fell apart. True, British antislavery gentlemen happily suspected that slavery would be vulnerable in a postwar southern nation, no longer sustained by the Union's prewar protection. They further suspected that the Confederacy's huge land mass could not be subdued. The Union's futile attempt to conquer, they fretted, strewed meaningless casualties across American battlefields.

When Lincoln issued the Preliminary Emancipation Proclamation, many English lords believed that the casualties would soar. Lincoln's Proclamation, Prime Minister Palmerston feared, sought to inspire servile insurrection and a southern race war. This widespread English misperception, illuminating again Anglo-American whites' terror of black violence, demonstrated again why slaves were shrewd to shun insurrection. While nonviolent fugitives won white allies on both sides of the Atlantic, Englishmen would have cheered if northern and southern whites together had smothered black insurrectionists.

Palmerston's fear of exposing British lads to American violence helped dictate his policy. As an economic nationalist, desiring trade with *both* North and South, and as a would-be international humanitarian, desiring a world without unnecessary carnage, he aspired to help end the allegedly unwinnable war as soon as he could. But he would not risk English lives, endanger Canada, and sacrifice Old World power to attempt New World mercies. Perhaps he could persuade the Union to concede defeat, as soon as the Lincoln administration would listen. But so long as Union leaders warned the British not to interfere, Palmerston would back off from playing referee.

Only briefly did U.S. Secretary of State William H. Seward have to issue warnings. In mid-1862, when a cotton shortage replaced England's cotton glut, the Palmerston regime became more anxious to end America's allegedly unwinnable war. The proposed means of termination, bruited about in London for the next half year, was to offer English service as mediators, possibly with a threat to recognize Confederate independence if Lincoln rejected mediation.

The gambit had to overcome Palmerston's edict that "a Rupture with the United States would at all times be an Evil."[6] The prime minister saw no purpose in offering mediation, so long as the Union would obviously reject the offer. Palmerston also saw no benefit from recognizing the Confederacy, unless "some direct active interference . . . followed." Any further English interference, Palmerston warned Parliament in 1862, would lead to "greater evils, greater sufferings, and greater privations."[7]

Foreign Secretary Lord John Russell, the cabinet's most important advocate of an English offer to mediate in late 1862, retorted that Lincoln's rejection of mediation would lead no further than England's recognition of the Confederacy, which would lead no further than Seward's verbal explosions. Russell favored an English recommendation that the Union quit the war, along with a pledge that we "shall take no part in the war *unless* attacked" [emphasis mine].[8] That *unless* would have little protected Britain against a possible tidal wave of events. While Lord Russell's proposed mediation would itself have been an innocuous intervention, Union leaders could have taken offense at the meddling, which could have led British leaders to take offense, which could have led. . . . Wars for national honor have exploded over even more milque toast beginnings than Russell's proposed mediation, even when more insistent national interests have mitigated against the blowup. A war between the United States and Great Britain would assuredly have counterbalanced southern anti-Confederates' damage to the Confederacy, just as French intervention had offset American Revolutionaries' internal defections.

But Lord Palmerston, not Lord Russell, controlled British diplomacy; and the prime minister saw no benefit that could justify his foreign secretary's risky *unless*. Palmerston called English mediation in the fall of 1862 as useless "as asking the winds . . . to let the waters remain calm." The "Bystanders" must remain "lookers on" and "the Pugilists must fight a few more Rounds" before the North would receive enough "pummeling by the South" to tolerate mediation.[9]

After the prime minister postponed mediation, the peeved foreign secretary aborted the October cabinet meeting, called to discuss his proposal. A rump meeting of cabinet members savaged Sir John anyway. As the Earl of Clarendon summed up the verdict, "Johnny always loves to do something when to do nothing is prudent."[10]

Russell's proclivity to do something imprudent had not quite been extinguished. At the subsequent November 1862 cabinet meeting, Lord Russell urged that Russia, France, and England together propose a temporary armistice, a cooling-off period. The requirement of unanimous European action illustrated perhaps the greatest obstacle to an English attempt to mediate, even if only to suggest a temporary armistice. Great Britain would not touch the New World hot spot unless all her Old World rivals equally risked burned hands. That prerequisite robbed Russell's proposition of any potential effectiveness, for pro-Union Russia would have aborted the plan. Palmerston's cabinet shot down Russell's final trial balloon anyway.[11]

Time would have worked against the foreign secretary's proposal, even if Russia, Palmerston, and the British cabinet had allowed the proposition to survive. The English cotton shortage, and with it English thoughts of mediation, did not begin until mid-1862. Not until November did the cabinet consider Lord Russell's mediation and temporary armistice proposals. Then Palmerston told Russell that such ventures must be postponed until the spring, for the forming ice precluded fortification of Canada. By the time the ice had melted, Lincoln's Emancipation Proclamation had spawned black freedom without black insurrection, to Palmerston's delighted amazement. The English, priding themselves on being the first emancipators, now favored the Great Emancipator. So illusions of an English rescue of the Confederacy flickered out after a few months of dim life, yielding what Robert E. Lee had anticipated: nothing.

3

While General Lee expected nothing from Englishmen, he did anticipate that massive defections from the North might save the Confederacy. As he envisioned it, spectacular military victories might yield northern war weariness. Then, to borrow Palmerston's boxing lingo, Yankees might throw in the towel. Lincoln's Republican Party, Lee knew, would never surrender. Only the opposition Democratic Party might admit defeat. If Northern Democrats secured a mandate to surrender at the polls, southern anti-Confederates' defection would indeed stand counterbalanced.

According to a widespread myth, as misleading as the myth that Maryland almost seceded, Democrats came close to winning at the polling places, thus bringing Confederates close to winning their independence on the battlefields. The 1862 congressional election hardly sustains that myth. While Democrats gained some House seats, Republicans still easily controlled that chamber and *gained* five seats in the Senate. So speculation about some northern surrender of the Union must focus on the presidential election of 1864.

Supposedly, if Confederates had defeated William Tecumseh Sherman on the fall 1864 Atlanta battlefields, or if rebels had at least stalled Sherman at the gates of Atlanta until after the presidential election, the Democrats' George McClellan might have defeated Abraham Lincoln. Then a President McClellan would supposedly have carried out the favorite strategy of his party's peace wing: a thirty-day armistice, to be used to persuade Confederates to reenter the Union. Even if the rebels had remained unpersuaded, climaxes the speculation, the war would have been over. Once the war-weary North had shut down the war machine, a President McClellan allegedly could not have restarted the monster.[12]

The endgame part of this fantasy has least credibility. As Carthage and Sparta and Napoleon demonstrated, belligerents restart wars all the time and with a vengeance, after a temporary truce and a failed negotiation demonstrate that combatants' differences remain nonnegotiable. As Lord Palmerston commented, a Civil War "armistice without some agreement" on "separation" of the Union "would only be like [the] breathing Time allowed to Boxers between Rounds of a Fight, to enable them to get a fresh wind."[13]

While a moment of breathing time would not have precluded Federals' fresh start in a war against disunion, some Peace Democrats believed that a Democratic Party victory in 1864 could generate a negotiated reunion, with or without a temporary truce and an English referee. In August 1864 at the Democratic Party's national convention, a compromise between Peace and War Democrats seemed to offer that prospect. The more numerous War Democrats, wishing to wage the war for Union more successfully, won the party's presidential nomination for their favorite, General George McClellan. The less numerous Peace Democrats, wishing to see if a temporary armistice might bring a negotiated reunion, wrote their idea into the party's platform. The document declared that "after four years of failure to restore the Union by the experiment of war, . . . immediate efforts [must] be made for a cessation of hostilities," so that "at the earliest practicable moment, peace may be restored *on the basis of the Federal Union*" [emphasis mine].[14] Not even most Peace Democrats, in other words, were willing to grant the Confederacy permanent existence.

The ink had scarcely dried on the Democrats' proposal to negotiate a peaceable reunion before the platform became irrelevant. Three days after the Democratic convention, Confederates surrendered Atlanta, ensuring Lincoln's reelection. But would the convention's compromise have led a McClellan administration to accept disunion, despite the insistence on "Federal Union" in the platform, if Atlanta had held out and if McClellan had won the presidency?

Not if the new president, a convinced War Democrat, could help it. McClellan, true to his favorite part of the Peace Democrats' platform, always insisted that a Federal Union must be the basis of peace. In his letter accepting the Democratic Party nomination, the general wrote like the good soldier: "I could not look in the face of my gallant comrades, who have survived so many bloody battles, and tell them that their labors and the sacrifice of many of our slain and wounded brethren had been in vain, that we had abandoned that Union for which we have so often periled our lives."[15]

While McClellan never waffled on abandoning the Union, he wavered momentarily, slightly, on whether he could tolerate a temporary armistice, as a means to negotiate reunion. On August 10, three weeks before Sherman strode into Atlanta, McClellan cursed that some Democrats want me to

The Last Illusory Rescuers

Union General George McClellan, who was a threat to rescue slavery but not disunion. *Courtesy of the U. S. Army Military History Institute.*

Confederate General Patrick Cleburne, who futilely sought to surrender slavery in order to rescue disunion. *Courtesy of the U. S. Army Military History Institute.*

"write a letter suggesting an armistice!!!! If these fools will ruin the country, I won't help them."[16] Yet while drafting his letter accepting the presidential nomination, McClellan briefly toyed with the fools' panacea. He might accept a temporary armistice, early drafts hint, *if* Confederates wished to talk about restoring the Union. McClellan's final draft, however, rubbed out all ifs, all armistices, all negotiations. He would fight until rebels surrendered disunion.[17]

The slight waffle offered no way for Confederates to win permanent independence. McClellan played with and swiftly rejected no more than a temporary armistice, conditional on Confederates' negotiations toward reunion. Rebels rejected precisely that basis of negotiations. "We are fighting

for Independence," Jefferson Davis insisted in mid-1864, "and that, or extermination, we *will* have."[18]

Davis's extermination of Peace Democrats' 1864 hopes demonstrates
that war weariness, by itself, seldom ends wars. Some politically viable basis
for terminating the combat must exist or combatants will trudge on
wearily, until one annihilates the other. Acceptance of disunion remained
political suicide for northern mainstream politicians in 1864. Politics aside,
few Peace Democrats considered surrender tenable. Acceptance of reunion
remained equally untenable inside the Confederate high command in 1864,
as Davis's intransigence showed. Lord Palmerston had it right (even if he
picked the wrong winner): Fisticuffs would have to continue until the
Union accepted disunion or until the Confederacy tolerated reunion.

With candidate McClellan adamant about securing reunion, time was
the enemy of any Democratic Party surrender of Union, just as Lord John
Russell had possessed too little time to secure British mediation. Robert E.
Lee's heroics had bought three years for some intervention from outside
white Confederates' ranks to turn around the Civil War. That was not
enough time. Lee would have had to buy at least two more years, until the
congressional election of 1866, or possibly four more years, until the presidential election of 1868, for Peace Democrats even to campaign for peace
with disunion, much less to win an election on that (in 1864) politically
suicidal basis.

Confederates probably could not have hung on until a President Mc-
Clellan could be inaugurated, much less until his successor could be
elected. In August 1864, Abraham Lincoln privately pledged a harder war
between the presidential election and the March 4 inauguration day, if a
Democrat was elected president.[19] Lincoln feared not a surrender (he knew
that McClellan would fight for Union) but a military disaster (he feared
that the Democrat would resurrect soft war tactics). While McClellan fa-
vors "crushing out the rebellion," Lincoln conceded, "the rebel army cannot be destroyed with democratic [party] strategy." Under some
Democrats' plan "to conciliate the South," the "200,000 able bodied" and
emancipated black troops now used "to hold territory" will be "returned
to slavery." If we were to "abandon all the posts now possessed by black
men, . . . we would be compelled to abandon the war in 3 weeks."[20]

The president had evidently forgotten that George McClellan had promised (August 9, 1862) that slaves received into the military service of the United States "in any capacity" would receive "permanent military protection against any compulsory return to a condition of servitude."[21] True, President McClellan could honor that pledge and still dismiss all blacks from military service. But a former general, if he had become commander in chief, would not likely have ripped apart his army on March 4, 1865, not with victory almost in hand. Nor would the instant dismissal of over 100,000 Union soldiers have likely mattered much that late in the Civil War, not with Lee's army a shadow of its once mighty self. On the question of whether the Confederacy could secure permanent disunion, the Union's election of 1864 can only be called, to borrow the historian William C. Davis's splendid phrase, the "turning point that wasn't."

On another vital Civil War question, the election of 1864 remained a possible turning point. Although a President McClellan would not have surrendered the Union or reenslaved black soldiers, he probably would have welcomed rebel states back into the Union without requiring them to ratify the emancipating Thirteenth Amendment. Republicans so required, and the requirement mattered. If seven rebel states had rejected the amendment, the requisite three-fourths state majority would not have been available. Then blacks' freedom in peacetime would have tottered on the foundation of Lincoln's proclamation in wartime.

McClellan probably would also have been open to negotiate a restored Union, with slavery's survival guaranteed (except for the reenslavement of black military personnel). In March 1865, despite their previous protestations that disunion was nonnegotiable, Confederate leaders just might have settled for an enslaved Union, with their war (and thus slavery) almost lost and with McClellan Democrats less antisouthern than Lincoln Republicans. Yet while a President McClellan might have rescued slavery in the Union, he joined Lord Palmerston as a noncandidate for rescuing an independent Confederacy.

4

After the Confederacy failed to secure British or Peace Democrat aid, the rebels had only one candidate left to offset southern defectors' reinforcement of the Union. The Confederates would have to arm their slaves. While several southwestern papers fleetingly proposed this incendiary proposition in September 1863, the moment of truth came on the second day of 1864. Then an important Confederate major general brought the improbable slaveholder panacea to a historic caucus of the Army of Tennessee, in one of the Civil War's most remarkable scenes. The drama's star, Patrick Ronaye Cleburne, wielded both the unchallengeable loyalty of a Confederate hero and the heretical mentality of an eccentric not to this civilization born. The combination gave Cleburne his chance to utter the unutterable for one southern evening, before the forces of orthodoxy gagged discussion of his panacea.

An Irish rather than southern upbringing prepared Patrick Cleburne for this drama. The future southern brawler was born near Cork on St. Patrick's Day Eve, March 16, 1828, the third child of a prosperous Irish physician. At age fifteen, the pampered lad had to depart the family's elegant house when his father died and his oldest brother inherited the estate. Patrick Cleburne supported himself as a druggist's apprentice and as a soldier in the 41st British Regiment before migrating to America in 1849.

Within months of arriving in the land of opportunity, the opportunity to become a drug store manager pulled the seeker in an unusual direction for an Irish immigrant: south toward home, to Helena, Arkansas. The immigrant arrived in Arkansas armed with only his Irish love for personal freedom and personal cronies, his experience at pharmacies, his British army sword, and (Lord Palmerston would have loved this) his boxing gloves.

The stranger brought ideal paraphernalia. Cleburne's propensity to fight for honor and friends swiftly made him a capital drinking companion of good old southern boys who raised their fists whenever anyone besmirched their reputations. Yet when too often raising his glass, Cleburne became too combative even for honor-obsessed Southerners. So the newcomer became that Irish anomaly, a teetotaler. The renunciation made him that further Irish anomaly, a crony with no blarney. Taciturn, serious, intense, Cleburne wasted no time on chatter as he climbed the Helena social ladder. In the 1850s, he ascended from drug store manager to owner, then from law apprentice to partner, then from land speculator to railroad capitalist. The ex-Irish private also rose to become captain of the Yell Rifles, the local volunteer militia.

The outsider, however, rejected the insiders' top rung of the ladder. "I never owned a negro and care nothing for them," Cleburne wrote his brother as the Civil War began. He would fight for black slavery because Yankees seek to enslave whites, to enslave *us*. They "no longer acknowledge that all government derives its validity from the consent of the governed." A liberty-loving Irishman must stand "with Arkansas in weal or woe," alongside "friends" who "have stood up [for] me all occasions," against "a tiranical [sic] majority."[22]

Cleburne stood up against the tyrants throughout Grant's western campaigns. The pugnacious rebel unhappily retreated from Bowling Green through Nashville to Corinth when Grant seized Forts Henry and Donelson. For Cleburne's subsequent heroics at Shiloh and especially at Perryville, Jefferson Davis made him a Confederate major general (only one other nonnative Southerner so ascended). After the major general's heroics at Chickamauga and especially his rout of Sherman at Chattanooga, Davis called him "the Stonewall of the West." But the new Stonewall scorned the role of much honored loser. On January 2, 1864, he asked to address the Army of Tennessee's officers, to explain how to snatch victory from defeat.

The commander of the Army of Tennessee, Joseph E. Johnston, called his officers to quarters that night to hear their Irish comrade. The orator immediately displayed why he had earned Confederate warriors' respectful attention, whatever he said. When engaged in debate, Cleburne's mouth filled with blood, the consequence of an almost fatal bullet he had taken for a friend in an Arkansas brawl. When his lungs pushed sound through the gore, exclamation came out as a hiss, the consequences of a Union minié ball that had pierced his cheek and exited his mouth, carrying two smashed teeth with it. (I "caught the ball" in my "mouth and spat it out," this brawler later bragged.)[23] Fellow officers sat in shocked silence as the short, emaciated Irish warrior, his very form seemingly consumed by anti-Yankee fury, urged surrender of slavery in his unsouthern brogue, while blood from his mouth trickled down the beard that barely hid his brutal scars.

"As between the loss of [white men's] independence and the loss of [black] slavery," this nonslaveholder instructed slaveholding officers, "every patriot will . . . give up the negro slave rather than be a slave himself."[24] Slavery, "one of our chief sources of strength at the commencement of the war, has now become" militarily "one of our chief sources of weakness." Because of slavery, "our struggles and sacrifices" have yielded "nothing but long lists of dead and mangled," and "we are hemmed in today into less than two-thirds of'" our territory. Meanwhile, our "enemy menacingly confronts us at every point with superior forces," and our soldiers, suffering "fatal apathy," desert as never before.

Because of slavery, Cleburne emphasized, the enemy has three sources of soldiers to our one. Where we enroll native-born whites, he recruits his "motley" whites, "our slaves," and immigrants fresh off the boat, fired "against us by fictitious pictures of the atrocities of slavery." Moreover, "wherever there is a slave to set free," black labor becomes "comparatively valueless to us" but invaluable "to the enemy" as a "spy system, . . . revealing our positions, purposes, and resources."

The solution: We must emancipate every black who risks "his life in defense of the State," and we must liberate his wife and children too. Because of emancipation, northern recruiting of slavery-hating immigrants "will be dried up," and "the enemy's negro army will have no motive to fight." Instead, our blacks will make our "armies numerically superior to those of the North." No longer will the enemy's army of occupation use our blacks as "ready guides" to "every neighborhood" and as a "cheap ready-made means of holding" our territory. The enemy will find instead, from our whites and blacks alike, "a common hatred and thirst for vengeance," preventing him from "settling our lands."

A southern-born analyst might have assessed blacks' impact on the Civil War similarly. But no native Southerner would have added that "for many years, ever since the agitation of the subject of slavery commenced, the negro has been dreaming of freedom. . . . To attain it, he will tempt dangers and difficulties not exceeded by the bravest soldiers." Equally heretically, Cleburne declared that "contrary to the training of a lifetime," our blacks have fought "bravely" for their freedom. Why doubt that black soldiers "would submit to discipline and face danger," if we offered them the further allurement of freedom for their families? Why doubt that we would whip our tormentors, with hundreds of thousands of black troops added to our ranks?

As Cleburne finished, soldiers shouted answers. Thirteen officers, including three brigadier generals, had previously endorsed Cleburne's speech.

Several more rebels now praised the Irishman. Others, however, called the "monstrous" proposal "hideous and objectionable," "revolting to Southern sentiment, Southern pride, and Southern honor," sure to excite "the universal indignation of the Southern people and Southern soldiers."[25] Cleburne's critics demanded that Joseph Johnston silence the debate, lest the heresy dissolve the army and the Confederacy. General Johnston obeyed. He ordered participants never to mention the discussion outside quarters.

Cleburne's critics occasionally defied Johnston's gag decree. Brigadier General Clement H. Stevens, upon hearing about the secret conclave, typified Southerners' reaction. Cleburne, according to Stevens, lacked "a proper conception of the Negro, he being foreign born and reared." Our justification "is the inferiority of the negro." If we give that up, "I take no more interest in the fight."[26] Jefferson Davis, also told about the secret caucus, agreed "that such a subject should [never] be mooted, or even known to be entertained." He ordered "suppression . . . of all discussion."[27]

The suppression of all discussion about black troops may seem strange, for some black Confederates served as sharpshooters in the rebel army. But those unofficial black soldiers were trusted body servants. Cleburne would have extended the trust to all slaves. Most slaveholders considered that extension of trust naïve. Their reaction showed again the limits of their paternalism. Some house servants did indeed love their masters, but did the great mass of slaves? The masters' own answer dictated that Cleburne be silenced.

Cleburne, good soldier, accepted the gag order. For almost eleven more months, he fought the Yankees. Then on November 30, 1864, a bullet pierced his heart at the battle of Franklin (Tennessee), as he was leading the Army of Tennessee's last suicidal charge. Thirty years later, when historians found his speech, his adopted nation discovered that a magnificent Irish warrior had been a Confederate seer.

Arguably, a full democratic debate on Cleburne's prescience would have, should have resulted in his defeat. But indisputably, a democratic system demanded that such a life-or-death issue must be debated, not repressed. Not one of Cleburne's critics doubted that the Confederacy was dying (after all, the oft-beaten Army of Tennessee had lately suffered the supposed Miracle at Missionary Ridge). Nor did soldiers doubt that blacks contributed to the imbalance of soldiers (and of spies). Yet routed soldiers could not tolerate extended consideration of their last conceivable lifeline.

It was a key moment for understanding not only slaveholders' distinction between body servants and the mass of slaves but also the distinction between white men's democracy up north and down south. Everywhere, white Americans shared constitutions, white male suffrage, elections, low or no property qualifications for office, and an unshakable determination that other whites must treat them as honorable equals, never as dishonorable slaves. But northern whites could discuss anything. Middle and Lower South whites could debate everything except the critical subject. By calling the most important discussion taboo, slaveholders robbed themselves of democracy's genius: its capacity to reexamine and reformulate the culture's deepest concerns. While the black troop puzzle tormented Northerners and Southerners, only the North could air the torment, examine it from all angles, resolve it. While a northern army order such as General Orders #3 came down from on high, without prior public debate, congressional discussion immediately engulfed it and public disapproval soon overwhelmed it. No democratic confrontation, in contrast, killed Cleburne's last best hope.

By burying Cleburne's proposal before discussion could even begin, silencers recalled prewar Republicans' great issue: The Slave Power, to protect slavery for blacks, shackled democracy for whites. The silencing of Cleburne stemmed from the same slaveholder impulses as the congressional Gag Rule, the proslavery Kansas legislature's repression of free discussion, South Carolina's strangled debate over secession in 1860, and the symbol of all these gags, Preston Brooks smashing Charles Sumner to the U.S. Senate floor. The Cleburne incident showed again that the path to war was also the road to Confederate defeat, that an understanding of the 1860–65 epic must begin as early as 1830.

Patrick Cleburne, while a latecomer to the South, probably understood that he had suffered an ironic imprisonment. He had fought as an Irishman should, not to perpetuate slavery for blacks but to liberate whites from tyrants—to free himself from Yankee enslavement. Now the major general occupied a democrat's no-man's-land, shackled by Southerners' version of democracy from taking his best shot at liberty from Northerners.

On November 7, 1864, a desperate Jefferson Davis removed the shackles on public discussion. With Grant besieging Petersburg and Lee's army evaporating, the president asked Congress to buy 40,000 blacks and promise them emancipation "after service faithfully rendered." For now, Davis wished to use blacks only as military laborers. But if "our white population shall prove insufficient," 40,000 black military laborers, because of "their preparatory training in intermediate duties, would form a more valuable reserve force."[28]

At the moment that Davis indirectly conceded that Pat Cleburne's proposed reserve force must be discussed, the Irishman had only twenty-three days left to live. If Cleburne ever heard of his indirect vindication, he likely cursed rather than cheered. Davis had caught up not with Cleburne's early 1864 plea for black soldiers but only with Benjamin Butler's 1862 plea for black laborers. Moreover, even Cleburne's vision had been almost too late. Davis's diluted version, ten months later, came impossibly too late. In November 1864, Lower South blacks could never have cut their way past Sherman to labor for Lee, even if the Confederate Congress had instantly called them forth.

Nor were Confederate congressmen willing to issue the call. Instead, the solons called Davis fanatical. "Even victory itself," warned Congressman Henry C. Chambers of Mississippi, "would be robbed of its glory if shared with slaves." Beyond Congress, Georgia's Howell Cobb intoned that "if slaves will make good soldiers our whole theory of slavery is wrong — but they won't make soldiers." The *Charleston Mercury* added that South Carolina soldiers "will not fight beside a nigger." To "hack at the root of . . . our institutions — our civilization" — is to "kill the cause as dead as a boiled crab."[29]

On February 18, 1865, Robert E. Lee wrote Congress that his army would be as dead as slavery, unless the Confederacy adopted Davis's stalled plan — and used freed blacks not as military laborers but as soldiers. In language that resembled Grant's,* Lee declared that "under good officers and good instructions, I do not see why they should not become soldiers."[30]

Lee's prestige legitimated Davis's proposition. Still, Congress stalled for another month, then barely passed an almost unrecognizable version of Cle-

---

* For Grant's parallel words, see p. 168.

burne's conception (by only one vote in the Senate). The belated law, enacted March 13, 1865, less than four weeks before Appomattox, enabled Davis "to ask" owners for black military personnel. If asking individuals failed, Davis could ask states to supply 25 percent of their black males of fighting age.

Having allowed the president only to ask and then ask again, Congress barred emancipation of any troops asked for, unless both the slaveowner and his state agreed. While that provision protected donating masters, another protected donated slaves. Blacks' "rations, clothing, and compensation," ordered Congress, must be "the same . . . as are allowed to other [white] troops."[31] The Confederacy's initially equal payments to blacks and whites put the Union's initially racist pay scale to shame.

Swiftly, Davis put the Confederate Congress's refusal to emancipate to shame. He announced that only freed slaves would be accepted in the army. In the few remaining Civil War days, a few dozen freed slaves donned Confederate gray. The law obviously provided too little, too late. But if Cleburne had convinced his adopted nation to go farther, sooner, would slaves have fought for masters?

The politically correct answer, then and now: No. Then, most Confederates considered blacks biologically incapable of fighting effectively for anyone. Now, many consider slaves ideologically incapable of fighting against emancipating Northerners. Confederates certainly erred about racial biology. But certainty is more elusive about slaves' potential willingness to fight for the Confederacy, if Confederates had adopted the Cleburne plan in early 1864. Most Confederate slaves lived in the Lower South. Most northern armies were far off, their promise of emancipation at best a vague rumor. Under the Cleburne proposal, Confederate recruiters, pressing the only opportunity in town, would have offered slaves quite an inducement: freedom not only for husbands but also for wives and children.

Perhaps suspicious slaves would have preferred enslavement. Perhaps recruits would have fled to the Union army, the minute Confederates brought them close to Yankees. But then again, perhaps slaves would have seized the best bargain they had ever been offered: support ex-masters in exchange for becoming gun-bearing freedmen and liberators of their own families. As one Union black soldier described that psychological lure, "I felt like a man with a uniform on and a gun in my hand."[32]

This much is certain: black men would have had more to gain if they could have become masters of themselves by shouldering masters' guns than Lord Palmerston had to gain in a third American land war or George McClellan had to gain by surrendering the Union. Yet this too is certain: Slaves came no closer to counterbalancing southern anti-Confederates than did Englishmen or Democrats. Without Cleburne's abolitionist inducements to lure canny slaves, slave enlistment was as improbable as politically correct folk now claim. And the Slave South felt compelled to make the Cleburne-style emancipation vanish faster than any magician's rabbit.

5

By fatally procrastinating about their last best hope, recruiting their own slaves, Confederate state whites restricted themselves to only their 90,000 white troops from the Border South, to offset the Union's 450,000 white and black soldiers from slaveholding states. Confederate states whites could not forever afford that five to one shortfall in aid from outside, not atop their four to one shortfall in whites residing inside, not when the Union's sieging/turning tactics took maximum advantage of rebel shortfalls. Confederates could not even afford their "winning" margin of three Federals killed for every two rebels slain, not in a long war of attrition. At the end of the exhausting contest, the Union states still had 2,000,000 potential whites to recruit (and 600,000 Lower South slaves), while the Confederates' replacement cupboard had been stripped bare.

During the last hundred days of the war, Lee's army stripped itself almost as bare. At the end of February 1865, Lee retained only 35,000 men to Grant's 120,000. In that month alone, 8 percent of Lee's troops deserted. In letters to the front, some soldiers' wives begged their husbands to come home and feed starving families.[33] Troops' empty stomachs growled a second to the motion. The terror of hopeless encirclement sped thousands more home.

The late war epidemic of Confederate desertions, when added to all the other elements of an increasingly lopsided balance of power, made the heavy demands of the Union's triple siege at last almost light and Lee's final plight absolutely crushing. As March 1865 ended, the offensive-minded defender had only the worst defensive option left. He had to cut out of encirclement and run. The Confederate hero sliced out of Petersburg on April 2–3. Outflanked Richmond then surrendered. First among the Union troops who marched down the Confederate capital's streets were Grant's contraband. First among the Union civilians who strode into the conquered city was Abraham Lincoln, come to try out Jefferson Davis's desk for size. It was a little small for the towering man whom black celebrants were calling the greatest messiah since Christ.

The general who had long been the Confederates' messiah remained on the loose for a moment. Lee and his men traversed the several dozen miles from Petersburg west to Appomattox Court House during April's first week. Grant's men moved faster. They snapped another circle around Lee. It was surrender time for the third Confederate army that Grant's sieges had captured.

The surrenders at Donelson, Vicksburg, and Appomattox netted the Union over 50,000 Confederate troops. That number added another perspective to the 25,000 extra casulties that Lee's seven offensive battles had cost the Confederacy. Those numbers showed again that the effective siege, not the ineffective charge, ushered in the Civil War's most killing disasters. Lee's offensive-minded defense forced Federals to encircle his Virginia theater by land and by sea before they could encircle him. He had thus arguably at least delayed catastrophe. Confederates' alternative master strategy had not even enjoyed that success. By unendingly retreating and daring Federals to do the charging, Joseph Johnston had secured almost no Union charges, just the fatal siege of Atlanta.

Grant and Lee met to finalize the Army of Northern Virginia's surrender at 1:00 P. M. on April 9, 1865, in Wilmer McLean's modest house near Appomattox Court House. McLean's parlor, seemingly small for a historic occasion, was big enough symbolically. Early in the war, when living near Bull Run, McLean had witnessed two epic battles almost on his lawn. He had also experienced a Yankee ball crashing into his kitchen. Fleeing the combat, McLean had come to out-of-the-way Appomattox village to reside. But at Appomattox, the war again chased down the noncombatant, then surged through his door. Like so many Upper South men, Wilmer

Wilmer McLean's house near Appomattox Courthouse, site of Lee's surrender and symbol of a war that neither McLean nor Lee nor their Middle South could avoid. Courtesy of the Library of Congress.

McLean could not escape the consequences of a secession that only the Lower South had wanted, or a combat that had barely touched vast Lower South areas. At McLean's house, Grant and Lee almost ended the war that had particularly ravaged Upper South men caught in the middle.

Because much of the Lower South remained uninvaded and Joseph Johnston's 20,000 man Army of Tennessee remained unconquered, Jefferson Davis sought to fight on. Some historians approve his tenacity. They observe that guerrilla warfare—taking to the hills and harassing conquering troops—has outlasted many supposedly victorious armies. Joseph Johnston differed. He surrendered to Sherman nine days after Lee visited Wilmer McLean's parlor.

Johnston was right. This was one of the worst wars for a purely guerrilla defense and the worst time in this war to mount that strategy.[34] The Confederacy had successfully used guerrilla harassment *after* conquering Union armies had penetrated the heartland. Yet to press guerrilla tactics exclusively—to invite Federals deeper inside to harass them ever more—would only have invited a more horrendous smashing. The Federals' conquering mathematics calculated on blasting inside—on penetrating black belts and inviting slaves to escape. As for Confederate guerrillas hiding out in white belts, irregular warriors must rally the countryside against invaders. The Border South countryside, white and black, largely sided with the invaders.

If the war had continued into May 1865, Lower South black belts would have been the countryside ravaged. No longer would Wilmer McLean's Upper South have been the battleground for other people's war. William Tecumseh Sherman would have reentered Lower South black belts. No rebel army could have deterred him. Many slaves would have joined him. The war of Southerners against Southerners, having massively aided the Union, now left unaided Confederate whites no way to continue.

The Taproot and Its Blight 10

The history of the southern house divided defies simple summary. The story's revelations transcend the question of why the Confederacy lost the Civil War, also throwing light on the nature of Abraham Lincoln, American racism, paternalism, slavery, emancipation, bureaucracy, whites' democratic procedures, and blacks' nonviolent resistance. So too, although Southerners' war on Southerners is the critical missing piece in the why-the-Confederacy-lost puzzle, no one piece provides the solution. Without Lincoln's political finesse, for example, fugitive slaves and border whites might not have so profoundly compromised Confederate state whites. So too, without Grant's and other Union generals' military skill, anti-Confederate Southerners' contributions to Union power might never have been killing. There is nothing impersonally deterministic about this story; at many points, men's personal errors could have blunted the power of the Slave South's crippling divisions.

Furthermore, southern anti-Confederates' aid to the Union only crippled disastrously because free labor states started out with greater resources than slave labor states. Virginia's George Pickett pithily summed up the most important reason that the Union won the Civil War, when asked why his famous charge failed. Pickett mildly replied that "I've always thought the Yankees had something to do with it." Yankee power had so much to do with the Civil War outcome that without southern anti-Confederates' added power, the Union might still have prevailed. "The North," Shelby Foote has famously observed, "fought that war with one arm behind its back."[1]

Yet without southern anti-Confederates' Unionism, Yankees' other arm would have been sorely tested. If all the South's inhabitants, white and black, Lower South and Border South, had been solidly pro-Confederate, the North would have had to conquer the defense-friendly Ohio River, the guerrilla-friendly West Virginia mountain passes, and Maryland, Kentucky, and Missouri, just to reach the latitude where the Civil War in fact began. Free labor states would have had to replace over half a million Union soldiers and military workers who came from slave labor states. Federals would have had to find substitutes for the borderland's industrial plants, especially Baltimore's railroad hospitals. The Union would have had to conscript many more Northerners, despite much more Yankee draft resistance. One southern anti-Confederate lost to the Union and empowering the Confederacy would have required two more Yankees fully enlisted in the war effort.

That arithmetic, Lincoln believed, would have defeated the Union. My guess: He was right. The North's other arm was not *that* strong. All historians must guess about the potential outcome, for no one can write the definitive history of what never happened. But one conclusion is no guess: If the North had won without anti-Confederate Southerners' reinforcements, victory would have come harder and taken longer, producing a very different Civil War narrative.

While both one-armed northern power and southern anti-Confederate power sustained Union victory, each was more effect than cause. Beneath both northern strength and southern defection burrowed the taproot of slavery, spreading physical blights that made Confederate state whites' half of the southern population too much weaker, compared to Northerners plus the other half of southern folk.

1

Free labor states possessed more battlefield power for one overriding reason: Slavery had blighted slave labor states' share of American population and industry. The U.S. version of slavery, not slavery per se, spread that blight. In other New World nations, slave labor grew faster than free labor, for the slave trade remained open and free labor immigrants scant. The nineteenth-century United States instead shut off the African slave trade and attracted massive numbers of European free laborers. In the 1807 act that shaped the U.S. version of slavery and emancipation, Congress barred American importation of overseas slaves. During the next half century, the first massive rush of non-English immigrants reached U.S. shores. Newcomers overwhelmingly preferred the free labor section.

With few new Southerners and many new Northerners arriving, the North's manpower plurality soared. At the beginning of the national republic, future slave labor and free labor states contained approximately equal shares of the nation's population (with future free labor states containing 61 percent of the whites). By 1860, the North possessed 61 percent of all American people (and 70 percent of whites). During the war, 175,000 immigrants arrived in the Union and almost none in the Confederacy. From wartime newcomers, the Union recruited an estimated 75,000 soldiers (and the Confederacy almost none).

The taproot also blighted the Slave South's share of American industry. Again, nothing in slavery per se necessitated the southern industrial lag. Slaves can be used profitably in industry, as a few southern masters demonstrated. But some patches of agrarian depression aside, the South's farming capitalists saw little reason to become manufacturing capitalists. Slavery usually little damaged these entrepreneurs economically; their profits sometimes rivaled those of northern industrial capitalists. So agrarian an institution, however, weakened the slavocracy's physical capacity to wage industrial-age war. To that comparative weakness in prewar population and manufacturing, the taproot of slavery added a crippling Slave South wartime social fracture.

2

The free labor states contained not only more people and more manufacturing but also a more integrated society. Slavery's roots became shallower in the Border South than in the Lower South. In contrast, free labor's roots deeply penetrated all northern states. So too, while slaves seized opportunities to depart their owners, free laborers showed scant disposition to flee their employers. Five hundred thousand Yankee wage earners would never have deserted the Union to join the slaveholders, any more than five free labor states would have seceded from the Union to join the Confederacy.

Again, nothing in slavery per se made a slave society splinter more than a free labor society. In some slave societies, privileged slaves side with masters, just as in some free labor societies, employees revolt against employers. Even in the Civil War, some body servants unofficially joined the Confederate army, just as some free laborers went on strike against northern employers.[2] Far more often, however, Civil War slaves sought to escape a southern slave system that they hated, while Yankee free laborers sought to find jobs in a northern wage system that they cherished.

So too, nothing in a slave society per se stopped slaveholders from reopening the slave trade, so that all its subregions stood equally committed to the system. Prescient southern extremists tried to achieve precisely that sea change in the 1850s. They failed. Their failure meant that the Lower South continued to draw slaves from the Border South, making the taproot of slavery shallower where it was shrinking and deeper where it was expanding. The South's regional split in commitment to the basic labor system, plus its racial and class split between lowly blacks and lofty whites, made U.S. slave society far more fracture-prone than the free labor North.

Everywhere one looks for the physical capacity to make war, including population size and industrial development, the U.S. version of slavery held back the South compared to the free labor North. Everywhere one looks for sources of defections in the Slave South, including slaves' resistances and the Border South's northern tendencies, the nature of slavery's U.S. development holds the key. By making the South less industrialized, less populated, more prone to losing its laborers and some of its states, slavery yielded both greater northern power and greater southern fragmentation. These fruits of the taproot, when expertly used politically by Lincoln and militarily by Grant, Sherman, and their legions, nourished a war of attrition that ultimately overwhelmed fanatically supportive Confederate whites.

3

Some might dwell exclusively on slavery's moral rather than its physical blight. Some might even see the Civil War as an epic morality play, with Providence directing the more moral North to victory. Not this native son of the North, who has spent most of his adult life in the South. With regard to democracy, slavery, and racial justice, neither my native nor my adopted region's Civil War record inspires soaring moral pride.

True, Federals fought for majority rule and the minority's acceptance of election results. But Confederates fought for the consent of the governed and the natural right to switch consent to another government. True, Lincoln called slavery wrong, always hoped for its ultimate extinction, and ultimately rejoiced to help slaves toward freedom. But neither the president's nor his constituents' antipathy for slavery sufficed to bring off emancipation. Before and during his presidency, Lincoln most consistently sought to free whites from the Slave Power's antimajoritarian governance. Lincoln only freed blacks after he concluded that otherwise, the white men's war for a majoritarian Union would be lost. So too, William Tecumseh Sherman's temporary gift of white men's land to black freedmen came largely to clear black nonlaborers from his white troops' path. Both racial advances vindicated John Quincy Adams's remarkable prophecy of a generation earlier: The federal government would someday strip away black bondage but only under its war-making powers, to fashion a winning military machine.[3]

Confederates crept slower than Lincoln (though arguably faster than Sherman) toward conceding that the winning military machine must arm black soldiers. But then again, Southerners had farther to travel to reach that realization. They too, albeit belatedly and incompletely, finished the journey. In both sections, racial progress most depended not on whites' passion for racial justice but on the governing race's vision of how to win *their* war for *their* version of white men's republicanism. With that moral blight afflicting both sections, American racial equality could not proceed much further than emancipation, not for another century.

It was the physical blight from the U.S. version of slavery, not the moral one, that finally made the Confederacy crumble, when emancipation applied the final lever. Once an invading army replaced local patrols, the taproot of slavery could be extracted with one arm tied behind the back, if Lincoln, Grant, and Sherman maximized their advantage. And so they did.

Notes

Preface

1. Published as Gary W. Gallagher, *The Confederate War: How Popular Will, Nationalism, and Military Strategy Could Not Stave Off Defeat* (Cambridge, MA, 1997), esp. pp. 3–4, 12. Professor Gallagher's analysis has led me to qualify the interpretation of white Confederate dissidence in my preliminary foray into the Why-the-Confederacy-Lost puzzle, "The Divided South, the Causes of Confederate Defeat, and the Reintegration of Narrative History," William W. Freehling, *The Reintegration of American History: Slavery and the Civil War* (New York, 1994), ch. 10.

2. The exceptions among Confederate whites do not necessarily contradict Gary Gallagher's subtle, guarded way of putting his thesis; he admits "substantial evidence of discontent" (p. 12). But is the issue whether *most* Confederate whites long supported the cause? If so, Gallagher's *most* stands invulnerable to critics who dwell on the "substantial" minority of Confederate white dissenters. Or is the issue whether the undermanned Confederacy could afford the "substantial" discontent among its own whites, particularly in view of the far more substantial discontent among other Southerners? If so, Gallagher's *most* stands partially vulnerable to several impressive analyses of white Confederate dissidence, cited below, ch. 8, note 5., p. 224.

My judgment that Southerners other than white Confederates must be brought into the South's Civil War story—including explanations of the military story—is hardly mine alone. Eric Foner anticipated some of my themes in "The South's Inner Civil War," *American Heritage*, 40 (1989), 47–56, as did David Osher and Peter Wallenstein, in "Why the Confederacy Lost: A Review Essay," *Maryland Historical Magazine*, 88 (1993), 95–108. Some of the best social histories of the Confederacy elaborate on southern internal divisions beyond the white Confederates, including Clarence L. Mohr, *On the Threshold of Freedom: Masters and Slaves in Civil War Georgia* (Athens, GA, 1986); James L. Roark, *Masters without Slaves: Southern Planters in the Civil War and Reconstruction* (New York, 1977); Joseph P. Reidy, *From Slavery to Agrarian Capitalism in the Cotton Plantation South: Central Georgia, 1800–1880* (Chapel Hill, 1992); and J. William Harris, *Plain Folk and Gentry in a Slave Society: White Liberty and Black Slavery in Augusta's Hinterlands* (Middletown, CT, 1985). As the notes below indicate, these are but the beginning of the fine studies of the Civil War that have eased my way. I also benefited from a conversation with Reid Mitchell, whose eagerly awaited Civil War volume will further demonstrate that "the Southerners" were not the same as "the Confederates."

Chapter 1. The Union's Task

1. All statistics in this book derive from Francis A. Walker, comp., *The Statistics of the Population of the United States* (Washington, DC, 1972); and from U.S. Bureau of the Census, *A Century of Population Growth; From the First Census of the United States to the Twelfth, 1790–1900* (Washington, DC, 1909).

For a superlative up-to-date guide to the Civil War literature, see James M. McPherson and William J. Cooper, Jr., eds., *Writing the Civil War: The Quest to Understand* (Columbia, SC, 1998).

2. I consider the emphasis on guerrilla warfare between the main battles, or to put it another way, the emphasis on the pacification of the countryside no less than on the big brawls of the armies, the most important recent advance in Civil War historiography. The critical volumes include Stephen V. Ash, *When the Yankees Came: Conflict and Chaos in the Occupied South, 1861–65* (Chapel Hill, 1995); Ash, *Middle Tennessee Transformed, 1860–1870: War and Peace in the Upper South* (Baton Rouge, 1988); Daniel E. Sutherland, *Seasons of War: The Ordeal of Confederate Community, 1861–1865* (New York, 1995); Michael Fellman, *Inside War: The Guerrilla Conflict in Missouri during the American Civil War* (New York, 1989); Noel C. Fisher, *War at Every Door: Partisan Politics and Guerrilla Violence in East Tennessee, 1860–1869* (Chapel Hill, 1997); James J.

Brewer, *The Raiders of 1862* (Westport, CT, 1997); and most recently Daniel E. Sutherland, ed., *Guerrillas, Unionists, and Violence on the Confederate Home Front* (Fayetteville, AR, 1999). To observe the progress toward a deeper military history, compare Benjamin Franklin Cooling's earlier, superlative example of the old battlefield genre, *Forts Henry and Donelson: The Key to the Confederate Heartland* (Knoxville, TN, 1987) with his later, even better example of the new major battle/guerrilla genre, *Fort Donelson's Legacy: War and Society in Kentucky and Tennessee, 1862–1863* (Knoxville, 1997).

I here seek to build on this historiographical advance in two ways. Because of the Union's necessity to tame guerrilla unrest, first of all, armies of occupation, with their oft-times disproportionately large percentage of black troops, seem much more important; indeed military service behind the lines seems as indispensable as combat duty. Second, because guerrilla warfare against Union armies consumed some southern areas, its absence in other areas helps measure comparative degrees of proslavery commitment. What did *not* happen in Maryland after April 19, 1861, and in Kentucky during Grant/Buell's preparations for Henry/Donelson illuminates why these states did not come close to seceding, just as what did *not* happen in Maryland and Kentucky after the Lincoln administration became an immediate menace to slavery illuminates why secessionists had worried about border proslavery slackness before the war.

3. While Raimondo Luraghi's *A History of the Confederate Navy* (Annapolis, MD, 1996) is the latest and fullest account, I have been more influenced by William N. Still, Jr.'s, *Iron Afloat: The Story of the Confederate Armorclads* (Columbia, SC, 1986) and *Confederate Shipbuilding* (Columbia, SC, 1987).

4. Quoted by Gary Gallagher in McPherson and Cooper, eds., *Writing the Civil War*, p. 27.

5. On southern railroads, books a half century old remain invaluable, especially Robert C. Black, III, *The Railroads of the Confederacy* (Chapel Hill, 1952); and George Edgar Turner, *Victory Rode the Rails: The Strategic Place of Railroads in the Civil War* (Indianapolis, 1953). On the Confederacy's railroad saboteurs, good biographies include James A. Ramage, *The Life of General John Hunt Morgan* (Lexington, KY, 1986); and Brian Steele Wills, *A Battle from the Start: The Life of Nathan Bedford Forrest* (New York, 1992).

Much recent work on the Confederate economy has been in the revisionist vein of emphasizing Confederates' brilliant, even revolutionary attempts to catch up with the Yankee industrial revolution. This revision has deemphasized the northern economic lead as a cause of the Confederacy's defeat. Some key works, in addition to William Still, Jr., on the Confederate navy, include Charles B. Dew, *Iron-master to the Confederacy: Joseph R. Anderson and the Tredegar Iron Works* (New Haven, 1986); Frank

Vandiver, *Ploughshares into Swords: Josiah Gorgas and Confederate Ordnance* (Austin, TX, 1952); and Emory Thomas, *The Confederacy as a Revolutionary Experience* (Englewood Cliffs, NJ, 1971).

I believe this revisionism must not be taken too far, for the Confederacy could never remotely catch up on the big-ticket items that controlled transportation, nor on the repair of those militarily crucial behemoths. If the Confederacy had caught up with the Union's navy and railroads, a different Civil War would have emerged. On this subject, I enjoy Roger Pickenpaugh's *Troop Transfer and the Civil War in the West* (Lincoln, NE, 1998). But on smaller-ticket items, especially shoulder arms, the Confederacy's remarkable efforts came closer to yielding parity.

6. The best works on the critical revolution in shoulder arms include Grady McWhiney and Perry D. Jamieson, *Attack and Die: Civil War Tactics and the Southern Heritage* (University, AL, 1982), esp. ch. 4; Jac Weller, "Civil War Minie Rifles Prove Quite Accurate," *American Riflemen* (1971), 36–40; John K. Mahon, "Civil War Infantry Assault Tactics," *Military Affairs*, 25 (1961), 57–68; and the judicious summary in James M. McPherson, *Battle Cry of Freedom: The Civil War Era* (New York, 1988), pp. 473–77.

7. I first came across the helpful *through/around* vocabulary in Craig L. Symond's excellent *A Battlefield Atlas of the Civil War*, 3rd edition (Baltimore, 1994).

8. On the crucial differences between the eastern and western fronts, see Richard M. McMurry's little gem of a book, *Two Great Rebel Armies: An Essay in Confederate Military History* (Chapel Hill, 1989). I agree with Mr. McMurry that the war was won in the west. While I think he slightly overestimates the generals in explaining why that was so, his ch. 2 superbly illuminates social and economic factors.

Chapter 2. Fault Lines in the Pre-Civil War South

1. Most of the notes to this chapter refer to the more elaborate, extensively documented discussion in my *The Road to Disunion*. Volume 1. *Secessionists at Bay, 1776–1854* (New York, 1990). For fuller discussion of the sources for and information on the three-tiered South, see *Road*, I, chs. 1–2.

2. For further material on black belt solidarity, see ibid., I, 39–49.

3. For further discussion of white belt slackness, see ibid., I, 49–50, 187–210, and passim.

4. Since *Road*, I, appeared, David Grimstead has published a massive elaboration of this key difference between versions of white men's democracy, North and

South: *American Mobbing, 1828–1861: Toward Civil War* (New York, 1998). For further discussion of the importance of this point, see above, pp. 34–35, 192–93.

5. Alison G. Freehling, *Drift toward Dissolution: The Virginia Slavery Debate of 1831–32* (Baton Rouge, 1982); *Road*, I, chs. 9-10.

6. On Kentucky and Missouri, ibid., I, 462–73, 537–44; on Maryland, Ira Berlin, *Slaves without Masters: The Free Negro in the Antebellum South* (New York, 1974), part III. My forthcoming *Road*, II, will contain extensive discussions of the reenslavement episode and of post-Kansas heresies in Missouri (especially Frank Blair's) and in Kentucky (especially John G. Fee's).

7. The best synthesis is still Eugene Genovese, *Roll, Jordan, Roll: The World the Slaves Made* (New York, 1974). For other important books in this vein, see my *Road*, I, note 32, p. 580.

8. The best discussion of this theme is still in Kenneth M. Stampp, *The Peculiar Institution: Slavery in the Ante-Bellum South* (New York, 1956).

9. Unfortunately, the best summary of fugitive slave activity ends in 1860 (and does not adequately emphasize fugitives' impact on white politics in the 1850s). John Hope Franklin and Loren Schweninger, *Runaway Slaves: Rebels on the Plantation* (New York, 1999). For an example of the way such omissions mislead superb historians of slavery, see Edmund S. Morgan's review of *Runaway Slaves* in *New York Review of Books*, June 10, 1999. "This form of resistance," Morgan erroneously concludes, "posed no serious threat to the system" (p. 31).

10. *Road*, I, 89–97.

11. Compare Stampp, *Peculiar Institution* with Genovese, *Roll, Jordan, Roll.*

12. Fellow historians will know that I here especially dissent from the famous wording, Significant Others, in Stanley Elkins, *Slavery: A Problem in American Institutional and Intellectual Life* (Chicago, 1959). Elkins's theory that masters were slaves' overpowering Significant Others seems to me to require more than the now commonplace (and true) correction that slaves often considered their family members more significant than their owners. The point is that slavery demanded not only private but also public authority; patrolmen, not masters, became fugitives' white Significant Others. But beyond Elkins, the unfortunate tendency to conflate white power with masters' power, thus missing the *public* power that sustained private power, suffuses all important studies of U.S. slavery.

13. Robert W. Johannsen, ed., *The Lincoln-Douglas Debates of 1858* (New York, 1965), p. 88.

14. *Road*, I, 489, 500–505, 536–37.

15. Ibid., I, chs. 30–31; James A. Rawley, *Race and Politics: "Bleeding Kansas" and the Coming of the Civil War* (Philadelphia and New York, 1969).

Chapter 3. The Secession Crisis

1. On the gag rule see *Road*, I, 289–352; on fugitive slaves and Kansas, ibid., I, 536–65; on Brooks-Sumner, William E. Gienapp, "The Crime against Sumner: The Caning of Charles Sumner and the Rise of the Republican Party," *Civil War History*, 25 (1979), 218–45; and for a broader summary Russel B. Nye, *Fettered Freedom: Civil Liberties and the Slavery Controversy, 1830–1860* (East Lansing, 1963). For a telling brief summary of the issue at stake here, see Larry Gara, "Slavery and the Slave Power: A Crucial Distinction," *Civil War History*, 15 (1969), 5–18.

2. In historians' dispute over the impetus behind the Republican Party, my own reading of Republicans' public speeches and private letters yields more agreement with Michael Holt's and William Gienapp's emphasis on containing the Slave Power than with Eric Foner's emphasis on economics or Richard Sewell's emphasis on antislavery morality. Holt, *The Political Crisis of the 1850s* (New York, 1978); Gienapp, *The Origins of the Republican Party, 1852–1856* (New York, 1987); Gienapp, "The Republican Party and the Slave Power," in Robert H. Abzug and Stephen E. Maizlish, eds., *New Perspectives on Race and Slavery in America: Essays in Honor of Kenneth M. Stampp* (Lexington, KY, 1986), pp. 51–78; Foner, *Free Soil, Free Labor, Free Men: The Ideology of the Republican Party before the Civil War* (New York, 1970); Sewell, *Ballots for Freedom: Antislavery Politics in the United States, 1837–1860* (New York, 1976).

3. Johannsen, ed., *Lincoln-Douglas Debates*, pp. 316–17, 319.

4. Ibid., p. 311.

5. The debate between southern secessionists and Unionists can be followed in William W. Freehling and Craig M. Simpson, eds., *Secession Debated: Georgia's Showdown in 1860* (New York, 1992). For fuller viewpoints, see Dwight Lowell Dumond, ed., *Southern Editorials on Secession* (New York, 1931); and Jon L. Wakelyn, ed., *Southern Pamphlets on Secession, November 1860–April 1861* (Chapel Hill, 1996).

6. George H. Reese, ed., *Proceedings of the Virginia State Convention of 1861*, 4 vols. (Richmond, 1965), I, 62–66.

7. John Hunt Morgan to Thomas Morgan, November 9, 17, 1860, Hunt-Morgan Family Papers, University of Kentucky, Lexington.

8. Roy C. Basler, ed., *The Collected Works of Abraham Lincoln*, 9 vols. (New Brunswick, NJ, 1953–55), IV, 263, 270.

9. A. P. Aldrich to James Hammond, November 25, 1860, Hammond Papers, Library of Congress.

10. I will discuss the quasi-manipulated nature of secession in South Carolina in *Road*, II. For the Aldrich-Hammond-militiamen part of the story, see Lawrence T. McDonnell, "Struggle against Suicide: James Henry Hammond and the Seces-

sion of South Carolina," *Southern Studies*, 22 (1983), 109—37; Stephanie McCurry, *Masters of Small Worlds: Yeoman Households, Gender Relations, and the Political Culture of the Antebellum South Carolina Low Country* (New York, 1995), esp. pp. 292—302.

11. Ralph A. Wooster, *The Secession Conventions of the South* (Princeton, NJ, 1962), pp. 58, 88, 104, 133.

12. Ibid., pp. 147, 163, 180, 193. On the reluctance of the Middle South, we have one of the best Civil War books, Daniel W. Crofts, *Reluctant Confederates: Upper South Unionists in the Secession Crisis* (Chapel Hill, 1989).

13. Wooster, *Secession Conventions*, pp. 213, 230.

14. On this knotty question, the prime disputants are David M. Potter, *Lincoln and His Party in the Secession Crisis* (New Haven, 1942); Kenneth M. Stampp, *And the War Came: The North and the Secession Crisis, 1860—1861* (Baton Rouge, 1950); and Richard Current, *Lincoln and the First Shot* (Philadelphia, 1963). While Stampp seems to me right to emphasize that Lincoln meant to have Davis fire a first shot, if there was to be a first shot, Current seems to me right to emphasize that Davis still had to decide to fire that shot. The truth is that neither president could decide not to shoot without symbolically sacrificing his theory of democracy. Furthermore, the army, because its members were Lincoln's only administrators inside rebel states, invested an indefensible fort with swollen symbolic force. If Union civil authorities had been present to enforce the laws symbolically in rebel states, Lincoln might well have evacuated doomed military installations

15. Basler, ed., *Lincoln's Works*, IV, 323, 423.

16. Wooster, *Secession Conventions*, pp. 149, 165, 188, 203.

17. Ibid., p. 188; McPherson, *Battle Cry*, p. 298.

Chapter 4. From Neutrality to Unionism

1. The latest books are not always the best. I relish two older accounts of this subject, both still remarkably accurate: Edward Conrad Smith, *The Borderland in the Civil War* (New York, 1927); and "The Great Border" in J. G. Randall and David Donald, *The Civil War and Reconstruction*, 2nd edition (Boston, 1961), pp. 227—42. Of the more recent work, nothing on the borderlands is as sweeping or important as Richard Nelson Current's analysis of Middle South dissidence, *Lincoln's Loyalists: Union Soldiers from the Confederacy* (Boston, 1992).

2. Basler, ed., *Lincoln's Works*, IV, 428.

3. The latest and best account of the Baltimore riot of April 19, 1861, is Frank L. Towers, "'A Vociferous Army of Howling Wolves': Baltimore's Civil War Riot of

April 19, 1861," *The Maryland Historian*, 23 (1992), 39–71. Towers corrects information on quantities of casualties and identities of mob members in otherwise useful older articles, including Matthew Page Andrews, "Passage of the Sixth Regiment through Baltimore, April 19, 1861," *Maryland Historical Magazine*, 14 (1919), 60–73; Charles B. Clark, "Baltimore and the Attack on the 6th Massachusetts Regiment, April 19, 1861," ibid., 56 (1961), 39–71; Matthew Ellenberger, "Whigs in the Streets? Baltimore Republicanism in the Spring of 1861," ibid., 86 (1991), 23–38.

4. Tyler Dennett, ed., *Lincoln and the Civil War in the Diaries of John Hay* (New York, 1939), p. 11.

5. Basler, ed., *Lincoln's Works*, IV, 341–42.

6. For placing the Maryland secession crisis in the perspective of the state's history, before and after, pride of place goes to Jean Baker, especially in her *The Politics of Continuity: Maryland Political Parties from 1858 to 1870* (Baltimore, 1973); and *Ambivalent Americans: The Know Nothing Party in Maryland* (Baltimore, 1977). Also useful is William J. Evitts, *A Matter of Allegiances: Maryland from 1850 to 1861* (Chapel Hill, 1980). Joining this elite group upon its imminent publication will be Frank Towers's fine study of Baltimore during the Civil War crisis.

7. Lincoln to Winfield Scott, April 25, 1861, Basler, ed., *Lincoln's Works*, IV, 344.

8. Lincoln's far-from-draconic repression in Maryland is nicely put in perspective in Mark E. Neely, Jr., *The Fate of Liberty: Abraham Lincoln and Civil Liberties* (New York, 1991).

9. For an amusing debate on this matter and an example of how easily the Maryland-almost-seceded argument is defeated, see Jean H. Baker's triumph over her protagonists in the *Baltimore Sun*, April 6, May 7, June 4, June 23, July 17, August 10, August 17, 1964.

10. An extremely useful little book is *The Civil War Book of Lists . . .* (Conshohocken, PA, 1993). For Maryland, compare p. 19 with p. 27. This book's lists are only as accurate as the surviving records permit, which means that its figures for the Union are never rock hard and for the Confederacy even less so.

11. We have an excellent new history of Kentucky, with a sound discussion of the Civil War years: Lowell H. Harrison and James C. Klotter, *A New History of Kentucky* (Lexington, KY, 1997), esp. pp. 189–212. For more extended discussion, see Harrison's *The Civil War in Kentucky* (Lexington, KY, 1975); and for still more information, see John Alan Boyd, "Neutrality and Peace: Kentucky and the Secession Crisis of 1861," Ph.D. thesis, University of Kentucky, 1999.

12. Harrison and Klotter, *Kentucky*, pp. 188–89.

13. *Civil War Book of Lists*, pp. 19, 27.

14. On Delaware, see Harold Hancock, "Civil War Comes to Delaware," *Civil War History*, 2 (1956), 29–56; and Patience Essah, *A House Divided: Slavery and Emancipation in Delaware, 1638–1865* (Charlottesville, 1996). On West Virginia, see Richard O. Curry, *A House Divided: Statehood Politics and the Copperhead Movement in West Virginia* (Pittsburgh, 1964). On Missouri, see William E. Parrish, *Turbulent Partnership: Missouri and the Union, 1861–1865* (Columbia, MO, 1963); Parrish, *Frank Blair: Lincoln's Conservative* (Columbia, MO, 1998). Christopher Phillips, *Damned Yankee: The Life of General Nathaniel Lyon* (Columbia, MO, 1990); and Phillips, *Missouri's Confederate: Clairborne Fox Jackson and the Creation of Southern Identity in the Border West* (Columbia, MO, 2000).

15. Margaret Ruffin to Edmund Ruffin, August 13, 1861, Ruffin Papers, Virginia Historical Society.

16. Davis to A. S. Johnston, March 12, 1862, to Kirby Smith, July 28, 1862, to Braxton Bragg, August 5, October 17, 1862, Linda Lasswell Crist and Mary Seaton Dix, eds., *The Papers of Jefferson Davis* (Baton Rouge, 1971–), VIII, 93, 305, 322, 448.

17. Quotes in Richard E. Beringer et al., *Why the South Lost the Civil War* (Athens, GA, 1986), p. 168. Joseph L. Harsh does not make as much of this difference between Davis and Lee as he could, in his otherwise excellent recent account of the two leaders' partnership in developing a Confederate offensive-defensive strategy. I especially admire Harsh's ability to stress Lee's virtues while still acknowledging that the general had not much chance of prevailing, so long as the Union used its advantages. *Confederate Tide Rising: Robert E. Lee and the Making of Southern Strategy, 1861–1862* (Kent, OH, 1998).

18. Quoted in another of the superb Civil War books, Barbara Jeanne Fields, *Slavery and Freedom on the Middle Ground: Maryland during the Nineteenth Century* (New Haven, 1985), p. 117.

19. Quotes in this and the next paragraph are from Beringer et al., *Why the South Lost*, p. 174. On the Perryville episode, the moment of truth for Confederate filibustering, see Kenneth A. Hafendorfer, *Perryville, Battle for Kentucky* (Owensboro, KY, 1981); and James L. McDonough, *War in Kentucky: From Shiloh to Perryville* (Knoxville, TN, 1994).

20. On these eastern Tennessee events, the latest and finest account is Noel C. Fisher's *War at Every Door*.

21. I must reemphasize that troop numbers on the Confederate side can never be as precise as the cold numbers look. I have here largely taken the most plausible numbers I have found, Roger L. Ransom's, corrected to factor out Ransom's implausible assumption that many 10- to 14-year-olds fought in the Confederate army.

Overall, Ransom's book is the most helpful analysis of political economy aspects of the Civil War. *Conflict and Compromise: The Political Economy of Slavery, Emancipation, and the American Civil War* (Cambridge, England, and New York, 1989), esp. pp. 189–93, 214–15. Also helpful are *The Book of Lists* and Thomas L. Livermore, *Numbers and Losses in the Civil War in America* (Boston, 1901).

22. Of the several excellent monographs on Baltimore's economy, I most benefited from Sherry H. Olson, *Baltimore: The Building of an American City* (Baltimore, 1980) and John F. Stover, *History of the Baltimore and Ohio Railroad* (West Lafayette, IN, 1987).

23. Quoted in Cooling, *Forts Henry and Donelson*, p. 33.

24. Ibid., pp. 23–24; John D. Milligan, *Gunboats down the Mississippi* (Annapolis, MD, 1965).

Chapter 5. The Jackpot

1. While the emphasis on the borderland's importance in the Henry/Donelson campaigns is my own, most of the details of the story are derived from Benjamin Franklin Cooling's superb *Forts Henry and Donelson*. Rather than continually cite Cooling, footnotes in this chapter identify only quotes and cite the stray bits of information gathered elsewhere.

2. Gideon Pillow to Adna Anderson, June 14, 1861, quoted in ibid., pp. 13–14.

3. On Johnston, we have an excellent biography: Charles P. Roland, *Albert Sidney Johnston, Solider of Three Republics* (Austin, 1964).

4. Johnston to Samuel Cooper, October 17, 1861, quoted in ibid., p. 263.

5. *Civil War Book of Lists*, pp. 19, 27. I calculate that about 26.8 percent of Kentucky whites were males of fighting age, using the same assumptions as in ch. 4, note 21.

6. Cooling, *Forts Henry and Donelson*, appendix; Frederick H. Dyer, *A Compendium of the War of Rebellion* (Des Moines, 1908), pp. 1189–1213; *The War of the Rebellion: A Compilation of the Official Records of the Union and Confederate Armies* (referred to subsequently as *O. R.*) (Washington, DC, 1880–1901), series 1, VII, 852–54. I am grateful to Luke Austin for this note.

7. For a good discussion of this critical Civil War tactic, see Herman Hattaway and Archer Jones, *How the North Won: A Military History of the Civil War* (Urbana, IL, 1991), esp. pp. 13–18 but also passim.

8. Jay Slagle, *Ironclad Captain: Seth Ledyard Phelps and the U.S. Navy, 1841–1864* (Kent, OH, 1996).

9. Quoted in Cooling, *Forts Henry and Donelson*, p. 162.

10. Quoted in ibid., p. 185.

11. James Lee McDonough, *Shiloh: In Hell before Night* (Knoxville, TN, 1979).

12. Quoted in Cooling, *Forts Henry and Donelson*, p. xiii.

13. McPherson, *Battle Cry*, pp. 306–7.

14. Allan Nevins, *The War for the Union*. Volume 1. *The Improvised War, 1861–62* (New York, 1959), p. 147.

15. Lincoln to Orville H. Browning, September 22, 1861, Basler, ed., *Lincoln's Works*, IV, 531–32.

Chapter 6. The Delay

1. During the last decade, new publications on Lincoln and emancipation have been especially rich, including David Herbert Donald, *Lincoln* (New York, 1995); Phillip Shaw Paludan, *The Presidency of Abraham Lincoln* (Lawrence, KS, 1994); Garry Wills, *Lincoln at Gettysburg: The Words That Remade America* (New York, 1992); David E. Long, *The Jewel of Liberty: Abraham Lincoln's Reelection and the End of Slavery* (Mechanicsburg, PA, 1994); Mark E. Neely, Jr., *The Last Best Hope of Earth: Abraham Lincoln and the Promise of America* (Cambridge, MA, 1993); Robert W. Johannsen, *Lincoln, the South, and Slavery* (Baton Rouge, 1991); William C. Harris, *With Charity for All: Lincoln and the Restoration of the Union* (Lexington, KY, 1997). Older but still useful volumes include Herman Belz, *A New Birth of Freedom: The Republican Party and Freedmen's Rights, 1861–1865* (Westport, CT, 1976); Belz, *Reconstructing the Union: Theory and Practice during the Civil War* (Ithaca, NY, 1969); LaWanda Cox, *Lincoln and Black Freedom: A Study in Presidential Leadership* (Columbia, SC, 1981).

2. Lincoln to Greeley, August 22, 1862, Basler, ed., *Lincoln's Works*, V, 388–89.

3. For the text of Halleck's order, see Ira Berlin et al., eds., *Freedom: A Documentary History of Emancipation, 1861–1867*. Series 1. Volume 1. *The Destruction of Slavery* (Cambridge, England, and New York, 1985), p. 47.

4. On black Confederates, the best books are James H. Brewer, *The Confederate Negro: Virginia Craftsmen and Military Laborers, 1861–1865* (Durham, NC, 1969); James G. Hollandsworth, Jr., *The Louisiana Native Guards: The Black Military Experience during the Civil War* (Baton Rouge, 1995); Ervin L. Jordan, Jr., *Black Confederates in Civil War Virginia* (Charlottesville, 1995); Charles Kelly Barrow et al., eds., *Forgotten Confederates: An Anthology about Black Southerners* (Atlanta, 1995); and Andrew W. Bergeron, Jr., et al., eds., *Black Southerners in Gray: Essays on Afro-Americans in Confederate Armies* (Redondo Beach, CA, 1994). This important subject is now needlessly embroiled in controversy,

with politically correct historians of one sort refusing to see the importance (indeed existence) of the minority of slaves who *were* black Confederates, and politically correct historians of the opposite sort refusing to see the importance of black Confederates' limited numbers.

5. Leon F. Litwack, *Been in the Storm So Long: The Aftermath of Slavery* (New York, 1979), p. 37.

6. Benjamin Quarles, *The Negro in the Civil War* (Boston, 1953), pp. 48–50.

7. Quoted in Litwack, *Storm*, p. 7.

8. Bell Irvin Wiley, *Southern Negroes, 1861–1865* (New Haven, CT, 1938), pp. 70–71.

9. Armistead Louis Robinson, "Day of Jubilo: Civil War and the Demise of Slavery in the Mississippi Valley," Ph.D. dissertation, University of Rochester, 1976, p. 172. Professor Robinson died before he finished revising this splendid dissertation for publication; I hope one of his many admirers will soon make sure that the manuscript is in print.

10. Quoted in Bergeron et al., eds., *Black Southerners*, p. 10.

11. The tale is well told in Quarles, *Negro in the Civil War*, pp. 58–60. For Benjamin Butler's version, see *Butler's Book* (Boston, 1892). For his correspondence on the early contrabands, see Berlin et al., eds., *Destruction of Slavery*, pp. 70–75.

12. Butler to Thomas H. Hicks, April 23, 1861, *O. R.*, series 1, II, 589–90.

13. Quoted in Quarles, *Negro in the Civil War*, p. 48.

14. U. S., *Statutes at Large, Treaties, and Proclamations* (Boston, 1863), XII, 319.

15. Quarles, *Negro in the Civil War*, p. 69.

16. Quoted in Berlin et al., eds., *Destruction of Slavery*, p. 26.

17. For a wonderfully (and rarely) balanced discussion of this subject, see Litwack, *Storm*, pp. 4–14.

18. Quoted in ibid., p. 6.

19. Quoted in Quarles, *Negro in the Civil War*, p. 65.

20. Grant to Jesse Root Grant, May 6, 1861, John Y. Simon, et al., eds., *The Papers of Ulysses S. Grant* (Carbondale, IL, 1967-), II, 20–22.

21. For the intriguing exception, see Winthrop Jordan's superb sleuthing in Jordan, *Tumult and Silence at Second Creek: An Inquiry into a Civil War Conspiracy* (Baton Rouge, 1993). The proposed timing of this atypical Civil War slave conspiracy was revealingly typical. The Mississippi conspirators' rare plan to murder and rape was to be set in motion only at that universally propitious Civil War moment for successful massive slave resistance: when the Union army came to the neighborhood.

22. Quoted in Robinson, "Day of Jubilo," pp. 244–47.

23. Both quotes in ibid., p. 407.

24. Quoted in ibid., p. 407.

25. Quoted in Litwack, *Storm*, p. 100.

26. Cyrus Boyd Diary, entry for August 24, 1862, quoted in Robinson, "Day of Jubilo," p. 406.

27. Quoted in ibid., p. 417.

28. O. M. Mitchel to E. M. Stanton, May 4, 1862, Berlin et al., eds., *Destruction of Slavery*, p. 272.

29. Both quoted in Quarles, *Negro in the Civil War*, p. 83.

30. *Harper's Weekly*, December 7, 1861.

31. Quoted in Quarles, *Negro in the Civil War*, pp. 82–83.

32. Berlin et al., eds., *Destruction of Slavery*, p. 294.

33. Quoted in Leonard Curry, *Blueprint for Modern America: Non-Military Legislation of the First Civil War Congress* (Nashville, 1968), p. 62.

34. Quoted in Robinson, "Day of Jubilo," p. 456.

35. Robinson in ibid., pp. 251–56, 482, has superb comparative figures, demonstrating this point better than he modestly claimed. Especially fine on *female* contrabands is Thavolia Glymph, "This Species of Slavery: Female Slave Contrabands in the Civil War," in Edward D. C. Campbell, Jr., and Kym S. Rice, eds., *A Woman's War: Southern Women, Civil War, and the Confederate Legacy* (Charlottesville, 1996), esp. pp. 55–61.

36. These two crucial laws can be found in *Statutes at Large*, XII, 589–600.

37. *O. R.*, series 3, II, 397.

38. For Grant and Sherman, see Berlin et al., eds., *Destruction of Slavery*, pp. 289–91. For the War Department/Halleck's inconsistency, see Ira Berlin et al., eds., *Freedom: A Documentary History of Emancipation*. Series 2. *The Black Military Experience* (Cambridge, England, and New York, 1982), pp. 37–73. For Lincoln's public mulling, at a meeting with "Western Gentlemen," August 4, 1862, see Basler, ed., *Lincoln's Works*, V, 356–57.

39. Ibid., V, 330.

40. Ibid., V, 48, 324–25.

41. Ibid., V, 324, paragraph 2 of the bill submitted to Congress.

42. Freehling, *Road*, I, 140, 500; Ward M. McAfee, "California's House Divided," *Civil War History*, 33 (1987), 115–30; Paul Finkelman, "The Law of Slavery and Freedom in California, 1848–1860," *California Western Law Review*, 17 (1981), 437–64.

43. Basler, ed., *Lincoln's Works*, V, 370–75.

44. James M. McPherson, *The Negro's Civil War: How American Negroes Felt and Acted during the War for the Union* (New York, 1965), pp. 92–95, contains good examples of the black response. Professor McPherson's book, published when we both were

starting out in the profession, first impelled me to see the importance of black history during the Civil War; the volume remains valuable, a third of a century later.

45. Basler, ed., *Lincoln's Works*, V, 317–19; Quarles, *Negro in the Civil War*, 143–45. The $400 per slave figure came from Lincoln's first practical proposal for emancipation (and the first such proposal of any sitting U.S. president), his draft bill of emancipation for Delaware of November 1861. *Works*, V, 29–30. The House "Select Committee on Emancipation," in its report of July 16, trimmed $400 to $300, with Lincoln's approval. Quarles, p. 144.

46. Basler, ed., *Lincoln's Works*, V, 318.

47. Lincoln to Cuthbert Bullitt, July 28, 1862, to August Belmont, July 31, 1862, ibid., V, 344–46, 350–51.

48. Ibid., V, 419–25.

49. Ibid., V, 433–36.

50. Ibid., V, 462–63, 470–71, 500. I am indebted here to Michael Holt, who first led me to see the importance of Lincoln's commissioner strategy.

51. Ibid., V, 529–537.

52. For Chase's warning, see Donald, *Lincoln*, p. 397.

53. Donald's superb discussion of this episode includes the Davis quote in this paragraph and the Browning epithet in the next. Ibid., pp. 397–98. The episode illuminates the persisting power, in Lincoln's imagination, of the secession crisis phenomenon so ably described in Daniel Croft's *Reluctant Confederates*. Or to put it differently, we have here another example of why prewar and war must be studied together.

Chapter 7. The Collaboration

1. Harris's *Lincoln and the Restoration of the Union* is one of the most important recent books on the Civil War.

2. Donald, *Lincoln*, p. 558, has a good discussion. See also Julian S. Carr, *The Hampton Roads Conference* (Durham, NC, 1917).

3. The document is reprinted in a new compendium of Lincoln's positions on slavery, perfect for classroom use: Brooks D. Simpson, ed., *Think Anew, Act Anew: Abraham Lincoln on Slavery, Freedom, and Union* (Wheeling, IL, 1998), p. 191.

4. Lincoln to Michael Hahn, March 13, 1864, ibid., p. 170.

5. The full text of the Final Emancipation Proclamation is in Basler, ed., *Lincoln's Works*, VI, 28–30. The best study of the Emancipation Proclamation is still John Hope Franklin, *The Emancipation Proclamation* (revised edition, Wheeling, IL, 1995; first edition published 1963).

6. The famous wording is Richard Hofstadter's in *The American Political Tradition and the Men Who Made It* (New York, 1948), ch. 5, esp. p. 132. The "bill of lading" phrasing aside, Hofstadter's is the most elegantly written essay on Lincoln and one of the most insightful.

7. Lincoln to John A. McClernand, January 8, 1863, Basler, ed., *Lincoln's Works*, VI, 48–49.

8. Quoted in Quarles, *Negro in the Civil War*, p. 31.

9. Quoted in Paludan, *Presidency of Lincoln*, p. 189.

10. Samuel J. Kirkwood to Henry W. Halleck, August 5, 1862, Ira Berlin et al., eds., *Freedom's Soldiers: The Black Military Experience in the Civil War* (Cambridge, England, and New York, 1998), pp. 87–88.

11. Lincoln to John A. Dix, January 14, 1863, Basler, ed., *Lincoln's Works*, VI, 94.

12. Subjects documented at great length in Berlin et al., eds., *Black Military Experience*.

13. Lincoln to Andrew Johnson, March 26, 1863, Basler, ed., *Lincoln's Works*, VI, 149–50.

14. Halleck to Grant, March 31, 1863, in Berlin et al., eds., *Freedom's Soldiers*, pp. 89–91.

15. Quoted in Brooks D. Simpson, *Let Us Have Peace: Ulysses S. Grant and the Politics of War and Reconstruction* (Chapel Hill, 1991), p. 39; and in Dudley T. Cornish, *The Sable Arm: Negro Troops in the Union Army, 1861–1865*, (Lawrence, KS, 1987; first published 1956), pp. 421–23.

16. Quoted in ibid., pp. 118–19.

17. Thomas to Edwin P. Stanton, April 1, 1863, Berlin et al., eds., *Black Military Experience*, pp. 487–89.

18. A story beautifully told in Willie Lee Rose, *Rehearsal for Reconstruction: The Port Royal Experiment* (New York, 1967).

19. Quoted in Hollandsworth, *Louisiana Native Guards*, p. 19.

20. The best book on contraband labor is now Ira Berlin, et al., eds., *Freedom: A Documentary History of Emancipation, 1861–1867*. Series 1. Volume 3. *The Wartime Genesis of Free Labor: The Lower South* (Cambridge, England, and New York, 1990). Among the other fine studies are C. Peter Ripley, *Slaves and Freedmen in Civil War Louisiana* (Baton Rouge, 1976); Louis S. Gerteis, *From Contraband to Freedman: Federal Policy toward Blacks, 1861–1865* (Westport, CT, 1965); Lawrence N. Powell, *New Masters: Northern Planters during the Civil War and Reconstruction* (New Haven, CT, 1980); and yet another proof that Armistead L. Robinson's premature death was a tragedy for all who love this field: Robinson, 'Worser dan Jeff Daviss': The Coming of Free Labor during the Civil War, 1861–1865," in Thavolia Glymph and John J. Kushma, eds., *Essays on the Postbellum Southern Economy* (College Station, TX, 1985), pp. 11–47.

21. Cornish, *Sable Arm*, p. 114.

22. As befits one of the great Civil War stories, this tale has been told many times, most recently in Russell Duncan, *Where Death and Glory Meet: Robert Gould Shaw and the 54th Massachusetts Infantry* (Athens, GA, 1999). Among the other helpful sources are Russell Duncan, ed., *Blue-Eyed Child of Destiny: The Civil War Letters of Colonel Robert Shaw* (New York, 1994); Peter Burchard, *One Gallant Rush: Robert Gould Shaw and His Brave Black Regiment* (New York, 1965); Luis F. Emilio, *A Brave Black Regiment: History of the Fifty-Fourth Regiment of Massachusetts Volunteer Infantry, 1863–1865* (New York, 1969; first published 1891).

23. I first saw this quote, one of the Civil War's most upsetting and revealing, in Joseph T. Glatthaar, *Forged in Battle: The Civil War Alliance of Black Soldiers and White Officers* (New York, 1990), p. 137.

24. Quoted in Cornish, *Sable Arm*, p. 145.

25. Wiley, *Southern Negroes*, p. 329.

26. Berlin et al., eds., *Black Military Experience*, p. 518; Quarles, *Negro in the Civil War*, p. 223; Cornish, *Sable Arm*, p. 147.

27. Quoted in Robinson, "Day of Jubilo," pp. 258–60; and in Litwack, *Storm*, p. 144.

28. The plausible guess is Joseph Glatthaar's, appearing in his passionate argument that black troops turned around the Civil War: "Black Glory: The African-American Role in Union Victory," Gabor Boritt, ed., *Why the Confederacy Lost* (New York, 1992), pp. 133–62, esp. p. 144. For a fine example of how slavery totally fell apart in the countryside, when federal armies marched in and slaves ran off, see Charles P. Roland, *Louisiana Sugar Plantations during the Civil War* (Baton Rouge, 1997; first published 1957), pp. 92–100.

29. Sherman to James B. Bingham, January 26, 1864, Brooks D. Simpson and Jean V. Berlin, eds., *Sherman's Civil War: Selected Correspondence of William T. Sherman, 1860–1865* (Chapel Hill, 1999), p. 591; Grant to Elihu Washburne, August 30, 1863, Simon et al., eds., *Grant's Papers*, IX, 217–18.

30. Berlin et al., eds., *Destruction of Slavery*, pp. 157–84, 334–35; Fields, *Middle Ground*, pp. 108–11. Also helpful on emancipation in Maryland is Charles L. Wagnandt, *The Mighty Revolution: Negro Emancipation in Maryland, 1862–1864* (Baltimore, 1964).

31. The stages of the unfolding War Department/fugitive collaboration are expertly traced in Fields, *Middle Ground*, pp. 122–30; and in Berlin et al., eds., *Destruction of Slavery*, ch. 6, and *Black Military Experience*, pp. 183–86, 197–226.

32. For example, the president sustained the Frank Blair faction with patronage early on, just as secessionists had predicted. Parrish, *Blair*, p. 89.

33. A process well traced in Fields, *Middle Ground*, pp. 121–22, 128–29.

34. For the Missouri story in addition to Parrish's helpful *Blair* and his *Turbulent Partnership*, see Berlin et al., eds., *Destruction of Slavery*, ch. 7, and *Black Military Experi-*

ence, pp. 226–51; and Michael Fellman, "Emancipation in Missouri," *Missouri Historical Review*, 83 (1988), 36–54.

35. The Kentucky story is well told in Berlin et al., eds., *Black Military Experience*, pp. 251–78; and *Destruction of Slavery*, ch. 8; and in Victor B. Howard, *Black Liberation in Kentucky: Emancipation and Freedom, 1862–1864* (Lexington, 1983).

36. *Book of Lists*, p. 28.

37. For choice examples of the controversy see Barbara J. Fields, "Who Freed the Slaves," in Geoffrey C. Ward, ed., *The Civil War: An Illustrated History* (New York, 1990); the debate between Ira Berlin and James McPherson in *Reconstruction*, 2 (1994), 35–44; McPherson, "Liberating Lincoln," *New York Review of Books*, April 21, 1994; Berlin, "Who Freed the Slaves: Emancipation and Its Meaning," in David W. Blight and Brooks D. Simpson, eds., *Union and Emancipation: Essays on Politics and Race in the Civil War Era* (Kent, OH, 1997), pp. 105–21. For a judicious plea for a truce (and an exaggeration of the cease-fire already achieved), see Peter Kolchin in McPherson and Cooper, eds., *Writing the Civil War*, pp. 247–50.

38. For a fine example of black soldiers who pushed hard for their rights, came close to issuing ultimatums, but drew back to fight simultaneously against both the rebels and the Union's racial discriminations, see Donald Yacovone, ed., *A Voice of Thunder: A Black Soldier's Civil War* (Urbana, IL, and Chicago, 1998). On the subject of blacks' role in the passage of the Thirteenth Amendment, I have especially benefited from Mike Parrish's counsel; I hardly know where his ideas end and mine start.

39. William James, *Memories and Studies* (New York, 1912), p. 40.

40. The best point in the best analysis of the sculpture, Kirk Savage, *Standing Soldiers, Kneeling Slaves: Race, War, and Monument in Nineteenth-Century America* (Princeton, NJ, 1997), pp. 193–207, esp. p. 202. Albert Boime, *The Art of Exclusion: Representing Blacks in the Nineteenth Century* (Washington, DC, 1990), pp. 199–219, emphasizes (may slightly overemphasize) Saint-Gaudens's racism, which is evident enough in the sculptor's own discussion of the work, *The Reminiscences of Augustus Saint-Gaudens*, 2 volumes (New York, 1913), I, 1331–35. A helpful collection of pictures, commentary, and bibliography is in *The Shaw Memorial: A Celebration of an American Masterpiece*, printed in Conschocken, PA, 1997, distributed by the Saint-Gaudens National Historic Site, Cornish, NH.

41. I am indebted to David Carlson for this suggestion.

Chapter 8. The Harvest

1. On the Confederate economy, I concur more with the grim conclusions of Paul W. Gates, *Agriculture and the Civil War* (New York, 1965) and John Solomon

Otto, *Southern Agriculture during the Civil War Era* (Westport, CT, 1994) than with the rosier mood of Confederate modernization in Emory Thomas, *The Confederacy as a Revolutionary Experience.*

2. On the effectiveness of the northern blockade, another heavily contested Civil War subject, I like the balanced view in McPherson, *Battle Cry,* pp. 380–82, better than the minimization of the blockade's power in Stephen R. Wise, *Lifeline of the Confederacy: Blockade Running during the Civil War* (Columbia, SC, 1988). The damage of the blockade, like the damage of Confederate draft resisters, involved not so much whether helpers outnumbered damagers but whether the Confederacy could afford any substantial damage.

3. The best book on refugeeing is Mary Elizabeth Massey, *Refugee Life in the Confederacy* (Baton Rouge, 1964). The damage to black families is best demonstrated in Robinson, "Day of Jubilo." The impact of refugeeing is nicely shown in Robert C. Kenzer, *Kinship and Neighborhood in a Southern Community: Orange County, North Carolina, 1849–1881* (Knoxville, 1987). Ulysses S. Grant often complained that Mississippi Valley planters were refugeeing their able-bodied males, leaving Federals to feed other blacks. See for example Grant to Lincoln, August 23, 1863, Basler, ed., *Lincoln's Works,* VI, 375. The Texas story can be followed in George P. Rawick, *The American Slave: A Composite Autobiography,* 19 volumes (Westport, CT, 1972), IV–V. A good short discussion with choice examples is in Wiley, *Southern Negroes,* pp. 2–7.

4. A story told best in Rose, *Rehearsal for Reconstruction* and extensively in the books cited above in ch. 7, note 20, p. 221.

5. The best studies of this controversial subject include Paul D. Escott, *After Secession: Jefferson Davis and the Failure of Confederate Nationalism* (Baton Rouge, 1978); Georgia Lee Tatum, *Disloyalty in the Confederacy* (Chapel Hill, 1934); Wayne K. Durrill, *War of Another Kind: A Southern Community in the Great Rebellion* (New York, 1990); James Marten, *Texas Divided: Loyalty and Dissent in the Lone Star State, 1856–1874* (Lexington, KY, 1990); and most recently and vociferously David Williams, *Rich Man's War: Class, Caste, and Confederate Defeat in the Lower Chattahoochee Valley* (Athens, GA, 1998). Professor Williams's advice on this point was particularly helpful.

6. Quotations in this paragraph are from ibid., pp. 134, 142.

7. Iver Bernstein, *The New York City Draft Riots: Their Significance for American Society and Politics during the Civil War* (New York, 1990).

8. Basler, ed., *Lincoln's Works,* VIII, 2.

9. Sherman to Ellen Ewing Sherman, July 5, 1863, to Lew Wallace, August 27, 1863, Simpson and Berlin, eds., *Sherman's Civil War,* pp. 449–500, 526. On the Battle of Vicksburg, I have learned from Samuel Carter, III, *The Final Fortress: The Campaign for Vicksburg, 1860–1863* (New York, 1980) and Peter F. Walker, *Vicksburg: A People at*

War, 1860–1865 (Chapel Hill, 1960). On naval/army cooperation, particularly good are Milligan, *Gunboats down the Mississippi,* and Joseph T. Glatthaar, *Partners in Command: The Relationships between Leaders in the Civil War* (New York, 1994). On Grant's military genius, I agree more with John Keegan, *The Mask of Command* (New York, 1987) than with Rowena Reed, *Combined Operations in the Civil War* (Annapolis, 1978).

10. Lincoln to Grant, August 9, 1863, Basler, ed., *Lincoln's Works,* VI, 374.

11. Grant to Henry Halleck, July 24, 1863, Simon et al., eds., *Grant's Papers,* IX, 110.

12. Cornish, *Sable Arm,* pp. 266–67.

13. Sherman to John Spooner, July 30, 1864, Simpson and Berlin, eds., *Sherman's Civil War,* pp. 677–78.

14. On the Battles of Chickamauga and Chattanooga, the helpful books include Steven E. Woodward, *Six Armies in Tennessee: The Chickamauga and Chattanooga Campaigns* (Lincoln, NE, 1997); Woodward, *A Deep Steady Thunder: The Battle of Chickamauga* (Fort Worth, TX, 1997); and James Lee McDonough, *Chattanooga—A Death Grip on the Confederacy* (Knoxville, TN 1994).

15. Fellow Civil War buffs will know that this account omits some fascinating aspects of the climactic scenes at Chattanooga, in order to sharpen the focus on the (I think) primary reason for the Missionary Ridge "miracle." I consider the Battle above the Clouds at Lookout Mountain secondary because far fewer Confederates there suffered defeats, because the defeat did not lead to rebel retreat from Chattanooga, and because the debacle occurred too far from Missionary Ridge to much influence the "miracle." I also consider such rebel tactical errors at Missionary Ridge as confusing orders to the riflemen below and poor positioning of artillery above as secondary because similar defects were endemic on Civil War battlefields and such faults almost never led rebels' stalwart defenders to flee before unprotected chargers.

For a suggestive parallel example of the primary matter, Confederates' very infrequent shaky backbone, consider the Battle of Nashville (December 1864). That combat featured one of the few other times a Union wild charge swept the battlefield, also by George Thomas's men, also after the Army of Tennessee had suffered a demoralizing defeat atop a hopeful advance (a defeat this time made more dispiriting by Cleburne's death).

For further perspective on the long-term travail of the Army of Tennessee see Thomas L. Connelly, *Autumn of Glory: The Army of Tennessee, 1862–1865* (Baton Rouge, 1971); Larry J. Daniel, *Soldiering in the Army of Tennessee: A Portrait of a Confederate Army* (Chapel Hill, 1991); and especially Richard McMurry's incomparable *Two Great Rebel Armies.*

16. On Sherman, the most valuable book is Brooks Simpson's and Jean V. Berlin's edition of Sherman's wartime letters, *Sherman's Civil War.* Other rich studies

of Sherman and his March to the Sea include Michael Fellman, *Citizen Sherman* (New York, 1995); John F. Marszalek, *Sherman: A Soldier's Passion for Order* (New York, 1993); Lee Kennett, *Marching through Georgia: The Story of Soldiers and Civilians during Sherman's March to the Sea* (New York, 1995); Charles Royster, *The Destructive War: William Tecumseh Sherman, Stonewall Jackson, and the Americans* (New York, 1991). Sherman is also at the center of Mark Grimsley's excellent *The Hard Hand of War: Union Military Policy toward Southern Civilians, 1861–1865* (Cambridge, England, and New York, 1995) and Glatthaar's *March to the Sea*.

17. Sherman to Ellen Ewing Sherman, April 11, 1862, Simpson and Berlin, eds., *Sherman's Civil War*, p. 202.

18. On the Atlanta campaign, we have one of our best histories of a single battle, Albert Castel, *Decision in the West: The Atlanta Campaign of 1864* (Lawrence, KS, 1992).

19. Quoted in Royster, *Destructive War*, p. 327.

20. The latest and best book on the Sherman/Thomas campaign is Anne K. Bailey, *The Chessboard of War: Sherman and Hood in the Autumn Campaign of 1864* (Lincoln, NE, 2000). I am indebted to Professor Bailey and her publisher for sending me prepublication galleys. Also helpful are Stanley Horn, *The Decisive Battle of Nashville* (Baton Rouge, 1956) and Wiley Sword, *The Confederacy's Last Hurrah: Spring Hill, Franklin, and Nashville* (Lawrence, KS, 1992).

21. Sherman to George H. Thomas, October 2, 1864, to Ulysses S. Grant, October 9, 1864, Simpson and Berlin, eds., *Sherman's Civil War*, pp. 730–31.

22. Sherman to Thomas Ewing, Sr., August 10, 1862, to Salmon P. Chase, August 11, 1862, ibid., pp. 264, 269.

23. Quoted in Randall and Donald, *Civil War and Reconstruction*, p. 387.

24. Sherman to Henry Halleck, January 12, 1865, to John Sherman, April 26, 1863, to William M. McPherson, ca. September 15–30, 1864, Simpson and Berlin, eds., *Sherman's Civil War*, pp. 796, 461, 727.

25. Glatthaar, *March to the Sea*, p. 57.

26. Sherman to Halleck, December 13, 1864, Simpson and Berlin, eds., *Sherman's Civil War*, p. 762.

27. Berlin et al., eds., *Wartime Genesis of Free Labor*, pp. 111–12, 331–40.

28. Thomas J. Morgan, *Reminiscences of Services with Colored Troops in the Army of the Cumberland, 1863–1865*, Third Series. Number 13, in *Personal Narratives of Events in the War of the Rebellion, Being Papers Read before the Rhode Island Soldiers and Sailors Historical Society* (Providence, 1885) is a superb primary source on this subject; the quote is on p. 48. I am much indebted to Professor Anne Bailey for her advice on this paragraph. For her own excellent account, see *Chessboard of War*, esp. pp. 149–54.

29. Sherman to John A. Spooner, July 30, 1864, to Henry Halleck, January 12, 1865, Simpson and Berlin, eds., *Sherman's Civil War*, pp. 678, 796.

30. Quoted in Simpson, *Let Us Have Peace*, pp. 57–58.

31. Sherman to Henry Halleck, September 4, 1864, Simpson and Berlin, eds., *Sherman's Civil War*, p. 700.

32. Joseph T. Glatthaar, *Civil War Alliance of Black Soldiers and White Officers*, pp. 275–80, usefully lists all black officers, 107 in number, and all black congressional medal winners (7 in South Carolina/Alabama combat in addition to the 22 in Virginia).

33. Quoted in Symonds, *Battlefield Atlas*, p. 89. The tale of Grant's final campaigns has been told many times. I enjoy the accounts in Noah Andre Trudeau, *Bloody Roads South: The Wilderness to Cold Harbor, May–June, 1864* (Boston, 1989); and in Richard J. Sommers, *Richmond Redeemed: The Siege of Petersburg* (Garden City, NJ, 1981). Fine on the excruciating impact on Lee's army are William A. Blair, *Virginia's Private War: Feeding Belly and Soul in the Confederacy* (New York, 1998); and Tracy Power, *Lee's Miserables: Life in the Army of Northern Virginia from the Wilderness to Appomattox* (Chapel Hill, 1998).

Chapter 9. The Last Best Hope

1. The capitalization in this sentence takes off from McWhiney and Jamieson's provocative *Attack and Die*. For an excellent introduction to the vast literature on this specific point and on Lee in general, see Gary Gallagher, "Upon Their Success Hang Momentous Interests, Generals," in Boritt, ed., *Why the Confederacy Lost*, pp. 79–108, 186–88. Gallagher's defense of Lee enhances his *The Confederate War*.

2. On Lee's realistic dismissal of the likelihood of British intervention, see Harsh, *Confederate Tide Rising*, p. 57. I am indebted to George Herring for his advice on this section, particularly on the cotton embargo.

3. Quoted in Howard Jones, *Union in Peril: The Crisis over British Intervention in the Civil War* (Chapel Hill, 1992), p. 32. Professor Jones's volume, and his subsequent *Abraham Lincoln and a New Birth of Freedom: The Union and Slavery in the Diplomacy of the Civil War* (Lincoln, NE, 1999) are at once among the most informative and the most curious recent contributions to Civil War lore. On the one hand, Jones scrupulously gives us the facts about the possibility of English (and French) interventions. I here rely on Jones's facts. On the other hand, Jones holds out a possibility of British intervention that his facts cannot support. While Jones's Lord John Russell and Napoleon III bruited about proposals for preliminary mild interventions that they

naïvely failed to realize could cause big trouble, Jones's Lord Palmerston would have none of it, and he soberly controlled both flitting adventurers.

Palmerston and Lincoln so totally dominated their respective government's diplomacy and so mutually believed that an English intervention, without Union approval, would be disastrously against their countries' national interest that only blundering folly could have brought off the debacle. But Jones also shows that Palmerston and Lincoln were superb at showing each other exactly how far it was safe to go, especially during the formative *Trent* affair. Any post-Jones historian who claims that Great Britain came remotely close to turning around the Civil War is going to have to get around those two realpolitik dominators, and especially the forbidding Palmerston, a feat that neither Lord Russell nor Napoleon came remotely close to bringing off.

For a more consistently sober (and equally well informed) recent estimate of the possibility of England intervention, see Charles M. Hubbard, *The Burden of Confederate Diplomacy* (Knoxville, TN, 1998).

4. Quoted in Jones, *Union in Peril*, p. 26.

5. Quoted in ibid., p. 50.

6. Quoted in ibid., p. 75.

7. Quoted in ibid., p. 135.

8. Quoted in ibid., p. 178.

9. Quoted in ibid., pp. 186, 191, 193. For illuminating perspective on Russell/Palmerston in 1862, consider Seward/Lincoln in 1861. Just as British Foreign Secretary Russell sought to mediate in the American Civil War, so U.S. Secretary of State William H. Seward earlier sought to pick a war with Spain (in hopes that Confederates would rush back into the Union to share the spoils). But just as Palmerston rejected his foreign secretary's potentially dangerous meddling, so Lincoln rejected his secretary of state's wild scheme. Historians tempted to speculate that England almost intervened in the American Civil War, because Russell wanted to, should ask themselves this question: Did the United States almost go to war with Spain, because Seward wanted to?

10. Quoted in ibid., p. 194.

11. Ibid., ch. 10. British rulers displayed a certain imperial sense of moral superiority throughout the nineteenth century, and an accompanying imperial obligation to intervene in the New World, to serve supposed moral progress. American rulers worried excessively about that side of British character because they saw less clearly the countervailing side: a greater inclination to stay out of the New World, if American rulers warned Britain away. This little drama, always in American hands to control, worked itself out exactly the same way in the 1840s, when Britain toyed

with helping the republic of Texas abolish slavery (an overture that had no chance after southern slaveholders protested), as in the 1860s, when the British toyed with intervention to mediate in the Civil War (an overture that also had scant chance, after the Union protested). For the intriguing Texas parallel, see my *Road*, I, part 6.

12. This position has inspired quite the continuing debate. On the side that McClellan's election could have yielded permanent disunion, see Long, *Jewel of Liberty* and Albert Castel, *Winning and Losing the Civil War: Essays and Stories* (Columbia, SC, 1996), ch. 3. On the side that a President McClellan would not have given up the Union, see William C. Davis, *The Cause Lost: Myths and Realities of the Confederacy* (Lawrence, KS, 1996), ch. 8; Larry J. Daniel, "The South Almost Won by Not Losing," *North and South*, 3 (1998), 44–51; Stephen W. Sears, "McClellan and the Peace Process of 1864: A Reappraisal," *Civil War History*, 36 (1990), 57–64. My own disbelief in a McClellan surrender of the Union, published in an earlier form in *Reintegration*, pp. 225–31, was (to my knowledge) first presented, extremely persuasively, in Randall and Donald, *Civil War and Reconstruction*, pp. 473–79.

13. Quoted in Jones, *Union in Peril*, p. 186.

14. Quoted in McPherson, *Battle Cry*, p. 772. McPherson, echoing wartime Republicans, claims that "this crucial resolution made peace the first priority and Union a distant second." I agree with wartime Democrats that the resolution's words do not sustain that reading. A few historians claim that Peace Democrats would have sacrificed the Union for peace. With very few exceptions, the Peace Democrats' speeches and papers seem to me to scream exactly the opposite: that peace would best gain the reunion goal that must be the basis of a negotiated end of the war. Some historians also claim that a President McClellan could not have ruled without his party's minority peace wing. But could he have ruled without Democrats' majority war wing or without the Republicans (two groups that made up around 90 percent of Union voters)?

That the War Democrats dominated the Democratic Party in 1864 is the burden of Joel H. Silbey's fine *A Respectable Minority: The Democratic Party in the Civil War Era* (Ithaca, NY, 1983).

15. Stephen W. Sears, ed., *The Civil War Papers of George McClellan: Selected Correspondence, 1860–1865* (New York, 1989), pp. 595–97.

16. McClellan to W. C. Prime, August 10, 1864, McClellan Papers, Library of Congress.

17. Charles R. Wilson, "McClellan's Changing Views on the Peace Plank of 1864," *American Historical Review*, 38 (1933), 498–505.

18. Robert F. Durden, *The Gray and the Black: The Confederate Debate on Emancipation* (Baton Rouge, 1972), p. 70.

19. Basler, ed., *Lincoln's Works*, VII, 514–15.

20. Ibid., VII, 506–7.

21. See above, p. 103.

22. Quoted in Craig L. Symonds, *Stonewall of the West: Patrick Cleburne and the Civil War* (Lawrence, KS, 1997), pp. 41, 44, 46, 182.

23. Quoted in ibid., p. 91. For Cleburne's earlier brutal wound and its continued impact, see p. 41.

24. Cleburne's whole speech is printed in Durden, *Gray and Black*, pp. 54–62.

25. Quoted in Symonds, *Cleburne*, p. 189.

26. Quoted in ibid., p. 190.

27. Durden, *Gray and Black*, pp. 66–67.

28. Ibid., pp. 102–6.

29. Ibid., pp. 129, 184, 233.

30. Ibid., p. 206.

31. Ibid., pp. 202–3.

32. Quoted by Joseph Glatthaar in Boritt, ed., *Why the Confederacy Lost*, p. 152.

33. An important new theme in Civil War studies, especially developed by Drew Gilpin Faust in "Altars of Sacrifice: Confederate Women and the Narratives of War," in Catherine Clinton and Nina Silber, eds., *Divided Houses: Gender and the Civil War* (New York, 1992), pp. 171–99. One of Professor Faust's conclusions, that "the Confederacy did not endure longer . . . because so many women did not want it to," seems to me plausible, much more so than her argument that "because of its women . . . the South lost the Civil War" (p. 199). The latter argument, among other things, is highly vulnerable to Gary Gallagher's big question: Did white Confederate home-front morale collapse before or after military rout?

34. Excellent on this point is George Frederickson, "Why the Confederacy Did Not Fight a Guerrilla War after the Fall of Richmond: A Comparative View," printed as the Robert Fortenbaugh Memorial Lecture, Gettysburg College, 1996.

Chapter 10. The Taproot and Its Blight

1. Quoted by James McPherson in Boritt, ed., *Why the Confederates Lost*, pp. 19–20.

2. A point well made in Grace Palladino, *Another Civil War: Labor, Capital, and the State in Anthracite Regions of Pennsylvania, 1840–1868* (Urbana, IL, 1990).

3. Samuel Flagg Bemis, *John Quincy Adams and the Union* (New York, 1965), p. 338.

Index